D1626105

THE POLITICS OF BRITISH FOREIGN POLICY IN THE ERA OF DISRAELI AND GLADSTONE

THE POLITICS OF BRITISH FOREIGN POLICY IN THE ERA OF DISRAELI AND GLADSTONE

Marvin Swartz

St. Martin's Press   New York

LONDIN. UNIV. SHL WITHDRAWN

© Marvin Swartz 1985

All rights reserved. For information, write:
St. Martin's Press, Inc., 175 Fifth Avenue, New York, NY 10010
Printed in Hong Kong
Published in the United Kingdom by The Macmillan Press Ltd.
First published in the United States of America in 1985

ISBN 0−312−62645−2

Library of Congress Cataloging in Publication Data

Swartz, Marvin.
   The politics of British foreign policy in the era of
   Disraeli and Gladstone.

   Bibliography: p.
   Includes index.
   1. Great Britain − Foreign relations − 1837−1901.
2. Great Britain − Politics and government −
1837−1901.   3. Disraeli, Benjamin, Earl of
Beaconsfield, 1804−1881.   4. Gladstone,
W. E. (William Ewart), 1809−1898.
I. Title.
DA550.S9 1985   327.41   84−17696
ISBN 0−312−62645−2

*To my sons
Jonathan and Reuben*

Contents

Preface

I must record my gratitude for permission to consult collections of unpublished papers in the list of Archival Sources to Lord Medway and the Suffolk Record Office (Cranbrook Papers); the Liverpool City Libraries (Derby Papers); the Directors of the Goodwood Estate Company Limited and the West Sussex Record Office and the County Archivist; Lord St Aldwyn and the Gloucestershire Record Office (Hicks Beach Papers); the Northamptonshire Record Office (Hunt Papers); the Hon. David Lytton Cobbold and the Hertfordshire Record Office; Lord Clarendon, Lord Harcourt, and the Bodleian Library; Lord Halifax (Hickleton Papers), the Directors of Matheson & Co. Ltd, and the University Library, Cambridge; the Birmingham University Library (Chamberlain Papers); the Library of the University of Newcastle (Trevelyan Papers); Times Newspapers Ltd; the Hon. David Smith (Hambleden Papers); and the National Trust (Hughenden Papers). Lord Derby, the Duke of Devonshire and the Trustees of the Chatsworth Settlement, and Lord Salisbury kindly allowed me to study family papers. Use of material from the Royal Archives is by the gracious permission of Her Majesty Queen Elizabeth II. Quotations from Crown copyright records in the Public Record Office appear by permission of the Controller of H. M. Stationery Office.

I can mention here only a few of the many people who aided me in my research. They include R. A. H. Smith of the Department of Manuscripts at the British Library; David Aronson; T. I. Rae of the National Library of Scotland; Robert Mackworth-Young and Jane Langton and her colleagues at Windsor Castle; Pauline Dower; Gordon Phillips of *The Times*; Barbara North, Barbara Tempest and Patrick Wall of the National Trust, Hughenden Manor; Peter Raynor and Diana Kay at Knowsley Hall; T. S. Wragg and Peter Day at Chatsworth House; and J. F. A. Mason of Christ Church, Oxford, and R. H. Harcourt Williams at Hatfield House. Other librarians and archivists helped me at the University Library and the Seeley Historical Library, Cambridge; the Public Record Office; the

British Library; and the Library of the University of Massachusetts at Amherst. The Graduate Council of that university gave financial support during the early stages of this project; and the under-standing of colleagues enabled me to take necessary leaves of absence.

I wish to thank the Master, President and Fellows of St John's College, Cambridge, for the privileges which they extended to me. For their hospitality, I remember the President and Fellows of Clare Hall, Cambridge, and especially Derrik and Sheila Adams.

To fellow historians I wish to record my debt. James Joll, Arno Mayer and Zara Steiner read all or large parts of an earlier version of the manuscript. Derek Beales and especially Henry Pelling made me welcome in Cambridge. F. H. Hinsley, despite more pressing duties, repeatedly took the trouble to assist me in important ways. The Warden and Fellows of St Antony's College, Oxford, par-ticularly Archie Brown, have been interested in my work. Agatha Ramm made numerous helpful suggestions. I alone, of course, am responsible for any errors and all interpretations.

Amherst,   M. Swartz
Massachusetts

List of Abbreviations

Balfour P.	Arthur Balfour Papers (British Library, British Museum, London)
Bright P.	John Bright Papers (BL)
B.T.	Board of Trade files (Public Record Office, London)
CAB	Reports of Cabinet meetings (PRO)
Cairns P.	Cairns Papers (PRO)
Card. P.	Edward Cardwell Papers (PRO)
Carn. D.	Carnarvon Diary (BL)
Carn. P.	Carnarvon Papers (PRO)
Carn. P. (BL)	Carnarvon Papers (BL)
Clar. P.	Clarendon Papers (Bodleian Library, Oxford)
C.O.	Colonial Office files (PRO)
Cr. P.	R. A. Cross Papers (BL)
Cran. P.	Cranbrook (G. Gathorne Hardy) Papers (Ipswich & East Suffolk RO)
D. Cab. Min.	Derby, Cabinet Minutes, February–March 1878 (Knowsley Hall)
D.D.	Derby Diary (Knowsley)
Delane Corr., or P.	J. T. Delane Correspondence, or Papers (Archives of *The Times*, London)
Dev. P.	Devonshire (Hartington, also Duchess of Manchester) Papers (Chatsworth House)
Dilke P.	Sir Charles W. Dilke Papers (BL)
Disraeli P.	Benjamin Disraeli Papers (BL)
D.P.	Derby (15th Earl) Papers (Liverpool City Libraries)
Escott P.	T. H. S. Escott Papers (BL)
F.O.	Foreign Office files, departmental and private (PRO)
Glad. P.	William Ewart Gladstone Papers (BL)
Goodwood Ms.	Richmond (6th Duke) Papers, in Goodwood Manuscripts (West Sussex RO, Chichester)
Gran. P.	Granville Papers (PRO)

List of Abbreviations

Hamb. P.	Hambleden (W. H. Smith) Papers (Archives of W. H. Smith & Son, London)
Hamilton P.	Edward W. Hamilton Papers (BL)
Harcourt P.	Sir William V. Harcourt Papers (Bodleian)
H.B. P.	Sir Michael Hicks Beach Papers (Gloucestershire RO, Gloucester)
Hick. P.	Hickleton (Halifax) Papers (microfilm, University Library, Cambridge)
H.O.	Home Office files (PRO)
H.P.	Hughenden (B. Disraeli, also Philip Rose) Papers (Hughenden Manor; now in the Bodleian Library, Oxford)
Hunt P.	George Ward Hunt Papers (Northamptonshire RO, Delapre Abbey, Northampton)
Idd. P.	Iddesleigh (Sir Stafford Northcote) Papers (BL)
JC	Joseph Chamberlain Papers (Birmingham University Library)
Lyt. P.	Lytton (Edward Robert Bulwer) Papers (Hertfordshire RO, Hertford)
M & B	W. F. Monypenny and G. E. Buckle, *The Life of Benjamin Disraeli, Earl of Beaconsfield* (London, 1910–20, 6 vols)
Mepol.	Metropolitan Police files (PRO)
Morley, *Gladstone*	John Morley, *The Life of William Ewart Gladstone* (London, 1903; 1906 edn, 2 vols)
P.H.S. P.	Printing House Square (*The Times*) Papers (archives of *The Times*)
QVL	G. E. Buckle (ed.), *The Letters of Queen Victoria*, second series, *1862–1885* (London, 1926–28, 3 vols)
RA	Royal Archives (Windsor Castle)
Ramm, *Corr.*	Agatha Ramm (ed.), *The Political Correspondence of Mr Gladstone and Lord Granville 1868–1876* (London, 1952, 2 vols), *1876–1886* (Oxford, 1962, 2 vols)
Ripon P.	Ripon Papers (BL)
R.P.	Rosebery Papers (National Library of Scotland, Edinburgh)
S.P.	Salisbury Papers (Christ Church Library, Oxford; now at Hatfield House)

Stanmore P.	Stanmore (Sir Arthur Gordon) Papers (BL)
T.	Treasury files (PRO)
Tent. P.	Tenterden Papers (PRO)
Trevelyan P., CET or GOT	C. E. or G. O. Trevelyan Papers (Newcastle University Library)
Walter P.	John Walter III Papers (archives of *The Times*)

NOTE: During the latter part of the nineteenth century contemporaries were sometimes careless in using and omitting apostrophes; quotations in this study follow the original.

Introduction

The interaction between domestic politics and foreign policy became increasingly apparent in Great Britain between 1865 and 1885. In this period traditional sources of political power retained their importance: the Foreign Office, the Cabinet, parliament and the parliamentary parties, and the Crown. Yet popular forces – an expanded electorate and party organizations, a flourishing newspaper press – presented new challenges. Party leaders tried to convince not only their colleagues but also the country to follow them on matters of foreign affairs. Although political opinion at Westminster continued to be of more significance than did public opinion at large, the latter was of growing importance.

The political dimensions of their office had been understood by the most prominent makers of British foreign policy since 1815. As Foreign Secretary toward the end of the Napoleonic wars and afterward, Castlereagh was especially concerned with Britain's commitment to the European continent. He was anxious to set Belgium free from French control and to establish 'a just equilibrium in Europe'.[1] Although he desired to cooperate closely with the allies after 1815, Castlereagh refused to sanction interference in the domestic affairs of other states unless they presented an immediate threat to the general peace.[2] In making his policy he was given a free hand by the Prime Minister, Liverpool, so long as he steered clear of political difficulties; nor did the Cabinet object. Castlereagh's leadership of the House of Commons was an onerous duty, but it enabled him to carry his own policies there. Yet he shrank from wooing parliament or public opinion. He gave arguments to support his position but would not appeal to the imagination or emotions of his audience. He remained a cold and aloof aristocrat.

In contrast to Castlereagh, his successor, George Canning, appealed to and was supported by public opinion. He gave speeches outside of parliament. He believed that if he could secure popular backing, the press was sure to follow. More traditional politicians complained of this indecorous behaviour of the Foreign Secretary and leader of the House of Commons, but Canning was not to be deterred. He insisted that the support of the country strengthened his foreign policy, and he relied upon it as a foundation of his own political position. In a largely aristocratic world Canning valued the stabilizing role of the middle class. Opposed in principle to extending its parliamentary power, he favoured administrative reform to promote its interest.[3] Canning's espousal of open diplomacy was viewed as revolutionary. He followed England's interest, but with a keen eye on public opinion.[4]

Palmerston was Foreign Secretary from 1830 until 1841, except for a few months, and from 1846 until 1851; Home Secretary, 1852–5; and Prime Minister, 1855–8 and 1859–65. He carried further Canning's techniques of influencing public opinion. He supported efforts to find new markets for British trade. He regularly supplied the press and parliament with information. He was an advocate of moderate constitutional government not only at home but also on the Continent, as a way of avoiding violent revolution; hence his adoption of a liberal foreign policy.[5] By threats and bluster he overawed weak foreign states, as in the Don Pacifico affair, and rallied nationalist opinion at home. But he failed to deter Bismarck from warring against Denmark in 1864. Palmerston's death the next year opened the way for domestic political reform and for a reassessment of Great Britain's international role.

These tasks fell to William Ewart Gladstone and Benjamin Disraeli. Neither man was of aristocratic origins; yet both contributed to preserving the traditional order of society while advancing the interests of the middle class and extending to workers the right to vote. Foreign policy was one of their political instruments.

When Gladstone introduced a reform bill into the House of Commons in March 1866, he conceived of it as a conservative, not a radical, measure. He had not been committed to this or perhaps any other political idea throughout his career. He had a passion for causes, and the object of his passion varied with time and circumstance. In the mid-1860s he was outspoken about his willingness to alter society to some extent in order to preserve the rest. 'I will never be a party, knowingly, to what I may call frivolous acts of disturbance,' he stated, 'nor to the premature production of schemes of change.'[6] He believed that 'it is sometimes necessary in politics to make surrenders of what, if not surrendered, will be wrested from us. And it is very wise,' he advised his eldest son in

1865, 'when a necessity of this kind is approaching, to anticipate it while it is yet a good way off; for then concession begets gratitude, and often brings return.'[7] For Gladstone electoral reform was a means of allaying political discontent, winning the gratitude of the lower orders of society and ensuring their continued deference to their superiors, 'their good conduct'.[8] He told an audience in 1865 that if 'all the feelings of the country are in the best and broadest sense conservative − that is to say, that the people value the country and the laws and institutions of the country − honesty compels me to admit that this happy result has been brought about by liberal legislation'.[9]

Disraeli adhered to certain political principles, perhaps with more constancy than Gladstone. Their contemporaries hardly recognized this fact, for they confused the manner of the men with the substance of their politics. Disraeli professed to believe almost from the beginning of his political career in the 1830s that the Tories were the representatives of the true interests of a majority of the English people. One of those interests, of course, was that the representatives themselves be holders of landed property. He argued that the hereditary aristocracy must be flexible in the exercise of power, governing not exclusively in its own narrow interest but in the broader interest of the nation, the latter subsuming the former. Once he had achieved a responsible political position, Disraeli remained consistent in his attempt to vindicate the 'English Constitution' by preserving the traditional part it assigned to the monarchy and aristocracy and at the same time ensuring the support of the electorate for his party. Politically, the flexibility of the means he used masked the steadfastness of his purpose; so too did the humour, sarcasm and flippancy which characterized his approach as leader of his party in the House of Commons. The hard shell of appearance protected the vulnerable personality beneath from the scorn of a society which needed his talents but despised his origins. He was not enough of a hypocrite to deny that politics was the pursuit of personal ambition as well as principle. Disraeli's aims were as conservative as Gladstone's. He asserted that the Conservative party should prevent 'considerable changes...both in Church and State which neither the necessities of the country require, nor its feelings really sanction'.[10] He felt, however, that timely reform could serve the interest of his party and maintain the social and political order.

The reform act of 1867 was a moderate measure. The number of eligible voters was nearly doubled, to about two million; some 40 per cent of adult males were now enfranchised, although the right to vote remained a privilege conferred by ownership or occupation of property.[11] The worst fears of opponents of a wider franchise did not materialize. Lord Carnarvon, who had resigned from the Conservative Cabinet over the issue of reform, later admitted that 'he had been overmuch frightened by it, and that it had worked out better than he expected'.[12] After a talk with A. J. Mundella, an influential Radical MP for Sheffield, Carnarvon noted: 'He is in many essentials very conservative, looks with horror & ridicule upon all interference with property & believes strongly in the necessity of a religious education. He fears a return to protection mainly on the ground that we sd. then be driven to manufacture mainly for our home consumption wh. wd. give us only about 4 months employment. He is very *imperial* in all his colonial notions.' Although sanguine as to the future, Mundella expressed concern that 'political leaders (mainly of extreme radical Party) may upset everything. Nevertheless he believes that in the workmen there is a respect for all property & a sense of religion.'[13]

Although the new voters were not radical, their very existence had a profound political impact. Working-class unrest during the first half of the 1870s affected the drafting of the labour laws of 1875.[14] To win the allegiance of the broadened electorate, Liberals and Conservatives strengthened their organizations in the country. Lancashire became a political battleground. Though the north-west of England did not return a number of MPs proportionate to its population, it had received the largest increase in seats of any comparable geographical area in the redistribution of 1867/8, as by that of 1832.[15] Gladstone had used his speaking engagements in south-west Lancashire in 1868 as a national platform, and lost the contest.[16] The Conservative party agent, J. E. Gorst, wanted Disraeli to follow Gladstone's example and speak in Lancashire. By doing so, Gorst argued, Disraeli would not only help the party in that county but also broadcast its appeal to the new urban and industrial electorate elsewhere. He would, the party agent continued, 'meet with the most enthusiastic reception to himself personally: he would meet an intelligent appreciative audience interested in public affairs & especially in foreign policy, beyond the mere sphere of their own physical wants'.[17]

Disraeli accepted the suggestion. Speaking at Manchester in April 1872, he criticized the Liberal government's dealings with Russia and the United States and emphasized the importance of the empire and of maintaining a policy of 'proud reserve' toward Europe. In June 1872 at the Crystal Palace he stressed that if the first object of the Tory party was 'to maintain the institutions of the country, the second is, in my opinion, to uphold the Empire of England'.[18] From Disraeli's perspective, British institutions made possible a strong empire and the empire helped to shore up the institutions. The two went together. Foreign policy was thus an integral part of politics.

From the mid-1860s, British policy-makers redefined their nation's commitments to its empire and to the European continent. Because the fate of the Ottoman empire seemed to involve both British imperial communications and the balance of power in Europe, the eastern crisis of 1875–8 provided a major test of prolonged debate over foreign policy for Gladstone and Disraeli. That debate included the questions of how best to protect British interests and of how to appeal to public opinion – or whether to appeal at all. Hence the agitation over the Bulgarian atrocities and the dispute over the proper response to the Russo-Turkish war were problems of domestic politics as well as foreign policy. Disraeli failed to turn his success at the congress of Berlin into a political triumph. Nor did Gladstone's Midlothian campaigns give him a clear mandate in foreign affairs. The purchase of the Suez canal shares and the occupation of Egypt demonstrated that political pressure generally reinforced British strategic interests. By the mid-1880s, it was apparent that neither Disraeli's Palmerstonian bluster nor Gladstone's pursuit of a European concert was an effective reply to the challenges of an era of 'economic nationalism and national imperialism'.[19] Yet their rivalry of the previous two decades had established that in an era of increasing mass participation in the life of the nation, the making of foreign policy was inseparable from politics.

1 Imperial and Continental Commitments

Great Britain had commitments both to its empire and on the Continent. For half a century after the congress of Vienna she, more than any other European nation-state, enjoyed a sense of security in external relations. The treaty of Vienna and the guarantee of Belgian neutrality seemed sufficient to contain the expansionism of France, and no other power threatened to establish a hegemony on the Continent which would endanger the safety of the British Isles. The British empire and commercial enterprise faced no serious competitor. From the mid-1860s, the government had to meet new challenges. In the eyes of the aristocracy as well as the middle class, trade, commerce and investment were crucial components of national strength upon which prosperity seemed to depend. After the Franco-Prussian war, the creation of the German Reich upset the balance of power in Europe and introduced a new sense of rivalry in international affairs. Great Britain responded to increasing competition by promoting trade, maintaining and extending the empire, and attempting to avert the formation of a strong Continental bloc. Political debate, within as well as between the Liberal and Conservative parties, served to rally the nation to defend Britain's imperial and Continental commitments.

Changes at home as well as developments abroad influenced British policy-makers. Increasingly the social outlook of the aristocracy combined with the economic vision of the upper middle class. As the latter came to value such ideals as the possession of land and country houses, education at public schools and at Oxford and Cambridge, and the concept of the 'gentleman', aristocrats accepted many of the tenets of capitalism. Men wealthy enough to sit in

6

parliament were likely to be investors of capital or connected, usually as landlords or directors of companies, with mining and industrial enterprises. Both Benjamin Disraeli and W. E. Gladstone made investments on the advice of bourgeois friends. Disraeli's solicitor wrote to him in July 1868: 'We have at length would up our For. & Col. Gov. Trust accounts, and I have just received my proportion of profit together with £320 (Three hundred and twenty pounds) for the share which I accepted under my own name for you. I will pay this amount to your credit at L & W Bank on Monday.'[1] In 1871, after losing 'upwards of 30,000£' on speculation in the Metropolitan District Railway, Gladstone, according to a staunch Tory, appointed the former banker G. J. Goschen his 'investor General', thus explaining the latter's rapid political rise. Whether or not he believed this rumour, Lord Salisbury did not doubt that Gladstone would seek profitable investments: 'I am glad G. has got somebody to invest his money. He is quite unfit to do it for himself.[2] The gulf between holders of political power and social prestige on the one hand and possessors of capitalist wealth on the other, which enervated public life in many continental nations, was of relatively little significance in England.

The Duke of Manchester was a good example of an aristocrat involved in capitalist and colonial enterprise. A former cavalry officer and Conservative MP, concerned with the militia and volunteers, his interests extended beyond the bounds of traditional territorial obligations. He was president of the Royal Colonial Institute from 1871 to 1878. He was a founder of the New Zealand Company and of the National Emigrants' Aid Corporation, which were not entirely benevolent organizations. The latter in 1878 'declared a dividend of 5% free of Income Tax. = 10s. on £10-'.[3] Frederick Young, a leader in the emigration movement, was pleased when, in 1882, Manchester extended a dinner invitation to Cecil Rhodes, 'a good specimen of diamond mining success'. For Young, as for the Duke, the question of the colonies involved 'vast future developments'. Young reported to Manchester that the Poet Laureate was a willing recruit to the growing army of imperialists:

> He is just now absorbed with the idea of Imperial Federation. He read to me some fine stanzas, he is composing about it, with the *true patriotic* ring in them.
> He wishes them to be set to music, & to be sung hereafter on

some great national occasion.

The adhesion of such men as Tennyson to the great cause is very important.[4]

To abet this cause the Duke could use social as well as political connections, although the distinction between them was perhaps artificial. His wife was the mistress of Lord Hartington, the Liberal leader in the House of Commons after the retirement of Gladstone, and she maintained a close relationship with W. E. Forster. The latter, seemingly on the Duchess's advice, took two hundred shares in a gold mine in 1884.[5]

Politicians acting in an official capacity were receptive to capitalist proposals. In 1874 the Chancellor of the Exchequer, Sir Stafford Northcote, granted an interview to two MPs who were spokesmen for shareholders in the Anglo-American Cable Company. They wanted to reduce the cost of messages to North America 'in the interests of Commerce generally' and 'to put a stopper on the proceedings of men of the Labouchere class, who worry the quiet Cyrus Fields and other Anglo-Americans.... If the Government would take the whole thing into its own hands and reserve to itself a monopoly of communication between the United Kingdom and Canada, the Shareholders would be assured of a certain fixed and moderate dividend, undisturbed by cares: the price of messages might be reduced: commerce would be greatly benefited: and the Government would lose nothing.' Although he ultimately rejected the idea of the government's purchasing the Atlantic cables, Northcote took it seriously enough to question both the Colonial and the Foreign Secretaries.[6]

In 1876 Northcote tried to persuade the Foreign Secretary, Lord Derby, to intervene on behalf of British investors in the Peruvian guano trade. The government of Peru was, he argued, 'perpetrating a gross piece of injustice, the effect of which will be to cause the loss of a very large amount of British capital directly, and possibly a still greater amount indirectly. The effect of such a loss upon our trade and financial position will be great; and the pressure which may be put on us to interfere for the protection of the British creditor, not only in Peru but elsewhere, will be severe.' When Derby refused to act, on the ground that Great Britain would in effect be guaranteeing the loan of a dishonest state, Northcote retorted that the question went 'beyond the rights and wrongs of individuals, and that some very important national interests are involved in it. Large failures affect Commerce and Revenue, and the wholesale bank-ruptcy of our debtors affects the demand for our produce and so cripples trade.'[7]

As the Secretary of State for India, Lord Salisbury was frequently concerned with commercial problems. In 1867 he had been 'strongly favourable' to the demands of chambers of commerce and trade associations for a survey of a possible trade route between Rangoon and western China, although officials in the region denounced the idea as impracticable.[8] A decade later he was anxious to placate the 'Manchester people' on the subject of cotton duties.[9] Salisbury expressed his views on capitalism when he pondered a scheme for the purchase of the East India Railway Company in 1878. He liked it, but wondered whether half a dozen City men would be superior to the government of India: 'To say that mercantile is better than Government management is one of those dangerous platitudes which mislead all the more because from one point of view they are quite true. The management of individuals looking after their own concerns is of course superior to anything else that can be got; but of that there is no question here.' The choice was rather between governmental departments and boards of directors, 'both of them being sets of men paid to look after the concerns of other people'. Directors had the advantage, Salisbury argued, of being 'free from the restrictions to which the Government must submit, and which are increasing every year in weight & number. One inconvenience of Government servants is that they belong to too high a social class. So that they require pay wholly in excess of the value of the work they do.' Although he knew that directors might 'be trusted to buy their own rolling stock', the government would have to see that they bought enough of it instead of swelling dividends. As for the warning from the City that the proposed company was not large or strong enough to attract 'directors of genuine...City standing', Salisbury retorted:

> I have ceased to believe in people of 'standing & position' as agents, when there is anything to be done. They have usually outlived the motives which make men work. Their principal mission is to act as figureheads: to get confidence and elbow room for workers who have still got to climb up to the altitudes of 'standing & position'. But for our purposes this kind of patronage is not required: and we shall get on very well with a humbler class of directors.[10]

Here was a clear recognition of the 'entrepreneurial ideal'.[11] Salisbury was not only to be thrice Foreign Secretary and Prime Minister; he was also a former chairman of the Great Eastern Railway.

Politicians, of course, dealt with problems of business and finance with political considerations in mind. As Chancellor of the Exchequer in 1867, Disraeli had rejected the employment of a French company for postal communication with China: 'So far as I can read opinion, I think it would be dangerous to hanker after the French arrangement.' The House of Commons and 'general public' would object to such an agreement as impolitic, he remarked, 'particularly as regards India' and because 'of the impossibility of establishing any fair competition with an Association' subsidized by its government. He advised making a settlement with the only British tenderer, the P & O, despite the high cost.[12] A year earlier he had jibbed at a proposed treaty with Portugal: 'The difficulties in this matter are no doubt very great, & I am not, myself, inclined to run any risk of injuring our revenue for the sake of a Portuguese expansion of our commerce. But Spain is another matter, &, to secure that market, would justify some hazard & prompt much invention in encountering difficulties.'[13] For Disraeli a small economic gain was not worth a political risk. Conversely, a large economic risk might be worth taking for political gain, as in the purchase of the Suez canal shares in 1875. When he could realize both political and economic advantages, the politician was bound to act.

Governments thus intervened on the Continent from 1860 to assist the growth of the British economy. 'For fifteen years after the repeal of the Corn Laws, England sought to promote free trade by example,' explained the Senior Clerk in the Commercial Department of the Foreign Office, Charles Malcolm Kennedy; 'but papers of argument and facts presented to foreign Governments failed to produce any result.'[14] Only, he asserted retrospectively, 'when a Commercial Treaty Tariff Policy had been established', with the conclusion of the Cobden–Chevalier treaty with France in 1860, did the total value of British exports substantially increase. He concluded

> that the rapid growth of English Export Trade was not the result merely of the adoption by this Country of a Free Trade Policy, nor of the impetus given to Commerce by the great Gold discoveries of this Century, nor of the facilities afforded by new

means of communication; but that this extension of the Export Trade is to be mainly attributed to a policy of Commercial Treaties, containing, as their essential provisions, Tariff stipulations to give effect to freedom of commerce.[15]

At the same time as the aristocracy accepted the importance of capitalist enterprise and the middle class participated increasingly in politics, commercial prosperity was an avowed object of governmental policy.[16]

Financial economy was an important consideration in the making of foreign policy. Successive chancellors of the exchequer had grown accustomed to varying the rate of income tax to cover budgetary deficits. Gladstone failed to win the election of 1874 on the issue of abolishing income tax. Northcote set the rate at 2d in the pound for the next two years. Then British involvement in the Near East, South Africa, Egypt and Afghanistan contributed to sending the rate up to 8d by the mid-1880s. From 1877 annual incomes of less than £150 (rather than the earlier £100) were exempt.[17]

To avoid unpopular expenses, British governments practised economy in administering the empire.[18] In 1869 Edward Cardwell, the Secretary of State for War, insisted that all colonies, except those which he regarded 'for the present purpose...as Imperial Stations', should make financial contributions in support of the British troops defending them. The strength of colonial garrisons declined from 35,000 in 1869 to about 25,000 in 1872.[19] The Conservative government in 1876 refused to reverse this trend, even if the colonies would pay the costs, because of a shortage of recruits for the army.[20] Northcote in 1875 had wanted to do away with the British force in Hong Kong to save £100,000 a year.[21] He later expressed the hope that the colonies would protect British commerce as well as their own territories: 'to show that our Colonies are supports to the Mother Country, – not as some would have it, causes of embarrassment and weakness to her'.[22] Lord Carnarvon, the Colonial Secretary, although exulting in the annexation of Fiji,[23] promptly warned the first governor of the islands, Sir Arthur Gordon, even before he had taken up his post, 'I see very strong reasons for avoiding all possible expenditure that is not necessary'.[24] A year later the Permanent Under Secretary at the Colonial Office exhorted Gordon: 'You are already well aware that the sternest economy will be necessary. This Government and Parliament will, as I have often said, look upon the Government of Fiji as a failure if it continues to cost Imperial money; and I sincerely trust that for your own & everyone's sake you will be able to cut down & keep down expenses.'[25]

Although economy remained a concern after 1865, other considerations began to have a stronger influence on the formulation of British foreign policy. Its makers often reacted to foreign challenges, commercial and industrial, colonial and diplomatic, in the manner of a board of directors responsible for maintaining the national corporation. They preempted competitors, outbid them, or where these methods were inexpedient, concluded the best deal possible, always with an eye to strengthening weak rivals and weakening strong ones. Increasingly the national interest forced upon British policy-makers a conscious awareness of the importance of finance and trade. They became imbued, perhaps subconsciously, with simplified ideas of competitive capitalism. They measured the value of colonial possessions not on the basis of their intrinsic merit but as investments which were worth holding to prevent their falling into the hands of competitors or as speculations against possible future returns. The doctrines of social Darwinism, when they became popular late in the nineteenth century, were a rationalization of attitudes already deeply ingrained in British – and European – society.

Under the impulse of international uncertainties and domestic pressures, ministers nervously watched the entire globe. In November 1874 Disraeli reported to the Queen the Cabinet's recommendation 'to dispatch a new expedition to the North Pole. The discoveries of the Americans, & especially of the Austrians, in this respect of Arctic navigation, have greatly attracted public attention to the subject. Many think [that if] we are on the eve of a solution of the problem it should be solved by England.'[26] In regard to the tropics, organized colonial groups and the press prevented governments abandoning territories which they considered useless. When Gladstone's administration tried to relinquish the Gambia to France in 1870, an inhabitant of that colony posted 'a furious letter' to the editor of the *Daily Telegraph*. The latter felt compelled to publish it, despite a recommendation to the contrary by Lord Clarendon, the Foreign Secretary, because the *Standard*, a Conservative and pro-imperialist daily, had 'been pegging away at the subject for some days past'.[27] Within a week Gladstone responded to colonial pressures and promised not to cede any colony without parliamentary approval.[28] In 1874 Carnarvon faced the same problem: he wanted to be rid of the Gambia.[29] Derby advised him that the House of Commons had opposed the idea before, 'and the present parliament is likely to be inspired with at least as much zeal for the integrity of the British possessions. This is really *the* question.'[30] Derby was right. Carnarvon failed to partition West Africa with the French.[31]

The Gold Coast provided an example of the way in which British governments not only retained colonies but also acquired new ones. A select committee had resolved in 1865 that 'all further extension of territory' in West Africa 'would be inexpedient'.[32] Four years later the Dutch offered to sell their holdings on the coast to Great Britain, and Clarendon was in some doubt 'whether I shd. encourage or throw cold water on the offer....I believe that Parlt. wd. prefer to sell our own to buying others altho trade is beginning to flourish & the French to encroach in those regions.'[33] Lord Granville, the Colonial Secretary, retorted: 'I have little doubt that whether we stay or go from the Gold Coast, it will be an advantage to get rid of the Dutch.' He lamented: 'They are in our way whether we stay or go.'[34] Clarendon agreed. Exasperated at delays in acquiring the Dutch towns, he exclaimed: 'I suppose that stupid pig, the King, will not part with his costly & useless African possessions.'[35] The negotiations bore fruit after Lord Kimberley became Colonial Secretary. He considered the Dutch claim for £24,000 as moderate, and looked forward to concluding a convention recognizing Dutch acquisitions in Sumatra in return for equal trading rights there for British subjects.[36] In April 1872 the British finally occupied the Dutch forts on the Gold Coast. Kimberley had not yet determined to retain them by the end of 1873, although he reckoned that 'we must either do more or give the whole thing up. ...a *half-measure* is what I am most afraid of.'[37] Carnarvon complained in April 1874, 'I have tried hard in many quarters to suggest the idea of abandonment: but I can get no response.'[38] A letter from the editor of *The Times*, J. T. Delane, had prompted this remark. He warned Carnarvon: 'I fear you will not be able to abandon the Gold Coast — now less than ever. Nor am I quite sure you should. The world is growing so small that every patch of territory begins to be looked upon as a stray farm is by a County magnate. Besides,' Delane continued wryly, 'the British Public will not excuse you from the task of civilising the Ashantis and will point out that in the Houssas and other tribes you have the means of raising an army of natives sufficient with a few European Officers for all contingencies.' Lord Derby acidly commented, 'Delane's communication is friendly, but unpleasant. Instead of making slaves of the black men, we seem to have become slaves to them.'[39] A month later, Carnarvon vigorously defended retention of the Gold Coast in the House of Lords.[40]

Domestic pressures and international uncertainties compelled colonial secretaries to retain territory in Africa. Kimberley declared in 1873 that 'talk about an African Empire &c &c &c is simply "bosh"'.[41] He condemned 'the crazy projects attributed to us in the newspapers...when I begin to entertain projects of an African Empire...I hope I shall be put at once in a strait waistcoat.'[42] Statesmen might dislike but they could not entirely ignore the imperialistic tendencies of a politically-active middle class and the press. Then, too, in an era of increasing international rivalry, the maintenance and expansion of the empire might well seem to be in the national interest.

The policy of protecting commerce and preempting rivals was more apparent in Asia than in West Africa. In 1875 Derby argued that, although England did not want to go to war with China, she must insist upon her treaty rights and prevent the closing of that country to her. 'We have asked nothing but what is moderate and just', he asserted, and he advocated avoiding either of two extremes which might lead to a conflict: unreasonable demands or 'an attitude so spiritless, as to lead those with whom we have to do into the belief that we are ready to submit to anything. Our business is to keep a just mean between these two errors.'[43] He believed that this approach to China was politically wise — 'If war is forced upon us, we can't help it, and public opinion will go with us: if we gain our point without war, it will give the government a lift. Any way we stand to win.'[44] British diplomatists carefully watched the actions of the other great powers in the Far East. The minister to Japan was concerned early in 1876 that if Russia occupied a commanding position in Korea, 'then our only *defence* will be to take the best... place ourselves'.[45] Two months later, a British ship began a survey of the Korean coast, though the secretary of legation at Yedo would have preferred to extract treaty concessions by despatching a strong military force, which would compel the Koreans to 'knock under without a struggle'.[46] Interest centred upon Port Hamilton, which was eventually occupied during the Penjdeh crisis in 1885, though later abandoned.[47]

The coastal and island territories bordering the sea passages of south-east Asia were a source of anxiety for the British government. The trade route through the Straits of Malacca, between Sumatra and Malaya, of particular importance since the opening of the Suez canal in 1869, appeared to be vulnerable to disruption. Some Conservatives grumbled about the Liberal government's arrangements with the Dutch, and Lord Cairns privately condemned 'the idiotic surrender' in regard to their annexation of territory in Sumatra. 'The key to our whole commerce to China & Japan lies through these Straits', he argued; '& if the Dutch (which of course means the Germans, or any European power to whom they may cede their rights) hold one side of the Straits, our commerce is at their mercy.'[48] The next year Carnarvon, as Colonial Secretary, feared that the Dutch might lose a local conflict in Sumatra: if so, 'their power will be grievously shaken not only in Sumatra but in Java – and if there in Europe'. To the Foreign Secretary, Derby, he suggested: 'What the effect of a serious weakening of their position colonially would be on European politics is a matter wh. you will fully & readily appreciate. It mt. lead to an appeal to a larger power to extricate them?' Of more urgency to Carnarvon was another consideration: 'Anyhow it mt. very easily lead to a stronger power becoming their substitute in the East and our next neighbor there – wh. wd. involve many questions of difficulty.'[49] At about this time Carnarvon, fearing foreign intervention, and following lines laid down by Kimberley, sanctioned the establishment of residencies in Perak and Selangor, thus ensuring the British hold on the Malayan coast of the Straits of Malacca.[50]

British sensitivity to foreign encroachment extended into other parts of south-east Asia. In 1875 Derby complained when he learned of a proposed Belgian colony in New Guinea: 'I don't like the notion of letting foreigners come so near us. We shall want New Guinea some day for ourselves. Carnarvon agreed with him.[51] In the 1850s the British government had refused to annex Sarawak, where an Englishman, James Brooke, had become rajah. But in 1866 Disraeli's secretary explained to him: 'The importance of acquiring Sarawak is enhanced by the fact that France, Spain, America and Holland have and are extending their settlements on the China Sea. This makes it desirable for us to have a settlement there also for purposes of commerce and war.'[52] A decade later, Carnarvon considered that the second rajah, Charles Brooke, held sway over a 'quasi-English state', and that the course of the British government in regard to the whole of Borneo was 'not favourable to the establishment of any foreign colony'.[53] Great Britain established a protectorate over Sarawak in 1888.[54] In north Borneo the government was guarding approaches into the South China Sea. In Burma, it was protecting the Indian border. Informed in 1877 that Germany contemplated establishing treaty relations with Burma, Derby warned his ambassador in Berlin 'that any clauses in such a Treaty, providing for the importation into Burma of arms and ammunition, or for the employment of foreign troops in Burmese territory, would be held to be prejudicial to British interests'.[55] In 1879 Salisbury advised his successor as Indian Secretary, Lord Cranbrook: 'I think you will have to take Burmah. As a matter of political convenience I should prefer to postpone it till after the general election: but I doubt whether you will have the choice. It certainly ought to be in our hands: though of course we ought to commit no act of aggression.'[56] Finally, in 1886, the Indian Viceroy annexed northern Burma as a buffer against French penetration from Indochina.[57]

India was the most important British colony. In terms of investment and particularly of trade, it was a vital component of Great Britain's economic strength after 1870.[58] India also paid a large share of the bill for maintaining British imperial forces, and hence for the defence of England's status as a great power. Great Britain held the subcontinent by force; yet two-thirds of her army there consisted of natives. A Liberal Viceroy, anxious to prevent parliamentary debates about his domain '& especially "fools from rushing in"', reminded a political ally at home regarding the Indian army that 'we cannot trust it as we can English troops & that this is the root of all the difficulties about organization &c which people write about − many of them forgetting the lesson of the Mutiny. Well, this cannot be said, and therefore upon many matters only second best arguments can be used.'[59] A Conservative Viceroy warned, during the eastern crisis of 1878, that 'in the event of England being involved in any European war, I fear it would be most unsafe to withdraw a single European soldier from India at the present moment'.[60] The Permanent Under Secretary at the India Office, Sir Louis Mallet, referred to 'the only rational ground for the panic with which Russian advances are regarded by a certain class of Anglo-Indians...the feverish dread of insurrection'.[61] The precarious nature of British rule in India made the home government chary of any display of weakness in the subcontinent and quick to defend its colony and the routes of communication to it against foreign encroachment.

Secretaries of state for India in the 1870s acknowledged privately that Great Britain held India to exploit it, but they warned their Cabinet colleagues not to carry that exploitation so far as to precipitate rebellion. Cardwell and Gladstone, among others, had wanted to charge India with the cost of abolishing the purchase system in the British army, asserting that 'India will share largely in the improvement which is effected in the Army by abolition'.[62] The Duke of Argyll protested against this idea in January 1871. He reminded his Liberal colleagues that the British government already charged India 'with the whole of its cost to us. Whatever benefit we derive from our possession of India is a benefit which we derive *gratis*.' He observed that if Britain's relation with India was a partnership, in which the benefits might be divided, 'we are to pay nothing. Our Indian partner is to pay the whole. I am not complaining of this system. It is the system which has always existed, and I suppose it is the system which a conquering nation will always act upon towards the conquered.' The home government charged India 'with the whole pay of the troops employed there, and with all expenses incident to their recruitment and transport', even with the cost of depots which were part of the garrison in England. Further exploitation, Argyll believed, would be impolitic as well as unprincipled. Indian finances were in a precarious state, he warned; and European and native taxpayers, already suspicious of 'Home Charges', could unite and work through the press to embarrass the government: 'Public opinion in India can no longer be denied with safety.'[63] Salisbury cautioned that to encourage the native press was a 'doubtful policy. The habit of taking their opinions from newspapers will come to the natives soon enough and when it comes will be terribly difficult to deal with: but we have no call to develop it prematurely.'[64]

Salisbury, like Argyll, was convinced that India should serve British interests. 'It was time to put a stop to the growing idea that England ought to pay tribute to India as a kind of apology for having conquered her:' he wrote to congratulate Disraeli on a speech in July 1875, '& you have done it effectively.'[65] Some months later he assured a member of the Viceroy's Council:

I have never gone with those who in this country have held the language that England ought to bear India's proper burdens because England is rich and India poor. This is a species of International Communism to which I cannot subscribe. The lowest English taxpayer is, if you measure poverty by suffering, quite as poor as the poorest Indian taxpayer. Let each state bear its own burdens.[66]

Of course one of India's burdens was to support the British economy. Salisbury himself promised in regard to the Indian cotton duties 'to set the tariff right in the sense desired by Lancashire'; and he sent out Sir Louis Mallet, who 'has the confidence of the manufacturers & Chambers of Commerce', to do the job.[67]

Salisbury was anxious that no differences should divide the parties in their treatment of India. For this reason, he recommended that Disraeli advance Lord Northbrook, a Whig, to an earldom when he retired as Viceroy: 'I would not forget that he belongs to an opposite party. It is so important everywhere, & especially in India, that our party conflicts should [not] paralyze the administration, that it is wise in the interests of the Empire, rather to lean in favour of a political opponent.'[68] Salisbury was worried because he had a difference of opinion with Northbrook about the cotton duty: 'I shall be compelled to modify his Tariff in some degree — not only to satisfy pledges given to the manufacturing districts — but also to remove a cause of animosity between Manchester & Bombay which ten years hence may be a serious political danger.' He wanted to avoid any impression 'that Northbrook had fallen a victim to his zeal in defending Indian manufacturers against Manchester selfishness'.[69] The question was one of politics as well as economics. 'All the feeling in England is in favour of the Lancashire manufacturers', Argyll remarked: 'The Tories have a great desire to make love to Manchester & dish the *Whigs*.'[70]

Lord Lytton, who succeeded Northbrook as Viceroy, was determined to use Queen Victoria's new title of Empress of India, which parliament grudgingly bestowed upon her in 1876, to strengthen the British hold on the subcontinent. He explained his scheme to Disraeli:

The proclamation of the new title can, I think, be made an immense and startling success in India, which will immediately react on public opinion at home. ...To the inconsiderate criticism so unscrupulously directed against the new title, there can be but one completely satisfactory answer: — viz the unmistakable enthusiasm of its reception by H.M. Indian subjects, with such marked and immediate improvement in the prestige and popularity of our rule, as will conspicuously demonstrate the wisdom of its adoption.

The Viceroy acknowledged that 'the enthusiasm of Asiatics is never spontaneous. It is easily cooked if you appeal to it in the right way.' Because 'the native population of India is politically dumb', he considered that the title was as yet only potentially popular. He intended to announce the title with great solemnity at a special durbar about 1 January 1877 (because of the climate). But these preparations would be of no use, according to Lytton, unless accompanied by other announcements specially affecting the princes gathered there – and

by a few very simple and inexpensive acts of liberality which will, I am convinced, be received throughout the whole of India with energetic demonstrations of enthusiasm. This enthusiasm will in the meanwhile have been secretly but carefully prepared to explode at the right moment in the right direction. For I must repeat that Asiatic enthusiasm, though by no means insincere, is never spontaneous.

Lytton's arrangements were 'dictated by a careful study of native character'. He wished to present guns and banners to the princes and initiate an Indian peerage, to appeal to their conception of family pedigree: 'Here is a great feudal Aristocracy which we cannot get rid of – which we are avowedly anxious to conciliate & command – but which we have as yet done next to nothing, to rally round the British crown as its *feudal* head.' Lytton believed that the Indian maharajah would do, or pay, anything to add an extra gun to his salute, 'and were we not such puritans we might ere this have made all our railways with resources thus obtained'. He proposed to establish an Indian privy council, which would 'be highly appreciated by them, & in no wise inconvenient to ourselves'. It would not give 'the least real power to the native chiefs' but would provide an opportunity for their visiting the viceregal court and paying obeisance to the supremacy of British power.

The Conservative government received Lytton's plans favourably, in part because of the partisan advantages they offered. The Viceroy was, he assured Disraeli, confident that he could easily create a native enthusiasm which would 'more than justify every argument by which you have defended the political sagacity of the Cabinet, in passing this measure'.[71] Salisbury confided to the Prime Minister:

> I think his principle is sound − that of classes in India, the
> aristocracy is the only one over whom we can hope to establish
> any useful influence. The masses are no use − the literary class,
> which we have unwisely warmed into life before its time, is of its
> nature *frondeur*. Whether the aristocracy themselves are very
> powerful may be doubted: & any popularity we may establish
> with them is not much to lean upon in a moment of trial. But it is
> good as far as it goes: & their goodwill, & cooperation, if we can
> obtain it, will at all events, serve to hide to the eyes of our own
> people &, perhaps, of the growing literary class in India, the
> nakedness of the sword on which we really rely.

Salisbury concluded by calling for secrecy until the adjournment of
parliament, 'as the idea will be pulled to pieces if the other side get
wind of it too soon'.[72] The Viceroy's schemes were, in fact, im-
practical, and he was unable to give effect to most of them. [73] But in
an elaborate ceremony at Delhi on New Year's day, 1877, Lytton
duly proclaimed Victoria Empress of India.

  Because it was believed that India made a vital contribution to
British military strength, economic prosperity, and social stability,
the protection of the empire and routes to it was a primary consideration in formulating foreign policy. India, of course, paid the
cost whenever possible. In January 1869 the Admiralty, India Office
and Foreign Office worked out 'an arrangement under which India
would bear her share of the cost of the East India squadron'.
Gunboats in the Persian Gulf would constitute 'the proposed local
Marine'. The British government was to pay for that part of the
squadron engaged in putting down the slave trade on the east coast
of Africa, according to the First Lord of the Admiralty, '& India the
rest. They would pay about £70.000 a year out of £100.000.'[74] In the
Red Sea, the British had, since 1839, occupied Aden, at the south-
western tip of the Arabian peninsula. Granville lodged a protest at
Constantinople in 1873 when a Turkish pasha claimed authority
over the tribes in the hinterland.[75] Argyll agreed with the Foreign
Secretary's reluctance to establish a protectorate over the tribes at
issue: 'it is better not to have more *Treaties* − because they limit &
hamper our discretion. But Treaty or no Treaty we must look to the
safety of Aden and of its supplies.'[76] In writing to Gladstone on this
subject, Argyll exposed the ruthlessness of the British imperial
commitment:

Aden has always been held to be a necessity for our communications with the East – and now with Australia &c.

We should be great 'muffs' to allow its possession to be endangered by these antiquate claims of Turkey to dominion over the Tribes and Territories on which Aden depends for its supplies.

What I would do is to *act*, with or without Treaties, and tell the Turkish Generals that we will not permit this aggression.

Argyll refused to recognize that the Turks might have some rights in this part of their empire: 'if Turkey sets up as Sovereign of all Arabia, she will come into collision with us'.[77] As Argyll's successor, Salisbury expressed his indignation that the Porte's 'especial object appears now to be to assert all territorial claims which can be in any way inconvenient to Great Britain'.[78] The Indian Secretaries apparently believed that Great Britain had to guard not only the routes to India and strategic points along them, but also all territory in propinquity to those points.

Lord Carnarvon displayed a similar concern with South Africa when the Conservatives were in office. He wanted to acquire Delagoa Bay. Portugal's refusal to sell its colony caused him to remark to the British minister at Lisbon: 'How curious by the way to observe the tenacity with which these wretched little countries cling to their Colonial possessions which they neither can nor try to develope.'[79] A few months later, when arbitration awarded Delagoa Bay to Portugal, he complained: 'This place was *the key of the position as* regards the Dutch States & the award has taken it away from us. ...I own I am very anxious to get hold of it if possible.' He hoped to lease the colony from Portugal for fifty or sixty years and to force the money out of South Africa without approaching parliament.[80] Nothing came of this scheme, but behind it lay the desire to safeguard the Cape route to India for its strategic and commercial value. 'Another Delagoa Bay mt. upset all my plans and do real mischief', Carnarvon complained; and he suggested to Lord Derby asserting English sovereignty all round the coast 'so as to preclude all intrusion whether from within or without?' – as quickly as possible. Derby, as usual, saw no need for action but added, 'Indeed I thought that we did claim a right over all that coast.'[81] When, in December 1875, the Secretary for War was contemplating the withdrawal of troops as an economy measure, Carnarvon informed him: 'My own notion is that the Cape – whatever other route we may possess to India – is of far too great a value to be lightly surrendered & if so the *political* bearings of the question must be studied as well as the merely military ones.'[82] When tensions mounted in South Africa in the summer of 1877, he warned the Prime Minister that the coaling station at Simon's Bay, 'which as I have often pointed out in the Cabinet is the most important one in an Imperial point of view', was unprotected: 'If I remember rightly 190.000.000£ worth of our trade pass the Cape every year. It is these considerations which ought long & long ago to have led to a moderate expenditure: but they have been neglected & we are absolutely defenceless in this part of the world.'[83] Although he counselled the severest economy in Fiji, Carnarvon had no intention of doing so in South Africa, where the route to India was at stake. The one was an outpost, the other guarded the very citadel of an empire which seemed vital to the maintenance of Great Britain's position in the world.

British governments relied upon diplomacy rather than force to guard their interests in Europe. Active intervention on the Continent, they knew, would require a large army, which in both economic and social terms would be expensive to recruit. They attempted to maintain the sanctity of treaties, especially the guarantee of Belgian neutrality, as a substitute for action. When, in 1868, King Leopold complained of French interference with his country's railway lines, the Conservative Foreign Secretary, Lord Stanley, commented: 'The Belgian government, backed by our Queen, desires to turn the European guarantee which now exists into what will be *de facto* an exclusive British protectorate.' For England, he declared to Disraeli, the results would be 'the loss of all the military advantage which our insular position gives us, and the erection of a second Hanover'.[84] A few months later, although Gladstone instructed Lord Clarendon to convince the French that Belgian independence was 'an object of the first interest to the mind of the British people',[85] he was not prepared to make any commitments in that regard. The Queen's private secretary, General Charles Grey, was, according to Gladstone, 'inclined to be valiant on the subject of fighting even alone for Belgium but I do not see how it is safe to go beyond making it known that the day when this nation seriously suspects France of meaning ill to Belgian independence will be the last day of friendship with that country, and that then a future will open for which no man can answer'.[86] Gladstone warned Grey of the domestic risks of involvement in a continental conflict: 'For though Europe never saw England faint away, *we* know at what a cost of internal danger to all the institutions of the country, she fought her way to the perilous eminence on which she undoubtedly stood in 1815.'[87]

When the Franco-Prussian war broke out in July 1870, words rather than deeds characterized British policy towards Belgium. Gladstone was reluctant to make proposals to augment the army and navy 'on account of the shock it would give to public confidence with regard to the position of this country'.[88] Conservative leaders insisted that the army 'ought not to be wholly unprepared'.[89] They wanted the government to secure Belgium against any threat from either of her two warring neighbours − without fighting.[90] It did so by signing separate treaties with France and Prussia guaranteeing Belgian neutrality.[91] These engagements seemed to Gladstone preferable to preparing the British army for a possible cross-Channel expedition.[92] Although parliament had approved additions to the army and a vote of credit, the Prime Minister wanted to remove any pretext for intervention on the Continent. He feared that if England merely armed she would worsen her relations with both belligerents and bring about a combination between them 'in the face of which our army would run the risk of becoming ridiculous'.[93] The government tried to give the impression that it would take sides against a violator of Belgian territorial integrity, but it had no intention of acting alone. The British interest was to prevent the hegemony of any power in western Europe. In 1870 the diplomacy of Gladstone appeared to be both cheap and effective. Such successes became more difficult to achieve in the future.

The unification of Italy and especially of Germany shifted the balance of power in Europe and deepened British suspicions of all the major Continental states. The German armies had, in the autumn of 1870, broken the strength of France.[94] Disraeli, informed by the war correspondent of the *Standard* that Bismarck would demand territorial annexations 'as a glacis',[95] mused, 'France seems rapidly falling into the state it was [in] under Charles the 7th,' concluding with the air of a roué grown old: 'There were no men then, but at least they found, in time, a maiden; a rarer animal now, perhaps, in all countries than in those days.'[96] The proclamation of a government of national defence in Paris on 4 September 1870, following the capture of Napoleon III at Sedan, caused British politicians some anxiety. 'French Republics are not agreeable neighbours,' declared Gathorne Hardy.[97] Granville owned to Gladstone that, though 'personally better inclined to the French than you are', he was apprehensive of any rumour of 'a red Republic at Paris'.[98] Salisbury, who regretted the German triumphs, declared: 'Whatever else Bismarck does I do hope he will burn down the Faubourg St. Antoine and crush out the Paris mob. Their freaks and madnesses have been a curse to Europe for the last eighty years.'[99] Underlying this hatred of the French Republic was fear that it could inspire agitation against the existing social order in England. Political meetings protesting against the government's policy toward France during the autumn of 1870 were the largest held in London since 1866.[100] Six months later, the Commune intensified the British animus against Parisian radicalism. Afterwards, even the Republic seemed preferable to 'the Reds'.[101] During the 1870s drawn-out negotiations over replacing the commercial treaty of 1860 hardly improved Anglo-French relations.[102]

Members of both British parties viewed with misgivings the ascendancy of Germany in Europe. Although bearing in mind 'how easily in supporting France we may be drawn into a support of republicanism for which the mob is already with its own natural instinct clamouring', Carnarvon was not 'insensible to the opposite dangers wh. arise out of the tremendous growth of German power'.[103] This consideration, reinforcing his sense of moral outrage, impelled Gladstone to condemn the annexation of Alsace and Lorraine.[104] Granville suspected that Bismarck 'has probably got some engagement with Russia..., may have views upon Belgium ..., may entertain a notion of a triple league with Russia & the United States to humble us'. He explained to the editor of *The Times*: 'My own belief is that Bismarck hates England abstractedly [sic], & 2dly because she is the great centre of liberal ideas.' He was ready to give credence to stories about 'the manufacture of hostile feeling against England' in Germany.[105] Granville advised Gladstone: 'The only weapon I know to oppose Bismarck's possible insolence to us, is moral support to German liberalism.'[106] On the Prime Minister's recommendation, he instructed the Permanent Under Secretary at the Foreign Office, Edmund Hammond, to send a translation of the speech of a German liberal to a London newspaper.[107] Anglo-German antagonism was evident even before the establishment of the second Reich in January 1871.[108]

Interests and political sentiment alienated Great Britain from Russia and Austria-Hungary as well as from Germany and France. In the minds of many Liberals especially, the two former states were enemies of freedom, oppressors of their own people and of other nationalities. Statesmen of both parties viewed Russian and Austrian diplomacy as unstable, subject to change with the will of an autocratic emperor. Russia seemed to menace the Indian empire. In central Asia her territorial expansion was encroaching upon the buffer state of Afghanistan. In the Near East she pressed upon the Ottoman empire, through which ran British lines of communication with India, the Far East and the Antipodes. Austria was disinclined to assist England in the Balkans or at Constantinople; she could not face a conflict with Russia without the sanction of Germany, and Bismarck refused to give it. Edmund Hammond commented on the Austrian Foreign Minister in November 1870: 'I am afraid it is perfectly impossible to expect that Count Beust will run straight upon any subject, for he seems to have a settled opinion on none; and I have no doubt would leave us in the lurch, if we assented to any proposal that he might make...; though perhaps he is not worse than his predecessors of 1855 when dealing with an Eastern question, which he does not understand. He has too many irons in the fire, and he can never weld them together.'[109] Hammond cared little for Count Julius Andrassy, who became Foreign Minister in 1871: 'He seems to be worse even than Beust.'[110] Andrassy's despatch of his predecessor as ambassador to London increased distrust there of Austrian diplomacy. The fact that Great Britain had little to offer Austria could not alter Hammond's obstinate prejudice. The formation of the Dreikaiserbund, linking Germany, Austria-Hungary and Russia, exacerbated British suspicions of the Continental powers.

The Continental and imperial commitments were the basis of British foreign policy. Salisbury was an astute politician who recognized that public opinion was an increasingly important factor in the maintenance of British interests in Europe and the empire. During the Franco-Prussian war a Danish correspondent suggested to him 'that, after the disappearance of the old party-landmarks in the home-policy of England, a new and more solid basis of the reconstruction of a Conservative or Tory party might be found in a firm and resolute foreign policy'.[111] Salisbury replied:

I wish that there was any chance of awakening England to the necessity or the duty of sustaining upon the Continent the position which she acquired and held in former times. Such a revival of feeling on her part would not only draw classes together in this country and purify our internal conflicts from the material element which is coming to be dominant in them; but it would prove an important guarantee for the maintenance of the present structure of Europe.

But Salisbury asserted 'that any such revival of feeling in England is chimerical'. He did not think 'the statesmen' were to blame:

> The fault really lies in the change in the nature of the spirit of the English nation. They do not wish, as they formerly did, for great national position, and they are glad to seclude themselves from European responsibilities by the protection which their insular position is supposed to give them. ...The great middle classes and the professional classes with whom power in this country really resides, have deliberately turned away from the ancient aims and policy of England in foreign affairs.[112]

These observations, though unduly pessimistic, were prescient. Salisbury had articulated some of the assumptions about foreign policy which were generally left unspoken.[113]

Gladstone and Disraeli tried to act upon them. In doing so, they had to take account of not only rivalries between the parties but also the divisions within them. Since Palmerston's death had extinguished the pole star of the parliamentary firmament, the two party leaders navigated the political seas largely by reference to one another. At the same time they had to work diligently to keep their party barques afloat amid the tempests of politics. Parties were the means through which sections of the middle, and later the lower, classes successively carried on their struggle for governmental recognition of their interests. Various and often competing social forces gathered round the banners of Conservatism and Liberalism.

Gladstone's calculations were difficult because Whigs and Radicals held divergent opinions on foreign affairs. The former generally favoured the active pursuit of British Continental and imperial interests. Lord Granville, the Whig Foreign Secretary, assured Gladstone in December 1870: 'A sort of sentiment that the bumps of combativeness and destructiveness are to be found somewhere in your head has helped us much during the last five months.'[114] The Prime Minister readily admitted as much: 'All know the mischief done by the Russian idea of Lord Aberdeen & the Opposition are in the habit of studiously representing me as his double, or his heir, in pacific traditions. This I do not conceive to be true.'[115] Gladstone acknowledged, despite his pleas for economy, that military and naval strength was a vital adjunct to the diplomacy of a great power. But he knew that many Radicals, already alienated by the government's legislation, objected to large military expenditures or a concentration on foreign affairs. Largely middle class and Nonconformist, they wanted satisfaction of their own social and political demands. Their most prominent spokesman was John Bright. On the verge of resigning from the Cabinet in November 1870, he warned Gladstone: 'Be strong for peace — and show a good front against the "services" and all who would urge you to military preparations. Every man added to the forces and every ship put into Commission strengthens your opponents and weakens your own power.'[116]

Gladstone's solution was to apply moral principles to international relations and to stress the concept of a concert of Europe. He adopted this approach when Russia denounced the Black Sea clauses of the treaty of Paris (1856) at the end of October 1870. Although the press raised a bellicose clamour which 'much disgusted' Gladstone, the Cabinet was 'very sensible'.[117] A Whig member described privately how it had dealt with the Russians: 'We have sent them a strong protest against the manner of this proceeding, but hinted that we might consent to a revision of the Treaty by all the powers. However it looks very nasty & I hope we shall not be too humble.'[118] Granville claimed to have been firm enough on one occasion to have sent the aged Russian ambassador '3 times to the water closet'; but he failed to convince his own Parliamentary Under Secretary, who resigned after advocating showing 'a bold front to Russia'.[119] The British government proposed a conference in London, which Granville believed would 'satisfy public opinion in this country'.[120] When the representatives of the powers met, the German ambassador warned that 'the question of Peace or War in the East was directly involved in the issue of their negotiations';[121] but the result was a foregone conclusion. The conference sanctioned the Russian action. Yet Gladstone could claim to have forced Russia to the bargaining table and avoided the expense and immorality of preparing for war, thereby hoping to placate both sections of his party. During the eastern crisis of 1875–8 and the Midlothian campaigns of 1879–80, he further developed his ideas of international morality and a European concert in an attempt to keep the support of Whigs and win that of Radicals on issues of foreign policy.

For Disraeli, as for Gladstone, foreign policy offered a means of uniting his party. Many Conservatives who held different opinions on religious or social matters were agreed during the Franco-Prussian war in their concern for the army and navy, and felt that 'the Governm[en]t appear to be in a state of bewilderment'.[122] Carnarvon explained: 'One thing at least is clear to me − if we are not prepared to place ourselves in a very different position of military defence & preparation we shall do wisely to withdraw from all corners [?] in the foreign affairs of Europe. But even then I do not believe that our present military preparations are adequate for bare self-defence.'[123] Lord John Manners informed Disraeli in October 1870 that the Liberal policy of economy was unpopular and advised that England should be ready to send fifty thousand men, out of a standing army of twice that number, to the Continent at the outbreak of a war: 'With an overpowering fleet, and that force available she would then be able to exercise an influence in Europe, of which since the Danish disgrace she has been deprived.'[124] In advance of the parliamentary session of 1871, the Conservative Chief Whip, Gerard Noel, took the pulse of the party and the country and reported to Disraeli:

> There is a general feeling among the influential men of our party that there should be a long Debate on the Address and that our leaders should speak out strongly both on foreign affairs and the state of the defences of the country. I heard from many quarters that the 'cautious utterances' of Lord Derby are doing us harm & that his Preston speech has excited considerable disapproval [?], I may say condemnation, in Lancashire. The mass of the people especially the working men there feel very [? strongly] on the question of foreign politics, and say that Mr. Gladstone has altogether neglected the duty of England in Europe.[125]

Disraeli appreciated Noel's advice and acted on it. Derby's position was of particular concern to him.

Derby was the major obstacle to Disraeli's adoption of an active foreign policy that would safeguard British interests abroad and strengthen the Conservative party at home. Many Conservatives, probably including Disraeli himself, considered that Derby would one day become Prime Minister. His low church views and the respect in which he was held in the party and by the new electorate made him a valuable ally for Disraeli, especially since Salisbury and

Carnarvon, both high churchmen, still distrusted him. Derby was supposed to exercise a strong territorial influence in Lancashire, an area crucial to Conservative hopes in the next general election. For Disraeli, losing his support might mean losing control of the party, either immediately or after electoral setbacks precipitated by reversals in Lancashire. Derby was a former Foreign Secretary as well as the Lord of Knowsley, and his speeches on foreign affairs attracted attention. Although he favoured proposals for strengthening the navy, reforming the army, and increasing the militia, his complacent attitude toward the international situation exasperated his chief. 'Where is the enemy?' he asked in January 1871.[126]

Disraeli tried to arouse in Derby an awareness of the domestic political aspects of foreign policy. He concurred in Derby's opinion that Great Britain faced no immediate foreign threat:

> I am not, however, sorry to see the country fairly frightened about foreign affairs. 1st, because it is well that the mind of the nation should be diverted from that morbid spirit of domestic change and criticism, which has ruled us too much for the last forty years, and that the reign of priggism should terminate. It has done its work, and in its generation very well, but there is another spirit abroad now, and it is time that there shd. be.

In this broad interpretation Disraeli adopted the role of the elder statesman, or perhaps the novelist. As a defender of the landed aristocracy and a party leader, he gave two more reasons for encouraging a revival of interest in foreign affairs.

> 2nd, because I am persuaded that any reconstruction of our naval and military systems, that is practicable, will, on the whole, be favourable to the aristocracy, by wh. I mean particularly the proprietors of land: and 3rdly because I do not think the present party in power are well qualified to deal with the external difficulties wh. await them.

Disraeli considered that the government had reduced military strength unjustifiably, 'completely blundered the business when the crisis arrived', and failed to 'comprehend our present position. On all these points I shall attack them,' he informed Derby, 'and I shall not discourage the country. And I hope you will not.'[127]

Through the medium of politics, Gladstone and Disraeli

responded to Great Britain's imperial and Continental commitments. Foreign policy, though formulated by the Foreign Office and
Cabinet in accord with British interests, was subject to political
debate at Westminster and in the country. By January 1876, when
Disraeli was Prime Minister, the purchase of the shares in the Suez
canal company and the controversy over the Andrassy note had
stimulated his interest and that of popular opinion in matters of
foreign policy. During a Cabinet meeting he passed a brief note to
his Foreign Secretary: 'As there are many special subjects, wh. must
be noticed in the Queen's speech, I shall so draw it as not to pledge
ourselves to much domestic legislation. We can't have too much
foreign. Its the taste of the day.'[128] The stage was set for the eastern
crisis.

2 Party Politics in the Eastern Question

After revolts against Ottoman rule in Herzegovina and Bosnia in the summer of 1875 focused the attention of the European powers on Turkey, Disraeli hoped to use the issues involved to strengthen his government at home as well as to further Great Britain's imperial and Continental interests. Believing that the support of Lord Derby, the Foreign Secretary, and to a lesser extent, Lord Salisbury, the Secretary of State for India, was essential to the unity of his party and government, Disraeli made diligent efforts to convince them, and other members of his Cabinet, of the necessity for an active foreign policy. When the Prime Minister accepted a peerage, as Earl of Beaconsfield, he chose a successor in the House of Commons in accordance with Derby's predilections and to avoid factionalism among Conservatives such as that which had rent the opposition. The contest for the Liberal leadership in the Commons after Gladstone's withdrawal was an indication of the divisions in the party which rendered its criticisms of governmental policy ineffective. Lord Hartington, who assumed that position, and Lord Granville, the Liberal leader in the House of Lords, were Whigs who were generally in agreement with the government's diplomatic objectives. They spoke out in opposition when pressed to do so by their own followers and in order to retain control over them. The agitation over the Bulgarian atrocities which began in the summer of 1876 was a challenge by Radical Nonconformists not only to Conservative policy but also to the Whigs and moderates who led the Liberal party. Gladstone's hesitant participation in the campaign represented an attempt to hold the party together. Beaconsfield assuaged his colleagues who were worried by the agitation and sent Salisbury as British plenipotentiary to a conference on the eastern question at Constantinople.

As Prime Minister, Disraeli remained what he had been as leader of the opposition, a politician. 'In legislation,' he believed, 'it is not

31

merely reason & propriety, wh. are to be considered, but the temper of the Time.'[1] He insisted that when his colleagues judged issues, especially those which attracted public attention, 'we must be careful to consider the *political*, as well as the *departmental*, side of questions'.[2] Some years later, Salisbury complained of Disraeli: 'his fault was want of firmness. The chiefs of departments got their own way too much – the cabinet as a whole got it too little, – and this necessarily followed from having at the head of affairs a statesman whose only fixed political principle was that the party must on no account be broken up and who shrank therefore from exercising coercion on any of his subordinates.'[3] Disraeli's method of conducting business was understandable. He remembered the difficulties of leading the party after the reform act of 1867. Among his present Cabinet of twelve members were a marquis, three earls, a duke, a duke's son, the Lord Chancellor and a baronet. Derby calculated in the summer of 1877 that, including Lord John Manners, the heir to the Rutland estates, half of his colleagues laid claim to more than 10,000 acres each, two others to more than 5000.[4] Disraeli was not in a good position to coerce his colleagues; he had, rather, to reconcile them not only to his own leadership but also to each other.

Disraeli treated foreign affairs in the same spirit as he did domestic. By speaking informally with Derby and Salisbury, the two ministers chiefly concerned in setting foreign policy, he tried to settle matters affecting their respective spheres of influence.[5] Sometimes he called the two of them together, as when in July 1876 he suggested to the Indian Secretary that the Russian ambassador 'shd. be a little checked in his reckless assertions. We need not bring it before the Cabinet, but I think you & Derby & myself might talk the matter over together.'[6] So long as the three of them agreed, the other members of the Cabinet were unlikely to oppose them. Reaching an agreement often posed a difficulty. Derby had a whiggish temperament, preferring pragmatism to principle, detesting initiatives, bowing to change when it was inevitable. Salisbury was a high Tory who tried to fix firm guidelines for action. Disraeli disliked both prevarication and rigidity. He wanted a foreign policy flexible enough to enable him, in any circumstance, to meet the needs of Great Britain abroad and the Conservative party at home.

The Prime Minister distrusted traditional diplomatists. In some cases he had reason. The Austrian ambassador, Count Frederick von Beust, and the Russian, Count Peter Shuvalov, were seemingly at odds with their respective Foreign Ministers, Count Julius Andrassy and Prince Alexander Gorchakov, whom they hoped to succeed. Disraeli was often exasperated with his own representatives abroad. He advised Derby regarding Sir Andrew Buchanan:

> I wish we had an other man at Vienna. He is most insipid. In the age of Bismarck, this post resumes something of its ancient importance...it is not age, which has enfeebled his intelligence or dimmed his powers. He was, and ever has been, a hopeless mediocrity....Buchanan should be confidentially communicated with, and told that he should resign.

Of Sir Henry Elliot at Constantinople, Disraeli complained, 'His conduct has seriously compromised, and damaged, the Government.'[7] He branded Lord Augustus Loftus in St Petersburg, against whom he had a prejudice of long standing, 'a mere mouthpiece of Gortchakoff' and a 'mere Livadian parasite...afraid even of G's shadow'.[8] Salisbury bore witness that these criticisms had some foundation: 'The feebleness of the service at all the Eastern Courts except Berlin is a positive calamity.'[9] Sometimes Disraeli did not admit even that exception.[10] The basis of his dissatisfaction with diplomatists was the unresponsiveness of their craft to the political concerns which were uppermost in his own mind. He seemed vexed that ambassadors were permanent officials, for he would have preferred that they change with every ministry.[11]

As Foreign Secretary, Derby served Disraeli's purposes poorly. Whether as cause or consequence of differences with his famous father, Derby suffered from emotional instability. He manifested an obsessive acquisitive instinct. His personality was unsuited for the rough and tumble of modern party politics. Despite his portliness, he enjoyed long walks in solitude or with his wife, Mary, the widow of the second Marquis of Salisbury and stepmother of the third. Socially, he felt more comfortable in the company of a friend than in large gatherings. Although intelligent, he was a ponderous thinker. In conversation, he gave an impression of indecisiveness. He admitted that 'writing clears one's ideas, and makes a subject familiar: which with me hearing other people talk about it does not'.[12] He took notes in Cabinet meetings and wrote, on average, more than forty letters a year to Disraeli, whom he met almost daily during parliamentary sessions, in the last decade of their political association. Derby approached politics with paternalism and anxiety. As the head of a great family, he imagined that he could serve the state disinterestedly, primarily as a minister not a politician. He was in sympathy with his permanent officials. Convinced of the supreme importance of the *haute politique* of diplomacy, they looked with condescension upon domestic politics. Petty aristocrats and gentry, they were mired in the bureaucratic routine of their department. Their hauteur was a defensive reaction against the world beyond Whitehall, where capitalism and the middle classes were altering the character of society and the new electorate was transforming the bases of political power.

Although Derby found the Foreign Office a convenient refuge from these forces, he could not ignore them. He recognized, for example, the importance of finance in the making of foreign policy.[13] In the initial stage of the crisis in the east he remarked,

> Opinion seems utterly confused & divided on the eastern controversy, and the only thing clear is that no real settlement is possible: only a temporary delay. Meanwhile we gain politically: petty questions of administration, and small subjects of criticism, are pushed into the background when a European complication occurs: and with tolerable management it is always possible to keep opinion favorable.[14]

Derby met journalists regularly at the Foreign Office. Especially with Edward Levy Lawson of the *Daily Telegraph* and Frederick Greenwood of the *Pall Mall Gazette*, he frequently held lengthy discussions. He explained his techniques to Frank Hill, editor of the Liberal *Daily News*, in January 1876:

> An editorial levee. Mr Hills' was a first visit, he came for information. I made him a little speech, disclaiming all wish to bias his judgment, but expressing willingness on public grounds to supply him with facts: he answered chiefly to the effect that foreign affairs are not now a party question: which is true enough.[15]

Yet at this very time Disraeli was determined to make political capital out of foreign policy. The end result was an open break between him and Derby.

In their methods of conducting foreign policy, the contrast between the Prime Minister and Foreign Secretary was apparent. Although both men read the private reports of British diplomatists abroad,[16] Derby, unlike Disraeli, spurned unorthodox sources of information. In May 1874 Lord Malmesbury, a former Foreign Secretary and now Lord Privy Seal, sent to the Prime Minister a report on French politics 'wh I think you shd send to Derby to read altho' I believe he holds private information & its *professors* cheap. I think one gets some corn out of their chaff & so did Metternich, Nesselrode, Pam, & Clarendon.'[17] Disraeli placed a great emphasis on the role of finance in determining the foreign policy of nations, as did Salisbury, who remarked to one of his Indian Viceroys: 'the effect of modern changes is constantly to diminish the value of strategic positions, and to increase the value of pecuniary resources'.[18] Disraeli prized intelligence from the heads of great banking houses, the Rothschilds and Gerson von Bleichröder, whose own fortunes depended upon their multifarious international connections, and he sometimes used them for confidential communications.[19] He turned these associations to diplomatic account: most obviously in purchasing the Suez canal shares, less so in practising a species of international blackmail *à la bourse*.[20] He lent an ear to society gossip. And he used the press for purposes of state and party more brazenly than Derby dared to do.

Considerations of both foreign policy and domestic politics compelled Disraeli to give his attention to the eastern question. Here, where Great Britain's Continental and imperial commitments were both at stake, he was determined to pursue a course independent of the other great powers. He reassured Derby: 'I think you will find, that public opinion will ratify your policy.'[21] To an inquiry from the Queen, he answered: 'your Majesty's fleet has not been ordered to the Mediterranean to protect Christians, or Turks, but to uphold Your Majesty's Empire.'[22] Toward the end of May 1876, he proclaimed to Derby: 'I am well satisfied with what we have done... and so far as I can judge, or learn, public opinion ratifies our course.'[23] The Prime Minister sought a diplomatic victory that would redound to British credit abroad and the government's at home.

By June 1876 Disraeli was under the impression that he had achieved his objectives of weakening the Dreikaiserbund and of winning domestic approval for his policy. 'Our refusal of the Berlin note is a success both at home & abroad,' exulted Derby.[24] Privately, he admitted that the government's display of naval force and its general attitude had also been 'a success. We are more respected & consulted than has been common of late years.'[25] Sir

Henry Elliot was delighted 'to find H. M. Govt. adopting the independent line they have followed, in which they seem to be approved by public opinion in [a] great part of Europe'.[26] Lord Lytton, the Viceroy of India, wrote in flattering terms from Simla to Montagu Corry, Disraeli's private secretary: 'Our recent foreign policy...is certainly the greatest international success England has had since the *early* days of Palmerston.'[27] In domestic politics, Disraeli bragged to the Queen, 'the Ministry, after all the struggles, is confessed by all parties, to be stronger than at the commencement of the Session; or indeed at any period since its formation'.[28] The Queen's private secretary, a Liberal in his sympathies, commented on this letter: 'he thinks Mr Disraeli is right in congratulating himself on the position of the Government which certainly stands better now than it did at the beginning of the Session. The Foreign Policy of the Government seems to receive general approval...and there does not seem to be any domestic question that is likely to cause trouble.'[29]

After enjoying apparent successes at home and abroad, Disraeli arranged with the Queen to take a peerage. Ill health and the work of the House of Commons so tired him that he had difficulty managing Cabinet sessions. Derby, as well as other ministers, noticed 'that there is less order & method in our Cabinets than there used to be: Disraeli often appears half asleep, takes no part, and much time is wasted in loose talk'.[30] Initially, Disraeli had suggested that he might retire altogether.[31] The Queen had been 'a little incredulous on this head', and urged him to remain as Prime Minister and go to the Lords. 'Having no heir...& in the sunset of life', Disraeli shrank from this course, he explained to a friend: 'So, I begged to adhere to my purpose, & to be permitted to enquire, whether it might not safely be fulfilled. The result proved that the Queen had a finer appreciation of the circumstances than myself & I found my withdrawal would lead to serious consequences.' He hoped that he had acted wisely: 'all I can say is I have done it for the comfort of my Sovereign, & for the welfare of the Party, that has so long entrusted to me their interests.' He had intended to delay the announcement until November 1876.[32] But when Malmesbury decided to retire from the Privy Seal Office in August, [33] Disraeli took that post and introduced Sir Michael Hicks Beach, the Chief Secretary for Ireland, into the Cabinet. The balance between peers and commoners in that body thereby remained the same.

Complete retirement was impossible for Disraeli, because he

seemed to be the only leader who could keep the government and the party together.[34] Questions of political and social change continued to divide Conservatives, as the acrimonious debate over the public worship regulation act had demonstrated two years earlier. Religion was a social more than a theological issue. The Anglican Church was a buttress of the traditional order. Its treatment was a matter of political controversy in much the same way that electoral reform had been a decade before. Within the Cabinet, Salisbury, Lord Carnarvon, the Colonial Secretary, and G. Gathorne Hardy, the Secretary of State for War, were high churchmen; Derby, low; and Cairns, the Lord Chancellor, evangelical. Disraeli wanted Hardy, a stiff debater and eloquent Tory moralizer, to succeed him as leader in the House of Commons. Lady Derby, supposedly without her husband's knowledge, warned the Prime Minister on 10 July:

> Stanley [that is, Derby] is quite upset at the thought of the smallest opening being given to Mr. Hardy to seize the leadership in the H. of C. He thinks he might ask for time to consult his friends & that perhaps a section of them — say the Oxford High Church party might press upon him the duty of not giving way to Sir S. Northcote.[35]

As a friend of Hardy, Frederick Stanley had told his brother's wife 'some months ago that H. knew Stanley [Derby] wd. be disinclined to work with him &c &c'.[36] This knowledge did not dispel the bitterness Hardy felt when Disraeli chose Northcote as his successor in the House of Commons.[37] Northcote was a pleasant man and diligent worker who did not antagonize any particular Tory faction; and the Queen liked him.[38] That he did not possess Hardy's fighting qualities hardly seemed to matter when Disraeli expected to leave the Commons in triumph. The selection satisfied Derby, who commented adversely on Hardy's 'somewhat extreme devotion to clerical interests — increased by his Oxford connection. ...His elevation would have been regarded as a triumph of the high-church & ultra section.'[39]

The Liberal opposition began to stir as evidence accumulated to support rumours of Turkish brutality and murder in Bulgaria. Disraeli, 'with[ou]t sufficient information' from the Foreign Office, had to postpone answering a question on the subject in the House of Commons.[40] The Permanent Under Secretary, Lord Tenterden, ill and overworked, was concentrating upon editing a blue book on the eastern question to 'read very well for the Government'.[41] He belittled an account of atrocities in Bulgaria contained in a despatch of the British consul at Rustchuk as a story told by a Turk in a café; and he affirmed that the Foreign Office had '*not had reports of the particular atrocities mentioned in the* "Daily News["]'.[42] He promised Disraeli a memorandum 'to take out of town at 3 *if you desire it* — so that you may be quite prepared on Monday'.[43] In a rage, the Prime Minister demanded of one of his secretaries: 'What does he mean with his "ifs" — ? Everything depends on my having papers now.'[44] Disraeli withstood the Liberals' parliamentary criticisms, which were poorly organized, during July and August 1876. He then retired from the House of Commons. If he hoped that the opposition would present no stronger challenge in the future than it had in the past, he was mistaken. The campaign over the Bulgarian atrocities had begun.

The atrocities agitation was, in the broadest sense, a political movement. Nonconformists in the north of England provided most of the volatile fuel for the fires of its passion. The agitationists couched their sympathy for the Bulgarians in religious and moral terms. Their dissent over foreign policy, ostensibly directed against Turk and Tory, was a challenge to the leaders of the Liberal party. In providing the only effective opposition to the government, the forces behind the new Radicalism were staking their claim to share control of the party with the social groups represented by Whigs and moderates. W. T. Stead, editor of the *Northern Echo* in Darlington and a principal organizer of the campaign, pressed Gladstone to join: 'It is still the cherished hope of the North Country that you may once more lead us to victory, & that hope has certainly not been weakened by recent occurrences abroad.'[45] The motives and enthusiasm of the agitation aroused the distrust of Hartington, Granville and most of their prominent colleagues. Lord Halifax, who was mainly concerned about the security of communications with India, asked Granville to impress upon Gladstone 'the wisdom of looking before he leaps'. The people were 'running a little wild on the Bulgarian atrocities,' he remarked: 'But a person in Gladstones position ought to look forward, & consider what policy this country is to pursue in regard to the Eastern question, & take care that he says nothing inconsistent with what we shd have to do if in power, or ought to urge on the existing Govt.'[46]

Gladstone was reluctant to participate in the agitation. He did not want to give the lie to his professed loyalty to Hartington and Granville; and he shared the Whigs' misgivings about the naive declamations of the agitators regarding British policy in the Near East. Perhaps most significantly, he rejected the ultimate common goal of the Radicals: disestablishment of the Church of England. He was anxious to avoid being ensnared by the Nonconformists for purposes inimical to his own beliefs and to the existing social order. He conceived, correctly, that for politically active Nonconformists disestablishment was the symbol of a desire to wield power. If they forfeited the symbol, he was willing to accept them as partners in the management of the Liberal party. He imagined that the bourgeois Radicals would be junior partners in a relationship dominated by the aristocracy and upper middle class.

To accomplish this purpose, Gladstone publicly emphasized the moral rather than the political aspects of the Bulgarian atrocities. He did so the more readily because this approach accorded with his own religious outlook. For him, ecumenical Christianity was the theological equivalent of the diplomatic concept of a concert of Europe. A crusade of Christians in defence of their fellow-religionists in the Balkans oppressed by Turkish infidels proved an irresistible attraction for Gladstone. He calculated: 'As a party question this affords no despicable material, but there are higher interests involved.' He reckoned at first that the issue might be a useful one for the opposition when parliament opened the next February.[47] Then, as the agitation in England grew and captured enough attention to warrant 'a meeting for the Bulgarians in Hyde Park', the inspiration of combining moral mission with political advantage affected Gladstone for the first time since the dispiriting disintegration of his administration. 'And altogether I feel more inclined to say something, during the recess, on the Turkish policy,' he warned Granville, 'than I have been for any such escapade during the last four years.'[48] Gladstone sympathized with the Duke of Argyll, who was 'so indignant with the tone of the F.O. and with the utter & abject selfishness of what they are pleased to call our "Policy", that I feel as if I must give tongue on the subject *somehow*, and *somewhere*, during the autumn or winter'.[49] Although Gladstone felt a similar sense of moral outrage, he gave vent to it with the carefulness of a consummate politician.

Gladstone attempted to use the moral fervour of the agitation for political purposes. His address at Blackheath on 9 September 1876 was an example of his craftsmanship. Its form was that of a revival meeting, with a 'respectable' middle class in attendance, and pleased the Radicals; its substance was so bland as not to frighten the Liberal leadership.[50] His pamphlet on the *Bulgarian Horrors and the Question of the East* was a contribution not only to the agitation but also to the Liberal campaign to capture the Buckinghamshire seat which Disraeli had held for three decades before his elevation to the peerage. Upon publication of the pamphlet, Gladstone sent '250 little ones' to the Liberal candidate, Rupert Carington; and obsessed by 'Bucks, Bucks, Bucks', he continued to give Granville gratuitous advice on marshalling votes in the constituency.[51] At the polls on 22 September, the Conservatives won a small majority: 'too near a thing to be pleasant' for them and 'a good result' for the Liberals.[52] Afterwards, Gladstone largely refrained from participation in the national atrocities campaign, which was beginning to falter. He claimed to be 'a follower & not a leader in the Liberal party' and 'to have done all in my power' to keep his role in the eastern question 'apart from the general course of politics & of party connection'.[53] His speech and pamphlet nonetheless identified him with the movement, gladdening the Radical Nonconformists and discomforting his former colleagues.

By the beginning of October 1876 Whigs and moderate Liberals had turned strongly against the atrocities agitation. Lord Kimberley considered that, although the government had blundered in its handling of both foreign policy and the reports from Bulgaria, 'the violent & unreasoning agitation renders the question immensely more difficult'.[54] Lord Spencer was 'amazed' at the anti-atrocitarian view taken 'by all men who I thought were staunch Liberals. They all are outspoken agst. Gladstone & are hot Russianphobists.'[55] W. V. Harcourt reported that 'the commercial men...who find their pecuniary interests greatly damaged by the present state of things' joined the Whigs in 'talking very adversely to the agitation'.[56] The Rothschilds, forced to back Carington in the Buckinghamshire by-election, soon reverted openly to being pro-Turkish, and seemed to have 'gone Tory altogether'.[57] The upper middle class, especially in London and the Home Counties, had never cared for the emotionalism of the movement.[58] The press soon followed the lead of its readers. The *Daily Telegraph* supported the government. *The Times* had backed the agitation but changed front after its manager warned the owner: 'It is now that the mischief done by allowing sensational influences to overcome reason in directing our Foreign Policy becomes manifest.'[59] Although the

Daily News defied the general trend of metropolitan opinion, it apparently suffered a decline in circulation, and its editor now rejected virulent contributions by atrocity-mongers.[60] The editor of the *Edinburgh Review*, a prestigious Whig journal, admitted: 'I am always desirous that the Ed. Review should express the deliberate views of the Liberal Party, but I never was more perplexed that [sic: than] I am at this moment by the extreme violence & extravagance of some of the opinions recently expressed by Liberal Statesmen of great influence.'[61] In mid-October, Granville described the situation succinctly: 'I believe our own party to be very much divided – one portion enthusiastic in Gladstone's sense, while the Whigs and commercial liberals think he has gone too far.'[62]

The agitation widened the rifts within the Liberal party and made concerted action impossible. Hartington's suggestion for calling an autumn session of parliament, which he had put forward in a speech at Sheffield early in September, was unfeasible, as he himself recognized within a month.[63] Granville explained: 'If we met it would require a vote of Censure on our part – which would be met by a counter resolution likely to be carried by large majorities in both houses. I am afraid we should have more defections on our side, than on that of the Conservatives.'[64] Most Liberals agreed with Granville on the futility of challenging the government.[65] W. E. Forster and Hartington returned from separate trips to Constantinople acutely aware of the complexities of the eastern question and with increased respect for the difficulties it posed for British policy-makers. Forster spoke in this vein at Bradford on 7 October 1876, and his moderation outraged the agitators.[66] Immediately after his arrival in London, Hartington, through his mistress, assured the Prime Minister that he was 'quite sound in his views, & he must consequently disagree with the conduct of his ex-colleagues, Messrs. Gladstone & Lowe, during his absence'.[67] Almost a week later, he promised Gladstone not to give the government as much credit as had Forster, 'but I do not think that I can go so far in condemning them as many of our friends, and, as I imagine, you would do'.[68] Hartington struck this note of compromise in an address at Keighley shortly afterward.[69] Because Radical as well as Whig MPs supported him and distrusted both Forster and Gladstone, Hartington's position was now 'stronger than ever'.[70]

The attitude of Sir Charles Dilke was a significant indication of feeling in the party. Author of *Greater Britain* (1868) and a distinguished traveller, he became a Liberal expert on foreign affairs.

Although he espoused Radical opinions, Dilke tried to maintain good relations with men of different persuasions, and claimed to judge issues on their merits. On the eastern question, he was prepared to have England chastise the Turks for misgovernment but not abandon them to the mercy of Russia. He assured Joseph Chamberlain in October 1876: 'I am not at all Gladstonian but short of bowing the knee in that quarter I will do anything possible to act with you.'[71] The new Radical MP from Birmingham replied: 'Thanks: I don't believe I am more Gladstonian than you, but at this time I can't help thinking he is our best card.' Chamberlain wanted to play Gladstone to trump the 'trimming' of Forster, whom he accused of 'trying to dish the Radicals by bidding for the Whigs and Moderates. Gladstone is the best answer to this sort of thing, and if he were to come back for a few years (he can't continue in public life for very much longer) he would probably do much for us, and pave the way for more.'[72] Harcourt wrote to Dilke on the same day as Chamberlain, 10 October 1876. He concurred in blaming Forster for speaking in 'the old Facing-both-ways style' at Bradford: 'his sham honesty is only the cloak of low cunning'. But Harcourt branded Gladstone's conduct as 'folly', and he condemned 'Chamberlain & Fawcett & the extreme crew' for 'using the opportunity to demand the demission of Hartington and the return of Gladstone. But you need not be alarmed or prepare for extreme measures,' he assured Dilke — 'There is no fear of a return from Elba. He is *played out*.' Gladstone's recent behaviour, according to Harcourt, had made 'all sober people' distrust him: 'He has done two great things. He has damaged the Govt. much & himself still more. At both of which I am pleased — most of all the last.'[73] Dilke sympathized not with Chamberlain but with Harcourt, to whom he stated: 'I, as you know, think Hartington the best man for us — the Radicals — because he is quite fearless, always goes with us when he thinks it safe for the party, and generally judges rightly — or takes the soundest advice on this point.'[74]

The differences between Gladstone and the Liberal leadership represented by Hartington were evident in their attitudes towards a 'national conference on the eastern question' called for 8 December 1876. Gladstone insisted that enthusiasm for the atrocities agitation ran high in the country, and' blamed 'the upper ten thousand' and the 'metropolitan press' for creating an impression of indifference.[75] To encourage the movement and retain his own standing with its organizers, he reluctantly agreed to speak at the conference.

Hartington opposed the gathering as 'almost sure to get principally into the hands of men of extreme opinions. ...I am afraid that the tendency of anything of this kind is to drive our best men, or at all events the Whigs, to the side of the Govt.'[76] The meeting at the St James's Hall turned out to be, as Hartington predicted, a demonstration by the pro-agitationists of the Liberal party.[77] He deemed the conference 'a failure', making many of his followers 'rather more inclined than they were before to support the Government. ...Gladstone might be supported in the country at a general election, though I doubt it; but I feel certain that the Whigs and moderate Liberals in the House are a good deal disgusted, and I am much afraid that, if he goes on much further, nothing can prevent a break-up of the party.'[78] Hartington knew that his followers in parliament, with whom he sympathized, viewed the Radical cohorts in the country with distrust tinged by fear. Gladstone believed that only by the incorporation of Radical Nonconformity could Liberals build a sound party structure. Without this shelter the Liberal aristocracy and upper middle class would perish politically, or seek protection with the Conservatives.

Gladstone's political mission was to reconstruct the Liberal party. He used the Bulgarian agitation as a means to this end. He explained to Granville: 'Now I have not your responsibilities to the party, but I have for the moment more than your responsibilities to the country. ...I regard myself as an outside workman, engaged in the preparation of materials which you & the party will probably have to manipulate and then to build into a structure.'[79] Gladstone's contributions to the atrocities campaign were a cement which, poured into the split in the party, would, he hoped, eventually harden and hold the factions together. If he did not gauge the proportions of the mix accurately, the shiftings on either side would tear the adhesive loose, leaving it to cling uselessly to one of them — or, worse still, to neither. The cement never set properly. Both Whigs and Radicals were displeased with the shape which Gladstone forced upon the party. Having no better plan, they hung together for another decade before coming unstuck. By December 1876, the political initiative had passed out of the hands of Gladstone and the agitators, and to the government.

The Bulgarian agitation made the Prime Minister, now Lord Beaconsfield, more determined than before to achieve a domestic political success through his foreign policy. He detested the agitators:

> None of these brawlers have any proposals, practical or precise.
> Gladstone, more absurd than any of them....As for calling
> Parliament together, such an act wd. deserve a vote of want of
> confidence. I shall not even assemble the Cabinet. There is
> nothing to consider. Our policy is unchanged, & an hysterical
> 'remodelling' of it will only make us contemptible.[80]

Despite his cynical bravado, the Prime Minister lamented to his
private secretary in mid-September 1876 that when 'the world went
mad as it does periodically...one keeper with a houseful of
lunatics is not enough'. For his difficulties, he blamed his erstwhile
rival: 'What a man is Gladstone! What a scoundrel!' He made plain
his primary objective: 'All I have felt throughout this storm is, that,
if we appear to have "modified" our policy, we are lost: we become
contemptible, & the Cabinet quarrels among themselves.'[81]

The atrocities campaign aroused misgivings about governmental
policy in the majority of Beaconsfield's colleagues. Although Lord
John Manners, the Postmaster General, remained staunchly
Turkophile,[82] the most influential ministers were apprehensive. The
Prime Minister coached Derby, warning him against 'timidity', and
advised him not to act 'as if you were under the control of popular
opinion'. He assured Derby that 'all this row will subside' once the
Turks had agreed to an armistice with Serbia and Montenegro,
although 'this Bulgarian bogey' had probably made a conference of
the powers necessary afterward.[83] The Foreign Secretary considered
the lesson 'hardly necessary, since I agree with him'.[84] He informed
the Home Secretary, R. A. Cross: 'If we can succeed in bringing
about an armistice and a peace, the difficulties at home will not be
serious.'[85] For making foreign affairs the focus of attention, Derby
blamed the 'absence of internal agitation...on any domestic
question'. According to the Queen, he said that '*sense alone* wd. not
stop this wild course of excitement, but...there shd. be a certain
amount of humbug with it to satisfy & calm the English public'.[86]
Northcote, Hardy, Cross, Cairns and especially Carnarvon were
uncertain about the political wisdom of Beaconsfield's stubborn
stand against the agitation and of Derby's diplomacy.[87] Beaconsfield
dismissed Carnarvon's fears as 'feeble & fussy' but tried to soothe
others of his colleagues as well as the Queen.[88]

The Prime Minister wanted to ignore the storm of opinion,
certain that it would blow over before parliament met. He shared
the philosophy, although not the haughtiness, of another political

veteran, Malmesbury, who deprecated the atrocities agitation: 'The usual autumnal "indignation meetings" have set in but it is a long way to February & doubtless they won't retain much edge by that time & get as blunt as the Vanguard & Slave circular did last year.'[89] As if to strengthen his master's resolve, Monty Corry wrote to Beaconsfield:

> I take it for granted that you would almost as soon give up your seals as have an Autumn Session. It would paralyse you abroad, and, at this particular moment, perhaps prove fatal at home. Of course they will drive you to it, if possible, − but I do not yet see the people pulling down the railings of Hyde Park, for an idea in Turkey.[90]

The Prime Minister had no need of such reminders. He refused even to hold a Cabinet meeting, despite the pleas of his colleagues. 'There is no use in calling the Cabinet together, for there is nothing to consult them about,' he explained to Cairns, a loyal ally whose judgement he respected. Derby, he insisted, 'is acting on the lines, wh. the Cabinet approved when we separated, & has not got beyond them'. The Foreign Secretary, Beaconsfield continued, had proposed the following terms to the powers: a return to the *status quo ante* in Serbia and Montenegro, administrative autonomy in Bosnia and Herzegovina, and consideration of 'what guarantees for fair government can be devised for Bulgaria'. He attributed to Derby 'an energy & fertility of resource, & fixity of purpose in the matter of wh. I never previously gave him credit', but he had not yet achieved any result requiring Cabinet discussion.[91] This explanation, following on the arrival of the Foreign Office print containing the proposals, satisfied Cairns, Hardy and most of their colleagues.[92]

By this time, the end of the third week in September, Conservatives were recovering their political confidence. They had won the Buckinghamshire by-election, and the agitation was less formidable. After delivering an address in Edinburgh, a Liberal stronghold, Northcote reported: 'It was the first time that the Cons. W[orking] M[en] had ventured on opening their doors, and they were greatly pleased to find themselves alive at the end of the day.'[93] Hardy chided Carnarvon for speaking of 'dissatisfaction everywhere. I am living in a corner where it does not reach me. The Press as a whole supports us and though I may wish many things otherwise our present policy is defensible.'[94] A leader-writer for the *Standard*,

Alfred Austin, had published *Tory Horrors* as a Conservative rejoinder to Gladstone's pamphlet. The Duke of Richmond cursorily dismissed the 'disturbance Gladstone has drummed [?] up about Bulgaria...solely [?] for party purposes'.[95] The Home Office, under Cross, devised 'a Stereotyped reply to numerous addresses wh. are coming in'.[96] The number of protests against the atrocities received at the Foreign Office fell sharply toward the end of September; and Derby remarked that the agitation was 'already subsiding, and [was] likely to subside rapidly, especially if peace is made'.[97] Northcote was able to describe gleefully 'a wonderful Anti-Atrocitarian demonstration' at Wakefield on 27 September.[98]

The Prime Minister felt that the trend of opinion was running in his favour. On 25 September 1876 he repeated for the Queen's benefit the advice he had already bestowed upon his colleagues:

> It has been, from the first, his primary object to defeat the purpose of the Opposition, which is to induce the public to believe, that the Ministry had changed their policy in consequence of the interposition of their rivals. If that idea were to prevail, the popular excitement might, to a certain degree, diminish, or even cease, but Yr Majesty's ministers wo[ul]d become contemptible, & soon fall. At present, Lord Beaconsfield feels confident, that, if we succeed in concluding a satisfactory peace, Your Majesty's Government will meet Parliament stronger than when it was prorogued.[99]

The failure of the agitators to raise large sums of money for their cause convinced the Prime Minister of their ineffectiveness: 'At present, notwithstanding the 2 or 300 meetings, & countless resolutions, no one will *subscribe*. There's the test.'[100] In this mood, Beaconsfield turned his attention to concluding the Balkan war in a manner creditable to his administration. The British Cabinet decided on 4 November 'to propose a conference at Constantinople' and, confirming a private arrangement made a month before between Beaconsfield and Salisbury, to send the latter 'as Plenipotentiary'.[101]

From the time of the Constantinople conference, the breach between Beaconsfield and Derby widened until neither friendship nor political interest could cross it. The Prime Minister believed that divided counsels and precarious finances would force the Russian government to shrink from waging war against the Porte in the face of British opposition. 'The disposition to "cave in" is strongly pronounced,' a Tory journalist reported to him in mid-November 1876 after an interview with the Russian ambassador.[102] This information prompted Beaconsfield to explain frankly to his private secretary: 'I think we shall win, if we clearly know the object we aim at, & then are becomingly firm. Clearness of vision & firmness of purpose will triumph, for I do not think, that Russia really has either quality, but is blustering with indefinite schemes.'[103] To 'win', to 'triumph', seemed imperative to Beaconsfield in order to strengthen the Conservative government at home even more than to protect any enduring British interest abroad. So long as he could achieve political success, he was prepared to defend the integrity of the Ottoman empire or 'to get the lead in our own hands & anticipate' its partition.[104] Ultimately he achieved something of both policies.

Derby's uneasiness at the conduct of Beaconsfield deepened into distrust. Before the atrocities agitation, the Foreign Secretary had acknowledged: 'A certain divergence between Disraeli's language & mine has naturally been made the most of: but it involves no difference of opinion on any practical question, and is really a matter of style & taste.'[105] The Prime Minister, Derby felt, was wont to excite or puzzle an audience with an air of mystery and to give an appearance of greater activity than was either shown or needed. Derby himself, by contrast, was disposed to make as little fuss as possible of any proceedings. 'But in regard to the action to be taken we are absolutely at one: and I see no reason', he had forecast hopefully in the summer of 1876, 'why we should not continue so.'[106] Now, at the end of October, he feared that Beaconsfield was promoting warlike preparations without consulting him: 'he is in an odd excited state, & talks carelessly about the probability of our being at war, and the steps to be taken, before people who repeat & probably exaggerate all his utterances. I foresee the probability, or at least, the chance of a breach between us.' Although no material differences had yet arisen,

> our points of view & objects are different. To the Premier, the main thing is to please and surprise the public by bold strokes and unexpected moves: he would rather take serious national risks than have his policy called feeble or commonplace: to me, the first object is to keep England out of trouble, so long as it can be done consistently with honor & good faith. We have agreed in

resisting the agitation got up by Gladstone: but if war with Russia becomes popular, as it may, we are not unlikely to be on different sides.[107]

More than an aversion to war prompted this accurate prophecy. Derby regarded diplomacy as a calling for a gentleman. An aristocrat at the head of an aristocratic department, he refused to accept that domestic politics should contribute to the formulation of foreign policy. His scruples, however sincerely held, were a rationalization of his own inability to pursue a strong policy abroad or to adapt the routine of the Foreign Office to the exigencies of the electorate at home.

Derby and his wife, moreover, developed a peculiarly intimate relationship with Peter Shuvalov. Derby, in his official dealings, weighed Shuvalov's character shrewdly. The ambassador, he observed, spoke cleverly, but in so discursive a manner that it was 'nearly impossible to catch his exact meaning, or to note it afterwards'.[108] Yet because of his uncertainty about Beaconsfield's policy, Derby, from the summer of 1876, increasingly placed his hopes for peace in Shuvalov: 'Schou. is not to be trusted, for he is a Russian, & an incessant talker, which last habit makes a man loose-tongued: but I am inclined to believe that he is well disposed as to the maintenance of peace, and opposed to the revolutionary party in his own country.'[109] The Russian probably sincerely desired a peaceful solution to the Balkan crisis for which he would gain the credit; he reckoned that such a success might elevate him to the Foreign Ministry in St Petersburg. By supporting his aims, Derby hoped to serve the cause of Anglo-Russian amity – and, incidentally, of counter-revolution. He and Lady Derby blundered in their private intercourse with Shuvalov. The Russian ambassador was ingratiating and clever, slipping as smoothly through English society as a snake through grass. He assiduously cultivated the press as well as politicians of both parties.[110] Derby, understandably, enjoyed the company of this suave and engaging member of the international aristocratic caste. Shuvalov could apparently drink prodigious quantities of alcohol without its affecting his diplomatic acuity. Under a pretence of jovial drunkenness, he probed less-talented imbibers, Derby among them, for secrets, or revealed information which might serve his purposes.[111] Mary Derby became deeply attached to Shuvalov.[112] Her personal inclinations, combined with a concept of patriotism, motivated her to meddle in foreign affairs, leak Cabinet secrets, and exacerbate differences between ministers.[113] Shuvalov duly transmitted the information he received to Gorchakov in St Petersburg.[114] As anti-Russian feeling grew stronger in England, Derby's position in the government became increasingly difficult.

As his relationship with Derby deteriorated, Beaconsfield's with Salisbury improved. Although the Prime Minister and the Foreign Secretary tried to maintain the political links which bound them together, their efforts merely postponed a break between them.[115] Derby had been willing to accept domestic changes, and had sided with his chief against reactionary tendencies within the Tory party in the decade after 1865. The timorousness which had prompted him to cater to demands for reform prevented him from cynically manipulating opinion from the Foreign Office. He feared that Beaconsfield's bluff and bellicosity might lead to war. Salisbury had detested reform as a surrender to the masses. He now appreciated Beaconsfield's active foreign policy in pursuit of British interests abroad and his attempt in this way to avoid further change at home. Although still suspicious of the Prime Minister, Salisbury admired his bold disregard of the atrocities agitation, and he did not countenance Carnarvon's criticisms of governmental indifference, based as they were on a morbidly sensitive morality.[116] He agreed to go as plenipotentiary to Constantinople because he believed that Derby's diplomacy was inadequate. Salisbury's mission was a sign of Beaconsfield's political astuteness. It was a means of by-passing the 'feeble and formal diplomacy' of the Foreign Office: 'Tenterdenism – which is a dusty affair and not suited to the times and things we have to grapple with'. It was also an implied promise to Salisbury that he might be Derby's successor: 'This is a momentous period in your life and career. If all goes well you will have achieved an European reputation and position which will immensely assist and strengthen your future course.'[117] Beaconsfield knew that policy as well as distance would separate Salisbury at Constantinople from the Foreign Office in London. He suspected that the conference, whatever its outcome, would widen the division between Salisbury and Derby and that he would be able to retain the services of at least one of them.

The meeting at Constantinople proved futile because of Turkish obstinacy. Beaconsfield then began to consider seriously the

SHL BIBL. LONDIN. UNIV. WITHDRAWN

possibility of gaining some material advantage for Great Britain, and political advantage for his government, should the Ottoman empire collapse.

The concentration of Beaconsfield and Gladstone upon foreign affairs during 1876 provided no clear victory to either Conservatives or Liberals, nor did it end strife within the parties. Many politicians resented their attempts to enforce party unity at Westminster by appealing to the country. The Prime Minister's active policy, which was meant to rally the nation behind Conservatism, met with opposition in the Cabinet. Gladstone's bid to win Radical support for Liberalism through the atrocities agitation alienated Whigs and moderates. A great foreign crisis or triumph might produce national unity; short of that, the politics of foreign policy reflected the existing divisions within and between parties.

3   The Stress of Politics

During 1877 foreign affairs became the focus of political attention. The Conservative Prime Minister, Lord Beaconsfield, and his Liberal rival, W. E. Gladstone, attempted to use the eastern question to unify their parties and to rally popular opinion behind them. They met with resistance from colleagues who did not share their perceptions, but found backing from public demonstrations. Although ultimately their views prevailed, during 1877 their success seemed doubtful, and the stresses of politics appeared to have 'split up' both the Conservative and Liberal parties.[1]

In the spring of 1877 the Foreign Secretary, Lord Derby, remarked: 'Since I have known parliament, attention has never been so fixed on foreign policy: which is in part owing to the interest felt in the east, partly·also to the total, & very singular, absence of agitation at home.' He acknowledged:

> the public craves for sensation, & will have it in some form. But after the incessant turmoil of change which with few intervals has continued since I entered public life, it is felt as a relief. − No sign of a reaction in radical sense has yet appeared: in fact the Cabinet is quite as strong as when we took office, & the Opposition not more united.[2]

Most politicians, including Derby and the official Liberal leaders, Lords Granville and Hartington, were unable or unwilling to turn the eastern crisis to party advantage. They could not gauge the passions of the masses, play upon them, and ultimately control them on behalf of their parties. That task fell to Beaconsfield and Gladstone.

Beaconsfield deliberately made foreign affairs the focus of attention at the opening of the parliamentary session in February 1877. The Queen's speech entered 'more fully than is usual, on such occasions, into our foreign relations', he explained to Victoria: 'But after the misrepresentations of the autumn, it was deemed necessary

51

to give a key note to the Country on the first & highest opportunity, & to show by a clear, & severly accurate, narrative, that the conduct of Yr Majesty's Ministers had been firm & consistent from the first.'[3] The consistency was a pretence. The Prime Minister recognized that he could no longer commit Great Britain to defend the Ottoman empire. The agitation over the Bulgarian atrocities during the latter half of 1876 had created a formidable anti-Turkish opinion in the country. Beaconsfield understood that, if Russia declared war on the ground of helping the Balkan Christians, the British government would find intervention on behalf of Turkey politically difficult, if not impossible. Yet many Conservatives especially continued to display 'a good deal of sympathy with the pluck of the Turks',[4] whom the Prime Minister could not abruptly abandon without enraging some of his staunchest followers and appearing to give in to the strictures of Gladstone. He framed the Queen's speech to avoid any international commitments: 'The remarks pledge us to nothing, for we are, now, indeed as free as air.'[5] Beaconsfield wanted to oppose Russian advances in the Balkans and Near East; but if the Turks suffered a military defeat, he warned, 'England must take what is necessary for the security of the Empire'. He did not think that a policy of 'simple *laissez faire* will go down with the public'.[6]

Derby was unsympathetic to Beaconsfield's approach to foreign affairs. As befitted his rank, he was a lackadaisical politician. He gave much attention, even when in office, to overseeing his private concerns, which included not only the Knowsley estate but also extensive rural and urban holdings in Lancashire and elsewhere. He sought security for his present possessions, safety for future investments. He spurned speculation. For economic and social reasons he wanted to keep the lower classes at bay.[7] Although Derby was a proud aristocrat, his financial interests and personality imbued him with the mentality of the bourgeois managerial class which was becoming increasingly prominent during the last quarter of the nineteenth century. Since he considered that the possessors of wealth and property had a common cause, he was more willing than most of his colleagues to encourage political cooperation between the aristocracy and bourgeoisie. He wondered at Beaconsfield's 'odd dislike of middle-class men, though they are the strength of our party'.[8] Derby suspected that the withdrawal of aristocrats from the parliamentary fray, though it would be fatal to their continuning as a governing class, was unavoidable, 'as the increasingly democratic spirit infused into English politics makes our public life rougher & more disagreeable'.[9] He felt that his own inclinations made him unsuitable for this new age: 'Distrust of loud talk & heated partisanship, dislike to sudden & hasty changes, desire for administrative efficiency rather than the assertion of any abstract principle of government, are my characteristics, if I know myself.'[10] Derby's personal traits, 'his increasing shyness — his dislike of religion — his dislike of all royal persons', probably debarred him from the Tory leadership. Lady Derby dreamt of 'an old Whig or Liberal combination' under her husband; but a friend warned her 'that there was little chance of any but a few discontented men who wd. only bring themselves & no followers'.[11] Aware that his disposition disqualified him from succeeding Beaconsfield as Prime Minister, Derby confessed: 'I am not interested enough in the questions which most conservatives have at heart to fight well upon them.' He found the routine work of his department more congenial than party politics; at least it helped him to avert 'mere vacancy & weariness'.[12] Politically unambitious, he clung courageously to admirable personal principles against great odds. To his colleagues he seemed, in effect, to have remembered the first part of the adage — *'Qui desiderat pacem'* — and forgotten the second — *'praeparet bellum'*. For this neglect Derby's suspicion of the masses in politics was in large measure responsible. He insisted that the Foreign Office should make foreign policy, and refused to risk war for the purpose which he thought his chief had in mind: to woo the electorate.

Lord Salisbury was closer to Beaconsfield than to Derby in his views on politics and foreign policy. The Indian Secretary desired to preserve the privileged position of the landed aristocracy and to limit the access of the middle classes to power. He had come to acknowledge, after the struggle over domestic reform, that Beaconsfield was working for the same end. Now he was apprehensive about the Prime Minister's use of foreign policy as a means. The atrocities agitation and his experiences at Constantinople had convinced Salisbury that British policy could no longer 'be framed on the theory of defending the Turkish Empire...we have not the political force to sustain it, even if we desired to do so. However we shall do what we can to keep Russia's hands off; but I am not sanguine.'[13] Whereas his friend Lord Carnarvon, the Colonial Secretary, opposed aiding Turkey on the ground that to help the persecutor of the Balkan Christians would be immoral, Salisbury argued that the Ottoman empire was of too little strategic value to

Great Britain to warrant defying a strong anti-Turkish opinion at home. When he became convinced that Beaconsfield had the intention not of defending Turkey but of containing Russian expansionism, and that a large section of the electorate favoured this course, Salisbury was prepared to back the Prime Minister. Ambition as well as pragmatism motivated the Indian Secretary. After the frustrations he had faced in dealing with Derby during the negotiations at Constantinople, Salisbury, perhaps inspired by his wife, began to comtemplate the possibility of becoming Foreign Secretary.[14] He naturally sought to give full scope to his considerable abilities, and even if only subconsciously, he probably felt a sense of rivalry with the husband of his stepmother. Most importantly, he came to believe that his presence at the Foreign Office would better serve the nation than Derby's. In mid-February 1877 he warned Derby that he feared criticism 'which would charge us with *insouciance* & inactivity − with having no definite policy − with deferring any definite determination to a more convenient moment, just at the time when matters are the most critical, & therefore a clearly-defined policy is the most required'.[15] Salisbury worried that public opinion might push governments without such a policy into an international conflict.[16] He felt that rulers in all countries had to control their peoples to preserve international peace as well as the domestic *status quo*.

Fearing war, the Foreign and Indian Secretaries both opposed the Prime Minister's attempts to implement an active policy in the Near East, but the chances of their cooperating politically were minimal. Derby's whiggism and Salisbury's toryism were incompatible; only a chief as practical and as uncommitted ideologically as Beaconsfield could keep them in the same government. 'I have no confidence in the party represented by Salisbury & Carnarvon; & altogether Conservative politics are assuming too much of a clerical complexion for my taste,' Derby admitted: 'Moreover, I do not believe the present Cabinet can hold together for a week if the present Premier retired.'[17] Beaconsfield crudely weighed the opposition to him on the scales of politics: 'Lord Salisbury, tho' a very able man, has no following in the country or Parliament. ...Lord Derby has a great following in country, tho' little in Parliament.'[18] During the first half of 1877, he tried to win the Foreign Secretary's support, but his arts of persuasion made no impression on a man to whom scrupulous adherence to principle meant more than personal ambition. Turning then to Salisbury, he met with success.

Before then the Cabinet had no consistent foreign policy. Beacons-field strove to strengthen the government at home by the appearance of a resolute diplomacy; Derby to avoid war, largely by working personally with the Russian ambassador, Count Peter Shuvalov; Salisbury to find a rational approach to guarding British interests without assisting Turkey. In March 1877 Derby insisted that Sir Henry Elliot return as ambassador to Turkey, despite strong parliamentary opposition to his doing so.[19] G. Gathorne Hardy, the Secretary of State for War, warned his colleagues on 17 March that 'he cd. not defend the step, & he believed the Ministry wd. be beaten on it'. Although Derby wanted to reserve the issue for the considera-tion of the Foreign Office, Salisbury, 'with some heat & solemnity', urged that it was one for the Cabinet, 'as their reputation & existence were at stake'. Beaconsfield 'felt it absolutely necessary to interfere' and, after a 'sharp discussion', Derby 'had to withdraw' his recom-mendation regarding Elliot.[20] This Cabinet meeting perhaps eliminated the chance of Derby's succession to the premiership. 'I doubt now if Salisbury wd. serve under him. I do not think I could,' Carnarvon noted the next day, 'and if we both withdrew, *as things now stand*, it wd. make such an event almost impossible.' The Chan-cellor of the Exchequer, Sir Stafford Northcote, agreed 'that Derby's temper was becoming impracticable'; he, like Carnarvon, was under the impression 'that Disraeli seemed to be now entirely under Derby's influence, that matters cd. hardly go on as they now are & that the situation was growing dangerous & very disagreeable to all of us'.[21] At about the same time, the Cabinet concurred in Derby's opinion 'in favor of the policy of acting in concert with the other powers' and agreed to a 'studiously inoffensive' Russian suggestion for reforms in the Balkans. As a result the six great powers signed a protocol in London on 31 March 1877. Beaconsfield had sanctioned this peaceful gesture, explaining to his colleagues: 'If the Ottoman Empire was about to fall to pieces, England could not, under such circumstances, be inactive, & it was better, that she shd act in concert than alone. He contrasted the position of this country, at the the time of the Andrassy note, when it was not even consulted, & the present state of affairs, when she was, avowedly by all the Powers, the arbiter of Peace or War.'[22] Derby believed that the Cabinet was 'vexed' by its chief's 'talking in his swaggering vein' about the deference paid to England — 'which to my mind is a mere matter of vanity, & of no real consequence: but he sees things in that way, & it cannot be helped'.[23]

The restraints imposed upon foreign policy by considerations of domestic politics irritated Salisbury, but he seemed more aware than Derby of the dangers of ignoring them. Probably with some exaggeration, he had described the political situation to his Viceroy in India:

> But the truth is we are obliged to watch our position here at home with exceeding care. The Opposition came up to town with sanguine hopes on the Eastern Question. To use their own expression, they were 'to have us out in a month'. In this expectation they have been foiled: but they are not in a better temper on that account. They are very much disposed to seize hold of any secondary question in order to inflict a defeat. Meanwhile our own side exhibit the effects of a three years campaign. They will stand by us on confidence votes: but on all kinds of by-issues – ecclesiatical, political [,] personal – there are many discontented individuals: and if their discontent was to select the same occasion for exhibiting itself...our position might be very awkward.

Under these circumstances, Salisbury concluded, 'English policy is to float lazily downstream, occasionally putting out a diplomatic boat-hook to avoid collisions'.[24] When in April the Porte rejected the London protocol and a Russo-Turkish war became imminent, this drifting seemed an inadequate method of running the political and diplomatic rapids.

The Liberals as well as the Conservatives remained divided over their approach to foreign policy. Whigs and moderates, led by Granville and Hartington, were more reluctant than Radicals, for whom Gladstone spoke, to attack the government over the eastern question. On the day of the opening of parliament, 8 February 1877, Sir William Harcourt had advised Hartington that 'it was impossible to stand still'. According to Sir Charles Dilke, Joseph Chamberlain '& some of the advanced party' insisted that England should join the other powers to compel Turkey to grant reforms. 'I am sure it is *of great consequence* that you should declare that view distinctly,' Harcourt warned Hartington, 'in which case I do not think any one on our side will desire to say anything.'[25] With this admonition in mind, Hartington addressed the House of Commons that evening, apparently successfully. 'Our people are delighted with Hartytarty, & not displeased with me, or our programme,' Granville informed the editor of *The Times* the next day. 'The Tories are indignant with the dulness and coldness of Derby', and Beaconsfield, Granville asserted, 'notwithstanding his immense power of sarcasm...will not be so formidable an opponent in the Lords as Salisbury'.[26] Despite their attempts at optimism, the Liberal leaders were convinced of the futility of any formal move against the government. The Conservative Chief Whip, Sir William Hart Dyke, stated that a question of confidence in the House of Commons would result in 'a Division composed of our own supporters in one Lobby, & our humanitarian opponents in the other & that a vast number of Liberals would not vote'.[27] Derby estimated that the government would win a division by one hundred votes. He believed that W. E. Forster spoke for 'the trading classes, who are the strength of the radical party', when he condemned the Duke of Argyll's idea of a war against Turkey. The German ambassador had told Derby that Hartington disapproved of 'Gladstone & his violence'.[28] Granville succinctly expounded the view of Whigs and moderate Liberals: 'To run our heads against the wall of a compact majority, would not only hurt our party, but would probably bring the progressive movement of the Gov. to a dead stop.'[29] He preferred to call attention to subjects of foreign policy in the House of Lords, without moving or dividing against the government.[30] Gladstone could find little support for raising a strident opposition in parliament. He had to settle for publishing another pamphlet, *Lessons in Massacre*. It was not a success.[31]

The distaste of Whigs and moderate Liberals for Radical criticisms of foreign policy helped the government to maintain its unassailable position in parliament. Toward the end of March 1877, Hartington denounced a motion by Henry Fawcett condemning the ministry's Turkish policy, and it met with a crushing defeat.[32] A fortnight later, Beaconsfield informed the Queen that the opposition had, 'at length, resolved to challenge the policy in Eastern affairs of Yr Majesty's Government'. He had no objection, he stated, so long as the discussions did not postpone the budget: 'After all the Opposition papers, & others, have prepared the country for the inevitable imposition of new taxes, it will be somewhat satisfactory to learn, that there is a surplus of half a million.'[33] Expecting a 'hot debate', the Prime Minister had 'no fears as to the result....He is persuaded that a vacillating or feeble policy wd. be fatal, & that it is in Yr Majesty's power to take a bold, but essentially secure course.'[34] The Liberal move for the laying of papers on Turkish affairs failed. The debate in the House of Commons on 13 April was, Hartington admitted, 'decidedly flat especially on our side'. He suggested to Granville: 'Somehow none of our great attacks ever come to much, & I begin to think we had better give them up.'[35] A few days afterwards, a discussion in the House of Lords 'collapsed'.[36]

Gladstone now forced the hand of the Liberal leadership. He wanted to introduce into the House of Commons five resolutions condemning Turkish conduct in the Balkans and denying the Porte, until it had introduced reforms, 'either the material or the moral support of the British Crown'.[37] Opposition within the Liberal party drove Gladstone 'to bed in disgust' on 26 April, according to Robert Bourke, the Parliamentary Under Secretary for Foreign Affairs.[38] The Liberal Chief Whip, in fact, asked his Conservative counterpart not to give Gladstone a day for debate.[39] Hartington had no desire to compromise on the resolutions simply because of an appearance of support for them in the country: 'I do not think that we ought to yield too much to outside pressure, which may turn out very deceptive.' Strongly backed by Harcourt, he worried whether 'any authority I might have would not be entirely destroyed' should he and Granville change course 'merely because so important a member of the party as Mr. Gladstone had decided to take his own line, and had met with considerable support on our side'.[40] Gladstone was determined to proceed, although he knew that he did not have 'a single approver in the *upper* official circle'.[41] His combativeness disgusted the Whigs and pleased the Radicals.[42] To avoid 'a serious split in the party', one of his supporters, Lord Frederick Cavendish, who was Hartington's brother, suggested that the leadership might approve only the first two resolutions.[43] This approach temporarily united the Liberal factions, and the debate opened on 7 May.[44] Granville and Hartington recognized that by pressing for a division which they could not win, and on which they themselves were not agreed, the Liberals would unite the Tories.[45] Beaconsfield understood the situation. On 14 May, after four days of debate, he explained to Northcote, the leader of the House of Commons: 'We seem to have different objects: you, rather to avoid a div., I deeming one absolutely necessary.' He discussed with his protégé 'how a division on Mr Gladstone's resolutions...should be forced tonight'.[46] Northcote followed directions, and the government had a majority of 131, which Beaconsfield proclaimed 'most satisfactory, & will have a great effect abroad'.[47]

Balked in parliament, Gladstone turned to the country, most notably in addressing the inaugural meeting of the National Liberal

Federation at Birmingham on 31 May 1877. Joseph Chamberlain dominated the NLF. He had an autocratic personality which permitted opposition only 'as a stimulus & protection from division in our own camp' and so long as it was 'neither dangerous nor offensive'.[48] He aimed to use the Federation to organize the political strength of middle-class Radicalism in the boroughs, hoping that it would attract broader support than its predecessor, the National Education League. Gladstone's presence in Birmingham, Chamberlain judged, would christen the new movement at its launching:

> it is a demonstration by the party of action amongst the Liberals in favour of more definite objects, and in support of the man who, more than any other at the present time represents a policy of action both abroad and at home.
>
> The future programme of Liberalism must come from below. It is evident we have no inspiration to expect from our present official leaders; and I hope that a result of the present movement will be to secure some greater unity of action and to give force and clearness to Liberal opinion.[49]

Gladstone had no intention of allowing Birmingham to set 'Liberal policy', but he was prepared to employ the 'electoral' organization of the National Liberal Federation to strengthen the party. He, like Chamberlain, held that 'the vital principle of the Liberal party...is action, and that nothing but action will ever make it worthy of the name of a party'.[50] Viewing the parliamentary party as static, he turned to the dynamism of the NLF in order to reawaken a sense of political mission which would both satisfy his personal moral craving and unite all Liberals. He looked upon Chamberlain as an instrument for the achievement of his goals. Although he appreciated the former screw manufacturer's 'tenacity of purpose', Gladstone had almost as little sympathy as the Whigs for his 'advanced policy'.[51] He wanted to hold the Radicals within the constraints of a Liberal party dominated by traditional politicans.

This aim was apparent in Gladstone's speech to the National Liberal Federation. Despite Chamberlain's assertion that the visit was 'not exclusively directed to the agitation in reference to the Eastern Question',[52] Gladstone concentrated upon that subject. He was aware that, although his parliamentary resolutions had won widespread approval among local Liberal associations, 'Dissenting communities' were less enthusiastic than he might have hoped.[53]

Rejecting the idea of disestablishment, he remained determined to use criticism of governmental foreign policy to bring the Liberals together. He could not see 'any other question of real magnitude likely to unite them'. He tried to justify this political strategy in terms of avowing that in this instance, 'as in so many other cases, the Liberal party alone is the instrument by which a great work is to be carried on'.[54] His address at Birmingham reflected the ambiguity of his position, as Sir Michael Hicks Beach, the Chief Secretary for Ireland, in attendance at Balmoral, explained to the Queen: 'The earlier sentences...appear to be, to some extent, a bid for the leadership of the Radical party. But some at least of his audience must have been disappointed by his subsequent avoidance of those "home" questions in which probably, they felt a more real interest.' Beach believed that, whatever their effect 'on the party with whom he is at present acting', Gladstone's views 'will not be approved by the country, nor by the moderate portion of the Liberal party'.[55]

At about the same time, Hartington tried a different ploy to effect the cooperation of Radicals and moderate Liberals. He decided in June 1877, despite some opposition within the party, to approve of the extension of household suffrage to the countries.[56] G. O. Trevelyan had apparently enlisted his support by expressing 'anxiety for the general interests of the party, which I believe would profit by your taking that course to a degree which would far outweigh any temporary disadvantage'. In Trevelyan's opinion, the Liberal leader would thus 'do an immense service to the party; and, as I believe, tide it over difficulties out of which I do not see any other way'.[57] After a division on the issue in the House of Commons, Derby noted: 'The Whig party, headed by Hartington, has taken a decided step, voting in favor of Trevelyan's motion on the reduction of the county franchise.'[58] This decision alienated some Liberals, among them G. J. Goschen, who feared that the lower classes would use their votes to manipulate parliament for ends inimical to the interests of the possessors of property and wealth.[59] The franchise question failed to rouse sufficient enthusiasm to eliminate the divisions within the Liberal party.

The Prime Minister believed that he could rally popular support for a policy of opposing Russia. A by-election at Salford on 19 April 1877 strengthened his conviction. The Conservative candidate held the seat there with an increased majority. In a long report to his master, Montagu Corry asserted that the contest 'turned on the

Foreign question, mainly' and 'that the feeling of the working class is neither for Russia, nor for Turkey, but thoroughly excited at the prospect of the interests or honour of England being touched'. He drew the conclusion 'that Lancashire is determined that England shall not kiss the foot of Russia'.[60] That county seemed to be a significant electoral barometer. Lord Barrington informed Beaconsfield that Sir Henry James regarded Salford as a great defeat for the Liberals, and 'Harcourt thought so much of it that, in his opinion, you wd. mould yr. Eastern Policy upon it!'.[61] The Prime Minister proclaimed to the Queen: 'The Salford Election is one of those critical events, that greatly affect political conduct. It has greatly strengthened the Government – checking, in a marked manner, the Home Rule delusion, & approving the foreign policy of Yr Majesty's ministers.'[62] A few days later, on 24 April, Russia declared war on Turkey. Within a month Corry went 'to feel the pulse of the holiday-makers' at the London Pavilion. 'There was one song, very badly sung,' he stated to Beaconsfield, 'but tumultuously cheered at the end of each verse, for the sake of the "refrain" –

"We'll give the Russian bear
A taste of what we are,
And fight to keep our empire of the seas." '[63]

The history of Russophobia was rooted in the past.[64] In the present, Beaconsfield was anxious to turn such patriotic xenophobia to political advantage.

The Cabinet was reluctant to conform to the Prime Minister's wishes. In mid-April 1877 Beaconsfield had postponed a meeting of his colleagues to avoid 'anarchy' and, to the Queen, had accused Derby of 'timidity' and Salisbury of 'false religionism'.[65] Governmental controversy was public knowledge. 'The debates in the Cabinet are of more importance than those in Parliament,' Lord Bath pronounced, 'and the difference of opinion there greater then between the opposing Political parties.'[66] One colleague shared and articulated Beaconsfield's concern: Earl Cairns, the Lord Chancellor. By late May 1877 the situation appeared 'deeply critical' to him, and he wrote confidentially to the Prime Minister: 'We have defined British interests, & said we would protect them: & we are not taking any *real* step for their protection.' Cairns feared that Russia might try to take Constantinople '& will snap her fingers at us'. The political consequences, in his opinion, could be disastrous:

> Then the Opposition will turn us, − & our own friends will join them − & no mercy will be shown, or allowances made, on the score of the difficulties in our way in the House of Commons. They will say you had a majority of 130, & might have done whatever was necessary.
>
> It would, in my opinion, be infinitely better for the Cabinet to determine on a strong & (as I think) a wise step; the occupation of Gall[ipol]i; & if we are thwarted in taking the step, to lay down the emblems of a power wch. we are not allowed to use. Were it not that I detest the appearance of a selfish disloyalty to the Colleagues of my whole public life, this is the course which, as an individual, I shd. be disposed to pursue.[67]

Beaconsfield, too, felt that the Liberals would make use of a 'disastrous defeat abroad', in the form of 'a ruinous war, or a humiliating peace', to turn out the government or force a dissolution. 'The country would still rally round British interests', he asserted: 'in three months' time, Brit. interests will be in the mud.'[68] He tried by quoting parts of Cairns's letter to brace Derby's will. The Foreign Secretary replied laconically: 'I am quite alive to the risk of Cabinet differences, and will do all in my power to avert them.'[69]

Derby, unlike Beaconsfield, did not conceive of the Russo-Turkish war primarily as a domestic political challenge. When told that one of the Liberal managers in the Salford by-election had said that either candidate might have been sure of return if he had declared openly for war with Russia, the Foreign Secretary had responded: 'Luckily, neither was disposed to buy popularity at that price.'[70] He recognized that the Prime Minister based his eagerness for action in the Near East upon 'his fear that unless something be done, the ministry will lose public confidence'.[71] During one Cabinet discussion on foreign affairs, Beaconsfield made a remark which struck Derby 'as significant, but imprudent, since it avowed an ulterior object. He said the upper classes & the working classes were united against Russia. The middle classes would always be against a war: but fortunately the middle classes did not govern.'[72] He thought that the Prime Minister looked upon war without British interference as a humiliation; 'and of the injury to finance & industry which would be caused by taking an active part, he either does not care to think, or considers that such sacrifices are a less evil than the playing of a secondary part'. Derby noted his personal anxiety about the situation: 'The new phase into which we have passed has the odd effect of placing me in a sort of antagonism to the Premier with whom I have hitherto acted in the closest union: & of putting me on the same side with Salisbury & Carnarvon, whose relations with me have been of late cool, though not unfriendly.'[73]

To counter the recalcitrant aristocrats in the Cabinet, Beaconsfield relied upon the Queen, to whom he exaggerated the significance of his differences with his colleagues. The opposition of Derby and Salisbury gave him an excuse for recruiting her support against them, and for not adopting the belligerent policy upon which she insisted. In hyperbolic language that blurred the distinction between reality and romance, he misrepresented the arguments of his opponents and revealed his own apprehensions:

Lord Derby seems for peace at any price, & Lord Salisbury seems to think, that the progress of Russia is the progress of religion & civilisation. Lord Beaconsfield does not believe, that this is the feeling of the British People, & that if they wake one morning to hear, that the Russians are in Constantinople, they will sweep the Ministers, who have counselled Yr Majesty, off the board of public life altogether.[74]

Toward the end of June 1877 Beaconsfield warned his royal mistress of the possible resignations of the Foreign and Indian Secretaries: 'their withdrawal, if it occur, would be when Lord Beaconsfield insisted on taking some active step to prevent the occupation of Constantinople by the Russians'.[75] Although Derby had recognized that 'a disruption seems not impossible', he did not consider it imminent before July 1877, particularly because he believed that the Liberals were incapable of forming a government. Receiving an appeal from the Prime Minister 'to stand by him' in the event of Salisbury's resigning, Derby replied that he doubted whether resignations were probable so long as the Cabinet was discussing preparations for action but not action itself.[76] Salisbury made plain that he was 'moderate & inclined to yield up to a certain point rather than make a split'.[77]

The real conflict in the Cabinet during the last half of 1877 was between the Prime Minister and the Foreign Secretary. The former made grandiose pronouncements to the Queen. He reported on 10 July that Hardy was 'entirely in favor of strengthening immediately Yr Majesty's Mediterranean Garrison, so that a force of ten thousand men may be directed, at any time, to a particular point in the Turkish Empire witht. delay. In six days, such a force might reach Gallipoli from Malta; in seven days, Varna; & in a very short time, Egypt.'[78] Beaconsfield also speculated on the possibility of the Porte's selling Egypt, Crete and Cyprus to Great Britain.[79] Derby feared that his chief 'had hopes of getting us into a war'; and he deprecated an idea, suggested by Cairns, 'of establishing a coaling station on a small island called Stampalia'.[80] Beaconsfield warned his Foreign Secretary as the Russian armies advanced in mid-July: 'If they got to Constantinople, there would be an outbreak of popular feeling against us, the bulk of the Conservatives would desert us, the Whigs would join, & Gladstone & his friends would say "if our advice had been taken, all this might have been averted". The ministry would be upset, & that with ignominy.' Seemingly possessed with the notion that a violent anti-Russian agitation was about to break out and carry public opinion before it, the Prime Minister wanted to declare a Russian occupation of Constantinople a *casus belli*. He thought that he could secure the agreement of all his colleagues, so he told Derby, except for Salisbury and Carnarvon, '& we could could get on without them'. He chose to ignore the fact that the Foreign Secretary had a 'strong conscientious objection to war, whether popular or not, unless its absolute necessity was proved'.[81] Derby refused to yield. He forced the Prime Minister to submit foreign policy to Cabinet discussion, a procedure Beaconsfield detested.[82] 'He has never before been exposed to the annoyance of having to waive or modify his ideas to meet those of his colleagues', Derby astutely observed: 'in my father's time he settled all with him, & what the two agreed on, the Cabinet always accepted.' Concerning his own relations with Beaconsfield, Derby added: 'I am afraid also he thinks my attitude ungrateful & unfriendly − though he has never said so. I owe him much, & have backed him to the best of my power, but questions of peace or war must override all merely personal considerations.'[83]

During July 1877 Derby grew increasingly apprehensive that his colleagues would, for the sake of appearances, take bellicose steps to avoid being blamed for inactivity in the Near East. The Cabinet, on 14 July, refused to make Russian entry into Constantinople a cause of war, to the disappointment of Manners, who was rabidly pro-Turkish, and Beaconsfield. At the same time, it authorized Derby to tell Shuvalov that, if the Tsar's armies approached the city with a view to occupying it even temporarily, the British government would be free 'to take any steps they may consider desirable to prevent an unnecessary & dangerous interference with interests wch. they are entitled to protect'. This formula averted an immediate risk of disunion in the Cabinet, the Foreign Secretary remarked, 'but the prospect is not pleasant'.[84] A week later, the Cabinet, with Carnarvon dissenting, decided that if Russia occupied the Turkish capital and did not arrange to withdraw immediately, Great Britain would declare war on her. It also ordered 3000 troops to Malta, despite some misgivings induced in Hardy by his military advisors.[85] Shuvalov was of the opinion that Beaconsfield wished to gain credit for preventing Russia from doing what she never intended to do; and Derby agreed with him.[86] At a meeting on 28 July the Cabinet listened to a suggestion of sending warships to Constantinople, and received from Hardy a plan for occupying Chanak. Derby lamented: 'the war fever is clearly getting hold of my colleagues, & they have the excuse that it prevails strongly in the party generally, & in H. of C. – Even Salisbury seems in part gained over. It would be strange, after all that has passed, if I were the sole seceder on a question of war or peace.'[87] To avoid that contingency, Derby concluded an 'alliance' with Carnarvon.[88] On 31 July, with the latter's backing, the Foreign Secretary, 'after the sharpest struggle I ever had on any political question', forced his colleagues to desist from sending the fleet to Constantinople on the pretext of maintaining order there. Although he did not threaten to resign, he 'let it be seen clearly that I did not mean to be overruled in my own department'. Salisbury had apparently surprised the Cabinet by his desire to despatch the fleet without the permission of the Porte: he objected not to fighting but to doing so for Turkey. Derby counted the day as a victory, but he expected to be obliged to wage battle again: 'I move, as it were, with my resignation in my hands.'[89]

Although the sense of immediate crisis dissipated at the beginning of August 1877, after the Turks held the Russians at Plevna,[90] the Prime Minister and the Foreign Secretary could not agree on a common policy. 'There is great disquietude, I am persuaded, in the country, & much discontent in our own party especially, at our uncertain tone,' Beaconsfield admonished Derby: 'It will not do.' He urged his younger colleague to 'try to touch a national c[h]ord' in dealing with the eastern question.[91] To Derby the widespread feeling that England should not appear to be playing a secondary role in the East was 'not a very intelligible one: as long as our interests are not touched, why should not foreigners settle their own affairs in their own way?'.[92] In the Cabinet on 14 August he was 'alarmed' by Beaconsfield's language:

> The fact is that we differ not about means, but ends. The Premier sincerely & really believes that it will be better for us to risk a great war, & to spend £100.000.000 upon it, than not to appear to have had a large share in the decision come to when peace is made. Most continental statesment would agree with him, & a considerable section of the English public. I do not think *prestige* worth buying so dear, & I feel sure that the majority are on that side.[93]

The Prime Minister now wanted above all to prevent a second campaign by Russia which might result in the fall of Constantinople. Balked in the Cabinet,[94] he secretly commissioned the British military attaché at the Russian court, Colonel F. A. Wellesley, to warn the Tsar that England would not remain neutral if his armies resumed the war during the next spring.[95]

With parliament adjourned, Beaconsfield devoted his attention to convincing his ministers to adopt this policy as their own. He made full use of the influence of the Queen. She wrote a memorandum in which she called upon the Cabinet to 'stop a second campaign' and '*at once* at any risk of disruption or other trouble come to a conclusion as to the points' on which the government would not yield.[96] On 16 September 1877 the Prime Minister explained his strategy to her:

> He has constantly pursued his purpose of preparing the minds of his colleagues for the decisive policy, which he trusts they may ultimately adopt. He circulates Yr Majesty's *memorandum* with discretion, wishing to obtain a considerable concurrence of opinion before he addresses himself to those on whose sympathy he can less depend. . . .
> *No second Campaign* must be the shibboleth of England.
> And it is of the utmost importance that Yr Majesty shd. use your Majys. influence & prepare the minds of Yr Majesty's Ministers, whom Yr Majy. may see in the interval for this great result.[97]

By the end of September Beaconsfield felt that he had broad support in the Cabinet. He had some hope of winning over Salisbury, to whom he expostulated: 'It seems to me we cannot meet Parliament again without a policy.' He cared little about the opposition of Carnarvon, who, except as a peer and friend of Salisbury, carried no political weight. But Derby's recalcitrance led him to expect 'a serious conflict' when he called his colleagues together.[98]

The Cabinet did not agree on any action when it met for the first time in seven weeks on 5 October 1877. Beaconsfield suggested that Great Britain offer to mediate between Russian and Turkey on the basis of the London protocol of 31 March and, if the former power refused, to aid the latter in defence of Constantinople. Only five other ministers favoured this approach. Salisbury put forward a compromise proposal by which Great Britain would remain neutral in return for a secret Russian pledge not to occupy Constantinople even temporarily; failing such an undertaking, the British government would prepare to take steps to intervene to protect the city. The Cabinet reached no conclusion, and suspended its discussions until it next met.[99] Salisbury later confided to Carnarvon that he had been amenable that day because 'I do not see very serious dangers ahead'. As for saving Contantinople, he believed that it was in no danger and trusted that, 'till the first week in February', it would not be:

> By that time many things may have happened; but in any case, the country will have very much changed if it desires any increase of taxation in order to help the Turk. My impression from what I have seen is that, though the feeling against Russia is strong, it no where rises nearly to Income-tax point. When Parliament has once met, we shall I trust be safe.[100]

Although his colleagues had expected an early resumption of their debate, the Prime Minister waited a month before reconvening the Cabinet. He had the excuse of a three-weeks' sojourn in Brighton for his health – which Carnarvon expected him to use 'to win over the hesitating element'.[101]

Beaconsfield was indeed anxious to settle ministerial differences before the next meeting of the Cabinet. The Queen demanded: 'Lord Derby must be *pushed* on, & we must be ready for action';

and she continued to hound her ministers on the subject.[102] Derby, unyielding, wrote to the Permanent Under Secretary at the Foreign Office, Lord Tenterden, whom the Prime Minister had summoned to Brighton: 'I have no doubt of the good effect of your calming counsels.'[103] Corry gathered that the Foreign Secretary 'is as resolute as ever to keep his hands in his pocket. And I am told that an insistance [sic] on a bold policy will lead to the secession of certainly four Secretaries of State.'[104] R. A. Cross, the Home Secretary, a Lancashire MP and an associate of Derby, complained that the work of the House of Commons had suffered during the last session because of the concentration upon foreign affairs by a Cabinet dominated by influential peers. Encouraged by the Foreign Secretary, he was 'very anxious still to put one or two things straight in which the mass of the people are much interested'.[105] Beaconsfield knew that domestic as well as foreign subjects required the government's attention. He intended to call the Cabinet for the first week in November '& then sit pretty continuously, till we have completely considered our situation, & the measures for next Session'.[106] Though witty, his description of '*seven* parties, or policies', in a Cabinet of twelve was exaggerated and of less significance than his determination 'that, in the first place, the Cabinet shall decide upon something'. After consulting with Cairns and Hardy, he devised a formula which he hoped all of his colleagues, except Carnarvon, would accept: 'an immediate – but secret & conciliatory – communication to Russia, requiring a written undertaking from Russian that she will not, under any circumstances, even occupy Constantinople'.[107] In separate interviews, Derby and Salisbury gave their assent to this proposal. 'It gives a better chance of keeping the Cabinet together than any scheme I have yet heard of,' Derby reluctantly admitted.[108] Salisbury viewed the scheme as a means of averting an Anglo-Russian war.[109] Both of them supported the Prime Minister in the Cabinet on 5 November 1877, to the 'evident surprise' of Carnarvon, who 'was routed. Otherwise, the Cabinet [was] unanimous.'[110] Its next three meetings were 'entirely on domestic affairs', concerned with business which Cross brought forward, and evidently helped to reconcile him to the Prime Minister's foreign policy.[111]

As Beaconsfield pressed the Cabinet to act during the autumn of 1877, the breach between him and Derby widened.[112] The latter considered that the former was 'constantly shifting his ground, & abandoning today the line which he seemed to have definitely adopted overnight'.[113] By the end of November Derby began 'to have great doubts whether we can get through the winter together'. He did not yet suppose that Beaconsfield wanted war, 'but he would run the risk of getting into one rather than take up an unpopular line in parliament'.[114] Derby suspected that the Prime Minister was trying to influence public and parliamentary opinion in favour of war through Algernon Borthwick, the editor of the *Morning Post*, and Bourke, among others. 'In "society" I have the certainty that war would be popular,' Derby admitted, 'as also, naturally in the army: probably the feeling would be the same among the mob: the middle class is almost to a man on the opposite side, but unfortunately the Premier neither likes nor understands the middle-class.' Although Derby, privately reinforced by his wife, refused to accede to the Prime Minister's wish to present Russia with '*an ultimatum*' against occupying Constantinople or the shores of the Dardanelles,[115] the Cabinet forced him to do so during the first week in December.[116] On 14 December, a few days after the fall of Plevna, Beaconsfield proposed to his colleagues an early meeting of parliament, a large increase in armaments, and British mediation between the belligerents. Following two stormy meetings and a hint that he might resign, the Prime Minister secured the approval of the Cabinet.[117] By now, Derby feared that his chief was 'looking forward to war as not only a probable event but one in a party point of view rather desirable than the reverse. I think he is wrong there, even if there were no larger issues involved.'[118]

By this time, Derby was isolated within the Cabinet. His temperament and conception of his duties plainly rendered him incapable of coping with the political strain of the eastern crisis. Steadfastly refusing to accept the Prime Minister's arguments, he did not believe that the issues of foreign policy should be at the mercy of the electorate. He preferred to attempt to answer the eastern question through diplomatic channels, and particularly through Shuvalov. On the eve of the outbreak of the Russo-Turkish war, Tenterden had clearly warned Derby of the departmental dangers of his exceptional treatment of the Russian ambassador:

I should point out to you that great inconvenience is arising from the communication to Count Schouvaloff of the proofs of the reports of his conservations. ...He is the only Ambassador who has this done for him. ...It is all the more disadvantageous because he systematically carries on business under the cover of 'private and personal' suggestions.... I shd think that the sooner he is relegated to the position of the other Ambassadors the better.[119]

This wise advice did nothing to interrupt the intimacy between Derby and his wife on the one side and Shuvalov on the other. The Foreign Secretary's conduct amounted to neither patriotism nor treason. It was the response of an aristocrat who believed that international affairs were the peculiar business of his class, and that issues of war and peace were too vital to be left to the masses, or to those who claimed to speak in their name.

During the summer and autumn of 1877 the leakages of Cabinet secrets by Derby and his wife, which had been suspected for some time, became the subject of angry comment by his colleagues and the Queen. Other Cabinet members resented the Foreign Secretary's practice, contrary to accepted precedent, of taking extensive notes at their meetings.[120] When Beaconsfield spoke to Derby about the matter, he replied:

> The notes which I generally take at Cabinet have never been seen except by Lady Derby, or my secretary. They have been kept merely for purposes of convenient reference, those of old date have been from time to time destroyed, and all will be. I have always understood it to be an unwritten rule of administrative practice, that no permanent record should remain of what passes in Cabinet. But to temporary memoranda, kept, while they exist, for personal use, I know of no objection.[121]

The Queen was incensed with Derby. She declared that, however firm the Cabinet appeared to be:

> Ld. Derby and his wife *most likely* say the *reverse right & left*, & Russia **goes on**! It maddens the Queen to feel that all our efforts are being destroyed by the Minister who ought to *carry* them out. The Queen must say she *cant* stand it! For Russia *will* have her own way, & *we be* humiliated if not ruined.[122]

The Queen wanted to replace the Foreign Secretary with Lord Lyons, the ambassador at Paris, with whom she 'lamented bitterly over Lord Derby's refusal, or at least disinclination, to do anything'.[123] Hardy scotched her idea that Derby might go to India if

Lytton retired, '& told her how strong Derby was in public opinion especially in the North though perhaps on grounds which wd. not bear examination'.[124] Anger at Derby's indiscretions eventually outweighed concern about his political influence, even in Cross's mind.[125] Early in October, the Queen ordered: 'Ld. Beaconsfield, must *insist* on the decision of the *Cabinet not* being communicated to **any Wives** & *above all* not to *Foreign Ambassadors*. This **must** be *insisted* on.'[126]

A crisis in the relations between Derby and his colleagues came two months later. The Foreign Secretary either did not know or did not want to know how Shuvalov obtained secret information. On 5 December 1877, the Russian ambassador told him that he had learned of the memorandum on which the Cabinet had agreed the previous day: 'how? or whence?', Derby noted; 'there must be a leak in the Cabinet'.[127] Before the Cabinet of 8 December, the Prime Minister had a few minutes' private conversation with Salisbury. He asked the Indian Secretary whether he should read to the meeting a letter from the Queen concerning leakages. Salisbury tactfully advised communicating the contents only to Derby, feeling that he would be receptive to the Queen's hints, 'but that he might be seriously offended, if such delicate matters, touching himself, were brought forward to be discussed by Mr Smith, Mr Cross, &c &c'. Derby himself, apparently suspecting Beaconsfield to be responsible for the leakages, mentioned the subject in the Cabinet. 'Ld. Salisbury, as the husband of the only other wife, who cd. interfere in such affairs, expressed himself without reserve,' or so the Prime Minister reported to the Queen.[128] The strictures in the Cabinet failed 'to arrest this evil', he remarked to Salisbury on Christmas Eve, '& I have been told, that Lady Salisbury, with the wise courage that distinguishes her, has, socially, expressed her sentiments to the great culprit. But more decisive means are requisite.'[129]

The Queen provided the means by prompting the Dean of Windsor to warn Lady Derby, who was at Knowsley for the holidays. He wrote 'a long and strong letter to Her. It will certainly check any confidences, if her friend is of the party there,' he assured the Queen. Lady Derby's reply contained no denial of the charges brought against her. She was vexed that stories on the subject could come to the attention of the Queen, 'in such a form as to induce H.M. to deem them worthy of attention; for had I done what would seem to have been imputed to me I must either have been guilty of a degree of imprudence & bad taste wh. I almost shudder to imagine, or I should be open to the still graver charge of betraying H.M.'s Govt or indeed my country to a foreign Ambassador'. Lady Derby asserted that she saw all the ambassadors three or four times a week, '& the *leakages* of the Cabinet have been so startling of late that I am not surprised it shd. have been found necessary to search for the source. The Ambassadors one & all are invariably the first recipients of these leakages.' The Dean considered these evasions so weak that he promised to see Lady Derby as soon as she returned to London.[130] Beaconsfield commented: 'The letter of the Lady is not satisfactory; but then it could not be.'[131] Apparently nothing could prevent Mary Derby's gossiping about state secrets.[132]

Derby gave no indication of knowing of the admonition addressed to his wife. She told him that Shuvalov blamed the Rothschilds for the leakages, claiming that they received information daily from Beaconsfield and used it for their own purposes. Derby appeared to be believe this story. He also suspected Montagu Corry and some of the Prime Minister's female friends of indiscretions.[133] Here he had reason. Through his private secretary, Beaconsfield had often given political news to journalists. They, and especially Borthwick of the *Morning Post*, frequently not only published articles which read like official pronouncements but also received visits from Shuvalov. Beaconsfield tried to mask his own conduct as well as to isolate Derby from his colleagues and the Queen by placing exclusive blame for leakages on the Foreign Secretary and his wife. He largely succeeded.

Salisbury was now more convinced than hitherto of the need to cooperate with the Prime Minister. He had been willing to defend British interests in the Near East, though not to ally with Turkey. In late December 1877 Russian advances seemed to demand a response from Great Britain. If the government failed to develop a coherent programme, he feared, gusts of popular emotion might sweep it into a disastrous course. In his mind, Derby's dilatoriness, which had served as a precaution against Beaconsfield's zeal, was no longer a restraint upon public passions but a goad to them. A minister as cautious as Northcote was ready, under certain circumstances, to sanction an occupation of Constantinople or Gallipoli:[134] Salisbury could do no less. Although to avoid precipitate action that might lead to war he did not openly back Beaconsfield, he understood that his chief was angling for his support and had practically abandoned hope in Derby.[135]

So too did Salisbury. On 23 December the Foreign Secretary had made a bid for his allegiance. Eight days earlier the Queen had demonstrated her confidence in Beaconsfield by visiting Hughenden.[136] Derby assumed that Salisbury shared his prejudice not only against the Prime Minister's belief in 'prestige' but also against 'the pressures of the Court'. He wrote to his wife's stepson: 'I am convinced that the Queen has satisfied herself that she will have her way (it is not disguised that she wishes for a war): and the conviction is universal among the diplomatists that she and the Premier will leave no stone unturned to accomplish their purpose.'[137] Aware of the indiscreet behaviour of the Derbys with Shuvalov, Salisbury would not join them in disparaging the Crown. On the contrary, he desired, as the Prime Minister had reported to the Queen many months before, 'to maintain Yr. Majesty's personal authority & influence, on which he sets great score...& which is an element in the government of this country, wh. it is most beneficial shd be cherished & strengthened'.[138] Although Salisbury might have cared little for the use of such flattery, he was more in sympathy with Beaconsfield's view of the political importance of the monarchy than with Derby's criticism of the Queen. He recognized that, by siding with the Prime Minister, he might eventually realize his ambition of gaining the office now held by Derby. Meanwhile, he was in a position to exert a considerable influence on the making of foreign policy. Prepared to seize his opportunities, Salisbury was in a sanguine mood. When he could get away from his duties in London, he enlivened the Christmas holiday at Hatfield House. During one of his electrical experiments, a guest was insensitive enough to ask him 'through 3 miles of telephonic wire why Parlt. was to meet on the 17th & received the answer "because we mean to invade Siberia"'.[139]

Although good spirit apparently prevailed at Hatfield, the mood at Highclere was one of discontent.[140] Carnarvon felt 'worn out... with the constant almost ceaseless strain politically of the last few months'.[141] Squabbles with his colleagues deepened the sense of depression which had afflicted him since the death of his wife in January 1875. Derby had observed the Colonial Secretary's 'tendency to rash and precipitate action, and a kind of restlessness, which have already led to one or two failures'. Colleagues noticed Carnarvon's 'peculiar' manner in Cabinet meetings, where he seldom spoke to anyone save Salisbury. They remarked upon his close association with the historian J. A. Froude, the Canon of

St Paul's, Henry Liddon, and other high churchmen who regarded the Russian war on Turkey as a religious crusade.[142] Under their guidance, Carnarvon seemed to feel that as a politician he should be 'morally just and single of purpose...one...in whose mind the conflicting pretensions of duty and interest never held debate'.[143] On 2 January 1878 he publicly aired his views on the policy under debate in the Cabinet. He told a South African delegation that England had drifted into the Crimean war 'and I am confident that there is nobody insane enough to desire a repetition of it'.[144] Carnarvon apparently had intimated beforehand to the delegation's spokesman, through Froude, that he was willing to say something about the situation in the Near East. He then read his remarks from a manuscript in which every word was written down. Seemingly 'the whole scheme was carefully prepared, and acted out'.[145]

In a Cabinet meeting the next day Beaconsfield strongly deprecated the speech, and Carnarvon indicated that he might resign.[146] Derby urged him not to do so, then slipped a note across to him: 'Don't weaken your own side by doing what your opponents (assuming them to exist) want you to do. Don't strengthen the war-party by secession. In the highest quarter (not in his room) no new member will be allowed in the Cabinet who is not for war.'[147] Later that day, although without referring to the Queen, Northcote tendered similar advice: 'Our position is so critical, and our relations with one another so delicate, that separate action is for the moment very dangerous. We differ greatly in opinion upon some important points, but we are able to concur as yet in a course of action which may lead to the issue which we all heartily desire, – a peaceful settlement not inconsistent with the honour and interests of the Country.' The Chancellor of the Exchequer then warned Carnarvon: 'If we Ministers, compromising men of varying sympathies, can maintain a course on which we can fairly agree, we may hope to keep the country together; but if we split, the country will split; and if the country splits, who shall say that the result may not be at least a temporary ascendancy of the War-party, – an ascendancy which may last long enough to do irreparable mischief?' To resign, he concluded, 'would be giving a most serve shake to the Cabinet and weakening its pacific elements very materially'.[148]

The Radicals, backed by Gladstone, wanted to arouse opinion in the country to press the government to remain neutral. Chamberlain reckoned that resolutions from municipal councils and chambers of commerce would be 'specially valuable as pointing to a general feeling against war amongst all parties'.[149] A. J. Mundella, Radical MP for Sheffield, thought that such an 'entirely spontaneous' movement would win adherents: 'Of course those of us who are connected with Commerce will do what we can to stimulate it, and to make use of it. It is valuable as proceeding from non-political bodies.' He commended the activity of the Nonconformists and of the arbitration and peace societies, 'but I can find nobody of authority connected with our Liberal organization in Parliament Street,' he complained to Gladstone: 'We shall do very well without them.'[150] Gladstone himself had a few months earlier written to Granville 'that chauvinism flourishes, and might prevail: though I am convinced that we have, at least like the the the Turks, the means of making a true and good fight'.[151] By December 1877 he declared to John Bright that 'we must in case of need stir the country from end to end against either war, or measures tending or looking to war'. He asserted that the struggle should not take on the 'character of a party question, which in a matter of war & of foreign policy is at the best a dangerous precedent'. For that reason he advocated that such ostensibly non-partisan bodies as chambers of commerce conduct the attack on the government.[152] To Chamberlain, Gladstone responded warily that he could see no public disadvantage in holding meetings and making declarations in favour of neutrality.[153]

Gladstone apparently hoped that the pressure of opinion in the country would force the Liberal leadership to take a strong stand against the government when parliament met. He wanted not only to keep the party together, but also to avoid becoming dependent exclusively on Radical support for his own dissent over foreign policy. By the end of 1877, a Conservative Whip had heard the rumour 'that Gladstone is canvassing Granville & Hartington with the view of stoutly opposing *any* action, which the Govnt. may think fit to take with reference to the Eastern difficulty, when Parliament meets'.[154] Lord Halifax also advocated this approach, explaining to Granville:

> I fully admit that the liberal party is not flourishing, but I don't believe that it is only capable of asserting itself against the Conservatives. The danger & difficulty is [sic] from within: & I am not sure that barring one man the difficulty may not increase as time goes on. The non-coms are likely to be more reasonable & easy to

deal with *now* than 5 years hence. I am not much afraid of the Russo-Turkish question.[155]

The Whigs had to adopt an active policy in order to preempt the Radicals. If they refused to do so, Gladstone was ready to act without them. He warned Granville that, if before parliament met 'there are evil symptoms, I shall probably...join the agitation in the interval: which hitherto I have refused to do, while not discouraging local and spontaneous meetings'.[156]

By mid-January 1878 both parties had roused opinion on one side or the other of the controversy over the eastern question. Liberals circularized the newspapers and attempted to get up a deputation of City merchants to interview Derby. Mundella accused Tory agents of spending money freely to induce workers to make bellicose declarations. Of one meeting on Clerkenwell Green organized for that purpose, he proudly reported to Gladstone that 'our friends succeeded in passing resolutions against war for Turkey'. He expected that Liberals would be able to achieve similar results at other gatherings.[157] Despite objections from Derby, who recognized 'that there is now less sympathy for Russia than there has ever been before', Conservatives staged their demonstrations, and accused the opposition of selfishly opposing the defence of British interests.[158] The metropolitan police detailed many hundreds of men on Sundays in late February and early March to watch the political gatherings in Hyde Park.[159] The governmental forces were strongest in London especially and in the West Midlands and Lancashire. The rowdyism in the capital seemed well organized.[160] Northcote tried to calm the Queen, who was apprehensive about the anti-war protestors: 'While he is only too conscious that the pursuit of wealth has become a more absorbing passion among certain classes, and has its baneful effect upon public spirit, he is on the other hand by no means willing to believe that the spirit of the country as a whole has really declined or is declining.'[161] Beaconsfield was doing his best to ensure that it did not: 'With regard to the Press, he can assure Yr Majesty that Mr Corry sees the Editors of the Telegraph, M. Post, & Pall Mall, every day, & guides, instructs, & inspires them. And the 'Standard' also, tho' the writers of that print are very dull. Nevertheless, the circulation of the paper is enormous.'[162] Some British diplomatists privately echoed the bellicose opinion at home. From Constantinople A. H. Layard advocated armed intervention: 'But in these days I fear that such heroic measures would not suit the spirit of Birmingham and Manchester. However, if Russia provokes John Bull too much he may arouse himself at last, and shake off the cotton bales under which he is smothered.'[163] The British ambassador at Rome, Sir Augustus Paget, had wanted to seize Gallipoli, ignoring the Turks had they complained: 'And if they had, and we had steeped our swords in the blood of a few Mahomedans why it would have been the very thing to suit the taste of the arch-"agitator" or howling maniac, as I venture to consider the ex-Prime Minister, and all his cohorts.'[164]

So unsettled was opinion that *The Times* had no firm policy. Its manager, J. C. MacDonald, had expressed the general attitude of the newspaper's staff when he admitted: 'If anything my sympathies are Russian in this Eastern war.'[165] Later he remarked: 'It is quite surprising how wrong headed the great majority of people in the south of England have been about the whole of this Eastern business — but a good deal of the feeling rested on a conviction that we ourselves would keep out of the struggle. The risk of our becoming embroiled has again brought forward the whole strength of the Peace party, & it becomes increasingly clear that however much we may sympathize with the Turk we cannot & will not fight for him.'[166] Unable to elicit guidance from the Liberal party, *The Times* opted for equivocation.[167] On 8 November 1877 the owner, John Walter, had cautioned his editor, J. T. Delane, about a proposed leader on the eastern question which dealt with the opening of the Dardanelles:

The only doubt I have is whether it be wise to publish it *yet*. Remember that tomorrow is Lord Mayor's day, and if such an Article were published in the morning, it would be almost impossible for the minister to avoid noticing it in his speech in the evening. If he should substantially endorse it, well & good, but how if he were to repudiate any such idea? That would be very mischievous, & even dangerous to the cause of peace.

Walter shrewdly suggested that Delane delay the leader a day, then tailor it to fit in with Beaconsfield's speech at the Guildhall.[168] In such fashion did he guard the Thunderer's reputation for omniscience. *The Times* articulated, rather than created, the views of its readers. MacDonald hoped in January 1878 that their opinion would soon coincide with that held privately in Printing House Square: 'The meeting of Parliament is looked forward to with intense

interest by the British Public and we shall soon have firmer ground
to stand upon, than has for some time been the case. High Society
in this Country at least is emotional to a wonderful degree & has
gone as wildly wrong about this war as it did about that in America.
But Public opinion is a very different thing.'[169] In fact it was not, as
MacDonald soon had to confess. He wrote to *The Times*'s correspondent in the Turkish capital:

> You are hardly more excited about the war in Constantinople
> itself than we are here; only in your case it is the break up of an
> Empire & the purpose [?] of the Conqueror which create the
> situation, whereas with us it is the conflict of not exactly *opinions*
> but rather *partizanships*. Everybody has taken sides & there is a
> degree of heat & passion on the subject such as has not been
> developed for a very long time.[170]

If it could devise a course of action, the government stood to profit
from this situation more than its opponents, or *The Times*.

In this tense political atmosphere, within a fortnight of meeting
parliament, ministers had not yet decided upon a policy. Derby and
Carnarvon deprecated any step that might lead to British involvement in the war. To avoid recriminations from his colleagues,
Beaconsfield did not deal personally with the Turkish ambassador
but employed Corry as a secret intermediary.[171] During a 'pleasant'
walk on 7 January 1878, the Prime Minister, according to Derby's
account, spoke of his trouble with the Queen, who 'threatens to
abdicate if her policy – which is war – does not find support'. She
wrote to Beaconsfield daily, or more often, 'always in the same
excited condition. He doubts whether there is not in all this a
beginning of insanity.'[172] On 9 January the Cabinet fiercely attacked
the Prime Minister's draft of the Queen's speech, eliminating
several bellicose passages on which Derby was prepared to resign.[173]
Northcote tried to plan for a vote of credit in coordination with the
War Office and Admiralty.[174] But as late as Saturday 12 January,
W. H. Smith, the First Lord since Ward Hunt's death the previous
July, was lamenting Derby's prevarication: 'If we cannot come to an
agreement on our policy on Monday in certain events, it is a
question whether it would not be more patriotic to break up and
resign now.'[175] In the Cabinet that Saturday Derby and Carnarvon
had fought against accepting Beaconsfield's proposal, prompted by
the heavy defeats of the Turkish armies, to order a fleet to the

Dardanelles and military force to the Bulair heights above Gallipoli. On Salisbury's suggestion, the Cabinet agreed to send only the fleet, with the Sultan's permission.[176]

Even against this compromise Carnarvon and Derby protested. The former, on 15 January, drafted a letter of resignation, to take effect when the Cabinet despatched ships to the Dardanelles.[177] Derby, confined to his bedroom by illness stemming from nervousness, insisted: 'I cannot put too strongly the objections which I feel to the sending up of the fleet.'[178] Incessant worry made him reluctant to continue in an office with which the Cabinet was constantly interfering: 'The fact is that a committee of 11 men occupied, & some overworked, in their own departments, is not & cannot be a suitable body for the transaction of diplomatic business.'[179] The Foreign Secretary was reluctant to cooperate with Carnarvon, whom he considered to be 'vain, touchy, & egotistical'. When well enough to receive his colleague, Derby 'heard him patiently, in the interest of the party, but gave little sympathy & no encouragement'.[180]

After the Cabinet meeting of 23 January 1878, Carnarvon and Derby discussed their situation and agreed to send formal letters of resignation to the Prime Minister the next day.[181] Carnarvon had 'the Queen's consent provisionally, & in the event of my finding it necessary to act on it'.[182] He asked Smith whether he had, in fact, telegraphed 'instructions to the Admiral to take the fleet up to Constantinople' and received an affirmative reply.[183] He and Derby resigned officially on 24 January 1878.[184] Salisbury later told his nephew, Arthur Balfour, 'that he could never get any reasonable account of his action out of Lord C. His conduct was probably largely due to personal motives. The fact that the names of Lord C. & Lord D. were so constantly associated together when they left the government is entertaining from the circum[s]tance that they were the two members of the Cabinet who got on least well together.'[185] Although they were in communication immediately after their resignations, Carnarvon and Derby failed to coordinate their activities.[186] The former insisted upon making a statement in the House of Lords on Friday afternoon, 25 January, perhaps to have the matter over with before the weekend. Beaconsfield managed to postpone Derby's doing the same; and the Queen's joy at his contemplated resignation was premature.[187]

The Foreign Secretary's colleagues were anxious to retain his services for reasons of domestic politics. As early as 24 January, Northcote was 'thinking over possible changes in the event of our two vacancies occurring', but he was 'far from clear about them'. He was especially concerned to keep Lancashire true to the Tory party. To call up Lord Sandon, MP for Liverpool and Vice President of the Committee of Council for Education, from the House of Commons would necessitate a by-election, and Northcote feared that 'we might lose Liverpool, – which would be fatal'. He wondered whether Lord Winnmarleigh, though 'rather old', might take the Privy Council Office: 'He is a good Lancashire man.'[188] Northcote was mindful that he would have to introduce the motion for a vote of credit on Monday 28 January. The previous Friday, he wrote again to Beaconsfield: 'I think it right to tell you that I hear alarming accounts of the effect which Derby's resignation might produce, especially on our Lancashire and Cheshire members. Dyke has not given me any names, but he says the feeling is much worst than he believed it to be when he spoke to you, and he thinks the division may be seriously affected by it.' In case of a bad division, the Chancellor of the Exchequer warned, the government must 'be prepared for a possible overthrow'.[189] The Chief Whip gave the Prime Minister similar advice:

> You asked me a question today with reference to the possible resignation of the Foreign Secretary. Since giving you my views I have heard much that confirms my opinion that he should at this moment be retained if possible in The Cabinet. The feeling in Lancashire is very strong & I have had many Telegrams on the subject, all expressing great anxiety. The Commercial element existing there, may also if thoroughly alarmed affect members in this House, & I am sure it would be well if no further change took place.[190]

Ironically, though by Beaconsfield's intention, Derby's brother, F. A. Stanley, was Parliamentary Under Secretary at the Treasury. His name appeared at the foot of the Command Paper printed that Friday asking six million pounds for 'Army and Navy Services': the vote of credit which the Chancellor was to request on Monday.[191]

Although Derby was persuaded to rejoin the Cabinet, his discomfort was understandable. The relationship between him and Beaconsfield was now based not on friendship but on temporary political expediency. The Foreign Secretary aimed at preventing an Anglo-Russian war, the Prime Minister at maintaining the appearance of governmental unity. Foreign affairs could not be entirely insulated from the buffeting of politics. During the previous year both Beaconsfield and Gladstone had appealed to and tried to manipulate public opinion through party organizations, the press and public demonstrations. They made agitation in the country a supplement to traditional parliamentary manoeuvring. The makers of foreign policy continued to pursue British interests, but they now had to find political support for their efforts in an era when millions of men had the right to vote.

4 The Politician as Diplomatist

For the Prime Minister, Lord Beaconsfield, foreign policy was an extension of politics. In aiming to fulfil Great Britain's imperial and Continental commitments, he was also trying to strengthen the Conservative government and party. Domestic opposition constrained him less between February and August 1878 than at any earlier stage of the eastern crisis. The Liberal factions were more at odds with each other than with the ministry. Within the Cabinet, Lord Derby alone continued to resist an active policy in the Near East; but the Foreign Secretary could merely delay the implementation of decisions over which he had no control, and by the end of March he had finally resigned his place. Lord Salisbury, who left the India Office to succeed him, worked closely with Beaconsfield to improve the diplomatic position of Great Britain after Russia's victory over Turkey had resulted in the treaty of San Stefano. Together they attended the congress of Berlin, where they obtained treaty provisions which were as favourable as possible, considering that the conflicting interests of the great powers prevented a definitive triumph by any one of them. In attempting to exploit his achievement at home, Beaconsfield discovered that diplomacy was of limited political usefulness.

Within a fortnight of his return to the Cabinet, Derby's colleagues forced him to acquiesce in sending warships into the Dardanelles. The Cabinet ordered the fleet commanded by Admiral G. P. Hornby to steam up the Straits 'whatever action the Porte might take'.[1] This decision caused some supporters of the Prime Minister to cancel a meeting which they had scheduled at the Carlton Club. Its purpose was to have been ostensibly to strengthen the ministers' hands, but really to effect the resignation of Derby and the assumption of the Foreign Office by Beaconsfield. The organizers now abandoned this plan, but they trusted that their intentions would be plain to Derby, who did not 'command either the respect or the confidence of his party'.[2] Indeed, 'the tail of the Party at the Carlton is furious against him', Carnarvon learned. He observed after a long talk with Mary Derby: 'Poor thing! I am very sorry for her, for she had courage enough to have made him *act* on former occasions & now she plainly sees that he has lost ground & is sinking in public opinion.' She suspected that her stepson, Salisbury, was driving recklessly along the road toward war 'with a view to the F.O.'.[3] Derby was in a weak position. According to his wife, he 'maintained his ground by stubbornness & his old plan of "wet-blanketting" each proposal as it is made. ...he felt absolutely alone'.[4]

Isolated from his colleagues, Derby lost his nerve. He complained to Beaconsfield on 19 March 1878 that the *Daily Telegraph* had published a Cabinet decision of the previous day regarding a com-munication to Russia. Such publicity violated the secrecy agreed upon and could, he argued, turn 'a friendly warning' into 'a public defiance'. He himself had told only Lord Tenterden in the Foreign Office and his own private secretary, T. H. Sanderson, 'both of them perfectly discreet'. He threatened 'to bring this subject before the Cabinet when it meets' — and in fact did so.[5] Salisbury pro-tested: 'I tell nothing of what passes in Cabinet to my Private Secretary. Why should Sanderson know.' He added: 'The occasion might be a fair one for protesting against the system of taking notes in Cabinet. You are never certain that they will not fall into hands for which they are not intended.'[6] The Prime Minister's reply to Derby was scathing:

> I can throw no light on parag. in D. Tel.
>
> My people are perfectly innocent of newspaper acquaintances; personally, I never see, or hear from, them. And I don't know, now that Carnarvon has gone, any member of the Cabt. who has such weaknesses.
>
> I always thought D.T. was devoted to you, but I suppose that's over.[7]

Over too was any semblance of friendship between Beaconsfield and Derby. The former, stung by the implication that he was responsible for the leakage — not an improbable assumption — had responded with a brazen distortion of the truth. If he meant to force Derby to recognize that he could no longer serve as a brake to the wheel of state, the Foreign Secretary did not admit as much.[8]

The Cabinet met on 27 March 1878. It now knew the details of the treaty of San Stefano, and suspected that Russia would refuse to allow the proposed European congress to pass on all its clauses, some of which were unacceptable to Great Britain. The Cabinet discussed delcaring a state of emergency, putting a force in the field, and sending an expeditionary force from India to occupy Scanderoon (that is, Alexandretta) and perhaps Cyprus. On the question of occupation, however, differences persisted as to which port to seize, and no firm decision was made. Salisbury thought Alexandretta more important than Cyprus, but the Secretary for War stated that the question had 'to be judged by military men'. Yet the 'only military plans...seemed to Lord Beaconsfield meagre'.[9] Salisbury was under the impression that his colleagues had resolved to take Alexandretta, and so telegraphed to India; he had sent engineers to survey the port, and considered that it ought to come under the Indian, rather than the Colonial, Office.[10] The Cabinet had, in fact, come to no definite conclusion on this point, except that, at last, something must be done.[11] In that tense meeting, each minister who had hopes or fears imagined that the discussion would lead to their realization. With no more reason than he might have had weeks or months earlier, Derby resigned. A few years later, after a conversation with his uncle, Lord Salisbury, A. J. Balfour made these observations:

> Why Lord Derby resigned is obvious enough. Why he did not do so long before is the only problem which requires solution. I suppose it was too great an effort even to form a decision which will for ever relieve him from the necessity of deciding anything again. The scenes in cabinet towards the end of his official connection with it, must have been highly curious. The issue of peace and war trembling in the balance. Lord Derby between overwork, alcohol, and responsibility, in a condition of utter moral prostration, doing as little as was possible and doing that little under compulsion. As the Ld. Chancellor told me the other day — 'During his last year (I think he said) of office all that Derby did was done at the point of the bayonnet [sic].' I believe during that period the Chancellor wrote many of the critical...despatches for him and, so to speak, put the pen in his hand and made him sign![12]

Perhaps, indeed, Derby's 'reason had suffered' during the previous two years of strain.[13]

Beaconsfield now reconstituted his Cabinet. Salisbury replaced Derby, thus ending the anomalous practice adopted during the latter's periods of withdrawal from his duties of sending telegrams and despatches, after Cabinet approval, 'merely "from the Foreign Office"', without the signature of the Foreign Secretary.[14] Gathorne Hardy, as Viscount Cranbrook, went to the House of Lords, a move he had desired since being denied the leadership in the Commons. He became Secretary of State for India.[15] Derby's brother, Colonel F. A. Stanley, joined the Cabinet as Secretary for War. Lord Sandon had been 'fidgetty' about his position as Vice President of the Council on Education. He agreed to accept the Presidency of the Board of Trade (vacated by Sir Charles Adderley's translation to the Lords), 'feeling that this is not a moment to even seem to quit the Government', but threatened to retire at the end of the session unless awarded a seat in the Cabinet.[16] He now got his wish. After Lord Carnarvon's resignation in January, Sir Michael Hicks Beach had become Colonial Secretary and the Duke of Northumberland had taken the Privy Seal Office. In a Cabinet of six peers and seven commoners, only two of the latter had neither a title nor a connection with the aristocracy.

The resignation of Derby was a significant indication of the transformation of British politics. The prestige of the house of Derby had helped to shelter Beaconsfield for three decades from the pelting criticism of being a *novus homo*. Now he dropped the guise of client of the family and became its patron. He included Frederick Stanley in the Cabinet, however, less out of sentiment than calculation. Many Tories believed that Derby determined the electoral course of large areas of Lancashire; they feared that if he abandoned the Conservative party, the county would do likewise. For that reason, and perhaps after a word of advice from the Prime Minister, the Queen wrote a particularly effusive letter of congratulation to Stanley's wife on her husband's appointment.[17] Beaconsfield also went out of his way to placate Sandon, for he felt that he could not afford to alienate this MP for Liverpool who was the son of the second Earl of Harrowby and had close political ties to the lord of Knowsley. These precautions were a sign that contemporaries, not unreasonably, still attributed much influence to landed magnates. Yet parties were becoming the predominant force in politics. Power lay with politicians who could command their allegiance and rally the masses in the country. Beaconsfield and Gladstone met the needs of this era of political transition, as Derby and Carnarvon,

Granville and Hartington could not. 'There is much relief & some joy, here at the resignation,' the Conservative Chief Whip reported from the House of Commons on the day Derby announced his decision: 'Some of the Rads are trying to make capital & say that the safe man has gone &c, but they will not *dare* say so in Public.' The Conservatives, W. H. Dyke exulted, had won a by-election at Worcester, and even a Liberal had admitted that Derby's departure would win them South Northumberland 'to a certainty'.[18] Derby's defection did no great harm to the Conservative cause. Beaconsfield controlled the party and commanded the attention of the country.

Salisbury, in contrast to Derby, was the kind of departmental head the Prime Minister liked: decisive, practical with a touch of imagination, cooperative, deferential. He managed the routine of the Foreign Office without getting bogged down in it. He was ready to implement decisions, as well as to help in making them; and he understood their domestic political implications. He accepted full responsibility for his office, was circumspect enough to avoid embarrassing his colleagues, and relieved his chief from the burden of worrying about the details of one of the great departments of state. As Foreign Secretary, Salisbury was a practical politician. He harboured no such inherent prejudices about international relations as he had a decade before about domestic issues. He appreciated, though he did not always sympathize with, Beaconsfield's calculations of the political impact of the conduct of British diplomacy. He knew, for example, that the question of withdrawing the fleet from the Dardanelles was 'not mainly naval, but political in its bearing. For actual *strategic* purposes the fleet is not of much value in its present position; and in fact it was sent up on political grounds *against* the advice of all the Sea Lords in the Admiralty – who saw considerable objections in a naval point of view to its being in the Sea of Marmora at all, with the Gallipoli peninsular in other than English hands.'[19]

Salisbury recognized the difficulties of formulating British foreign policy. A month before succeeding Derby, he had responded to a severe critic:

I do not complain of the language in which you describe our policy – as being intelligible only to a man who 'has the head of a pin, and the heart of a hen'. As I have more than once admitted during the past two years I think it is open to criticism. But I am afraid it is not indicative so much of the shortcomings of the individual[s] who have the shaping of it, but of a more deepseated and inaccessible evil. In the first place to ask us to pursue a bold policy towards the military powers of Europe, when we have no conscription, is to ask us to make bricks without straw. Diplomacy which does not rest on force is the most feeble and futile of weapons, and except for bare self defence we have not the force.

Turning his attention to domestic politics, he continued:

There are other reasons which make it improbable that anything approaching to a consistent and reasoned policy can ever be pursued by Great Britain. Other countries whatever their political constitutions are governed by one man, as far as foreign politics are concerned: or at most by two or three. Great Britain is governed by a Cabinet varying from twelve to sixteen: and I need not tell you how such a Government is likely to conduct itself in emergencies....So that without admitting the resemblance of the Cabinet to hens or pins, I can understand the construction which is put upon their doings.[20]

To compensate for these shortcomings, Salisbury, immediately upon taking up the seals of office, concisely formulated the bases of British foreign policy. He embodied his thoughts in a circular despatch, officially dated 1 April 1878, for the benefit of his colleagues as well as the diplomatic corps and the European powers.[21]

Bowing to political necessity, Salisbury endeavoured to gain the approval of the Cabinet for his policy. Unlike Derby, whose nervousness had fanned the fire of suspicion of the Continental powers in the breasts of Beaconsfield, other ministers and the Queen, Salisbury's calmness damped them down. 'I do not believe there is the slightest danger either of German or Italian hostility,' he assured the First Lord of the Admiralty: 'It is wholly unlike German policy which studiously abstains from active interference in matters not concerning Germany: & Italy has far too large a seaboard to make a deadly enemy of England. We should be able I suspect to help in such case in "rectifying" both her North Western & North Eastern frontiers.'[22] Less than a month after Salisbury had assumed his new duties, W. H. Smith was able to inform Admiral G. P. Hornby of 'a sensible relaxation of the tension here'.[23] The Lord President of the Council, the Duke of Richmond, wrote gratefully to the Foreign Secretary: 'I am glad you think things look tolerably peaceful.'[24] Salisbury carefully guided his colleagues when they had to make public statements about foreign affairs. To the Home Secretary, R. A. Cross, at the end of April 1878 he gave a full account of the current state of negotiations with both Austria and Russia, concluding: 'Of course all this is quite confidential – & is rather to put down to show what you should not say than what you should. Courteous but very firm, is the language I should recommend.'[25] Salisbury congratulated Cranbrook on a speech at Bradford, which 'answered admirably & contained nothing to which any one could object'.[26] As the Cabinet had not met during the Easter recess, both Cross and Cranbrook were relieved, for as the latter remarked, 'I was badly afraid of errors of ignorance.'[27] By his frankness Salisbury helped them to avoid this difficulty. He soon enjoyed the confidence of his colleagues.

With the backing of the Cabinet, Salisbury clarified Great Britain's policy in the eastern question. He disliked depending on the chance of an agreement with Austria-Hungary.[28] Northcote refused to consider a governmental guarantee for a loan to that power. But without one, he asked rhetorically of Salisbury, 'what can we do with "English capitalists". They won't advance their money to please us.' He did not think that the Austrians stood much chance of raising money in England: 'Nor do I see very clearly what our interest in the matter now is. I would have gone a long way in December to help her to mobilise and to arrest the Russians at Adrianople: and even now, if we had a common policy and were openly agreed upon a certain line of action involving costly sacrifices on her part, I should be willing to consider whether anything could be done for her. But she is still a weight on us, and a dangerous friend.'[29] The Prime Minister declared: 'Ct. Andrassy is an eel. However quick our glance or firm our grasp, he slips away, but it is hoped we shall transfix him at last.'[30] Suspicious of 'Andrassy's Penelopean negotiations',[31] Salisbury dealt directly with Russia. Through Bismarck's offices he arranged for a mutual withdrawal of the British fleet from the Sea of Marmora and the Russian army from the vicinity of Constantinople.[32] Shuvalov, who had staked his career on finding a peaceful solution of the eastern crisis through Anglo-Russian negotiations, proved cooperative. Salisbury relied not on his trustworthiness but on the strength of his ambition. 'Count Schouvaloff proposes shortly to go back to St Petersburg,' the Foreign Secretary informed the Queen on 1 May 1878, 'nominally to discuss with the Russians the English view of the treaty of

San Stefano: really to look after his own chances of succeeding Prince Gortchakoff.'[33]

During the fortnight preceding the opening of the Berlin congress on 13 June 1878, Salisbury strengthened the British government's diplomatic position. Shuvalov had returned from St Petersburg on 22 May. Eight days later he and Salisbury signed a secret protocol. By it, Great Britain recognized Russia's annexation of Bessarabia and Armenia, including Ardahan, Kars and Batum; and Russia agreed to limit the size of Bulgaria. A reference to England's duty of protecting the populations of Asiatic Turkey provided a cover for secret negotiations underway at Constantinople. Having decided to seize Cyprus, the British government forced the Sultan to grant it the right to occupy the island, should Russia retain any or all of the places in Armenia which the secret protocol of 30 May had already conceded to her. The Cyprus convention was formally signed on 4 June. On 6 June, Great Britain and Austria reached an agreement on mutual diplomatic support at the congress of Berlin.[34]

The success of Salisbury's diplomacy influenced the Cabinet's choice of delegates to the congress. Originally, it had designated Lord Lyons, the experienced ambassador at Paris, for that role.[35] Later, the Prime Minister evinced a desire to attend, but his colleagues were sceptical about the idea. As late as the last week in May Northcote wrote a brief note to him, apparently in a Cabinet meeting: 'I have had a few words with Cairns, Cranbrook, Cross, and Smith. They all seem to hesitate much about your going. Better not decide without further consideration. SHN' The next day, 28 May 1878, Northcote offered Beaconsfield similar advice:

Confidential
The upshot of my conversation is
1. That we had better wait a few days before deciding.
2. That if matters can be substantially settled beforehand, so that there are no outstanding points of importance left, you or he [Salisbury?] should go.
But that if there is much to be discussed Lyons should go.[36]

After the signing of the Anglo-Russian protocol of 30 May, Beaconsfield decided that he would represent Great Britain at Berlin, and that Salisbury would accompany him.[37] By 3 June when the government officially notified the German Chancellor, Prince Otto von Bismarck, that it would participate in the congress, the

Prime Minister felt certain that he would be able to present its outcome as a British victory—at the expense of either Russia or Turkey. As plenipotentiary, he expected to reap the political benefits of satisfying, in Cairns's words, 'the public, at home & abroad'.[38]

The Liberals were unable to launch a serious attack on the government during the spring of 1878. Joseph Chamberlain admitted at the end of March that 'in my deliberate judgment the majority of the constituencies are against us at this moment and the Government has it in its power to take us where it pleases. ...The rowdies in all the constituencies and that portion of the electors which calls itself non-political have gone over bodily to the enemy.'[39] Reports of jingoism among the working classes in Birmingham demonstrated the narrow social basis of the caucus. Chamberlain commented to Jesse Collings: 'It is curious if this be true, that no hint of such a feeling came out at the meeting of the 600, but of course there may be an underground current of which we know nothing because it exists amongst a class which is not represented on the Liberal association & which ordinarily takes no part in politics.'[40] As during the atrocities agitation, the financial and commercial men, of whom G. J. Goschen was a leading political representative, rebelled against criticisms which they considered 'inopportune and unpatriotic at this critical moment'.[41] Lord Carnarvon heard that any bellicose move by the government would cause 'a very great defection of the Liberals in the H. of C: that they fear for their seats — and that a large part of the middle class who before were all in favour of peace have now been converted to war'.[42] When, in April 1878, Sir Wilfrid Lawson introduced an amendment opposing the calling out of reserves, Gladstone, in a minority of sixty-four, voted for it while Hartington abstained. The result, according to Granville, was 'one of the heaviest blows to the possible discipline of a party I had ever remembered'.[43]

In May Chamberlain — 'that impudent fellow' Northcote dubbed him — gave notice of a vote of censure on the bringing of Indian troops to Malta.[44] Hartington complained to Sir William Harcourt: 'Chamberlain's motion appears to be remarkably ill-timed, & I presume that there is no wish to support him; but one can never tell what our erratic party may wish to do.'[45] His hand forced, Hartington himself eventually proposed the vote of censure, which centred on the constitutionality of the government's action. In this way he hoped that 'a number of Liberal Members who have been supporting the Govt. on the general Eastern Policy' could vote together 'on a point which does not commit them against that Policy, and yet one on which their vote will please constituents who do disapprove of the Govt. on other grounds'.[46] After the division turned out badly, he refused to join the Radicals in further opposition until the end of the Berlin congress.[47] Chamberlain himself became cautious. 'Amongst other things he described himself in the course of conversation as a radical but as no revolutionist, and as having been greatly alarmed at the risks which war with a divided public opinion would entail on the older & settled institutions of the Country,' Carnarvon recorded: 'He said he did not believe that there was much socialism in any class and he praised the singular absence of envy in all classes of Englishman.'[48]

Jingoism was in the ascendant, but it held perils even for its proponents. The manager of *The Times*, J. C. MacDonald, grumbled: 'Unfortunately in this crisis public feeling seems to be getting quite the upper hand of every prudent consideration.'[49] The desire to 'crumple up' Russia was 'fast becoming uncontrollable', he ruefully acknowledged in writing to his correspondents abroad.[50] *The Times* drifted with the tide of opinion, and Chamberlain accused it, not altogether wrongly, of having 'ratted completely' to prevent any loss of circulation.[51] The Prime Minister and his colleagues had encouraged a belligerent reaction in the country in order to forestall any campaign along the lines of the atrocities agitation as well as to strengthen the government's hand in dealing with Russia. Yet the Salisbury–Shuvalov protocol of 30 May 1878, despite a few face-saving clauses, conceded most of the Russian gains embodied in the treaty of San Stefano, against which the British government had vehemently protested. When he learned of the terms, Derby, who was now cooperating with the Whigs, expostulated to Granville: 'A more complete surrender of all that the Cabinet professed to stand for could not be. ...There was no moment when Russia would not have made this bargain with us, without pressure or intimidation. In fact she has got all she wants.'[52] Beaconsfield wished to announce the occupation of Cyprus simultaneously with the Berlin congress's public confirmation of the Asian arrangements of the secret protocol. He hoped thereby to avoid incurring the odium of his most fervent supporters in the country and to preempt Liberal criticism. In this objective he nearly failed, because the traditions of the Foreign Office took little account of the cupidity of 'new Grub Street'.[53]

Charles Marvin performed the duties of a copying clerk in the Foreign Office. He was paid 10d per hour. Salisbury's private secretary, Philip Currie, carelessly left the Anglo-Russian protocol for ordinary copying, and Marvin, who did the work, made a short abstract on 30 May. He gave it to the editor of the *Globe*, which published a summary of the main points of the secret agreement the next day. Denials of the authenticity of the account by Salisbury probably prompted the editor to press Marvin to produce the actual document. After rummaging through papers at the Foreign Office, he found the text a fortnight later, and the *Globe* printed it. Marvin received £40 from the paper on 15 June 1878 − 'for literary work' his solicitor later asserted − and deposited that sum in his savings account. The whole transaction was common knowledge in the offices of the *Globe*. Through a compositer, the story reached Cross, who, because of Salisbury's absence in Berlin, was acting Foreign as well as Home Secretary. On the morning of 26 June he met with the Treasury Solicitor, Law Officers and Lord Tenterden. They arrived at the opinion that Marvin could be charged with larceny and the *Globe* as an accessory after the fact. The same night, detectives arrested the clerk at his house in Plumstead, where 'a quantity of papers in Russian and letters to the "Globe" was found'. Charged with larceny and conspiracy, Marvin went free on bail, part of which a *Globe* sub-editor supplied. Cross had not consulted the Cabinet, and most of its members were surprised to learn of the apprehension of a suspect. Salisbury thought Marvin 'too small game to be worth flying at', but wanted to threaten him with prosecution 'to extract from him evidence against the Russians or the *Globe* manager'. Beaconsfield, who detested misguided zealousness on the part of his subordinates, referred to Cross as 'the inspirer of this folly'. Tenterden, well aware of the Prime Minister's disdain for permanent officials, wrote an apologetic letter to explain that Currie had handled the protocol as a personal negotiation between Salisbury and Shuvalov, that the Foreign Office had not treated it 'officially' and had nothing to do with it. Northcote nonetheless feared that there would be 'some disagreeable questions put as to the manner in which business is done at the F.O.'. He and his colleagues felt, correctly, that Marvin would not be convicted and were disappointed that he did not break bail, 'as we have been expecting'. The government could not discontinue the proceedings, once started, especially as by the beginning of July the story was widely known. German and Russian diplomatists had heard of it; so too had Henri de Blowitz, the notorious special correspondent of *The Times*, then at Berlin. The Russians in particular were unlikely to keep silent, for the original assumption had been that they had leaked the protocol in order to embarrass the British government.[54] Although this incident had some effect on British diplomacy, its ultimate importance lay in the stimulus it provided for the preparation of an official secrets act.

By rousing jingo feeling in England, the *Globe*'s publication of the protocol of 30 May caused ministers anxiety. 'The Jingos are all furious,' one informant wrote to Montagu Corry, who had accompanied his chief to Berlin: 'But they do not see further than the tail of their initial letter J so they will reconsider their own impulsive error.'[55] From the India Office, Cranbrook explicitly warned Salisbury:

> I am afraid that you are meeting with some difficulties not lessened by the rascally publication which excites so much attention here. It is astonishing how some are irritated by it but all seems to resolve itself into Batoum which is supposed to be the Highway to our Indian possessions. We are not fortunate in defenders as regards our own friends for the support of the Times aggravates the case against us. It is amusing to see the Ministry wh. was 'dragging the country into war' now blamed for an exactly opposite policy.

Cranbrook concluded with a phrase which Beaconsfield later used, in altered form, to define his accomplishment at Berlin: 'Wishing you rapid & safe progress & a speedy return with an honourable peace.'[56]

That outcome seemed to depend upon saving as much of Armenia as possible, and particularly the port of Batum, from the Russians. Cross admitted: 'Batoum is a sore point'; and Cranbrook told the Cabinet, in effect: 'Batoum is what our friends care about.'[57] Northcote wrote humorously to Salisbury: 'If you can save Batoum, you may do anything you like, and will only have to buy a slave to remind you that you are mortal.'[58] Lord John Manners, the Postmaster General, warned Beaconsfield of the intense interest in the fate of the port, and of a certain Moslem tribe in Armenia, the Lazes: 'Save it and them, and you come home triumphant; sacrifice them, and you will be regarded as having failed.'[59] Dyke reminded the Prime Minister that the government was at the end of its fifth session, and that both he and his Liberal counterpart listened daily to enquiries regarding a possible dissolution — 'however I let them gossip & spend there [sic] money too in preparing if they like, on the other side'. In the present state of affairs the Conservative Chief Whip recognized that the fate of Batum was of electoral significance: 'I believe many sacrifices would be thought of little consequence if the place were not allowed to fall totally into Russian hands.' The local organizer from Bristol, speaking to Dyke about constituency business, 'interrupted me quite suddenly with — "mind no giving up of Batoum, or it is no use your sending a Candidate to Bristol"'.[60] The Cabinet was wary of a 'renewal of hostilities'; and Tenterden remarked that 'our Admirals are Crying for an excuse to fight & it wd be a thousand pities if it was now afforded to them'.[61] Beaconsfield acknowledged that 'something must be done about Batoum', but he was not sanguine 'after that unfortunate Schou-Sal: Mem-[oran]dum'.[62] He suggested to Salisbury that they might issue a threat: 'I think we shall have to tell Schou: that if Russia is not wise, they will have a Jingo Govt. & war with England in a month. It looks very like it.'[63] The Foreign Secretary, though he did not regard popular outbursts of opinion with great seriousness, acquiesced: 'Evidently there has been some revulsion of feeling in our party. I believe it is the hot weather. I will do all I can to frighten Shou.'[64]

At Berlin Beaconsfield and Salisbury were not the only negotiators trying to coordinate their diplomatic efforts with political exigencies at home. The powers had decided the most pressing issue: they had avoided war. Now, although they had already traced the general outline of the settlement, their plenipotentiaries had still to work out many details, some of them of considerable importance.[65] The leaders of each major European delegation were politicians of the first rank who understood the possible domestic consequences of their proceedings. Political considerations dictated much of the conduct especially of the Russian and Austrian, as well as the British, representatives.[66] When Salisbury tried to force Gorchakov and Shuvalov to yield over Batum, he had little success in 'shaking out of their mouths this bone'.[67] Of his proposal to open the Straits to British warships, the Cabinet in London, with the exception of Manners, disapproved, though it sanctioned his 'using the question...as an argument in Congress to preserve Batoum or to have it made a free Port'.[68] Cross wrote that if Salisbury and Beaconsfield could achieve this object, 'we shall feel eternally grateful to you'.[69] The treaty of Berlin finally recorded the Tsar's intention of making Batum a 'free port, essentially commercial' (article LIX). This compromise was the best that the British delegates could hope for in the light of the Anglo-Russian protocol of 30 May.[70]

The Conservative leaders hoped that the acquisition of Cyprus would serve as a political palliative to Russian successes, but the problem of revealing the news vexed them. To spare Beaconsfield added nervousness, Northcote, who was in charge of the government during the absence of the Prime Minister, did not inform him of all the difficulties at home.[71] Relying upon Salisbury's calmness, he wrote pessimistically to the Foreign Secretary on 20 June 1878 – 'The Globe has cast down the spirits of our men in a most extraordinary degree' – and supplied him with full details:

> I cannot help feeling nervous as to the manner in which the other Conventions [sic] may be brought out. If it were to be betrayed, and given to the world irregularly, it might do infinite mischief. You will have to exercise all your skill in launching it; and pray don't forget to keep us well informed, so that we may know how to answer on the instant it should become necessary. We are already twitted with being ready to give up B.[atum] and K.[ars], and if we could be charged with selling them for C.[yprus] we should be out before you could get home. Your original plan of making as good a fight as possible for the frontiers of Armenia, and only falling back on the other scheme after failing in this, is damaged by the revelation of what looks like a foregone conclusion. We shall be said to have sold the battle. It would, I think, be well for us to make the announcement here contemporaneously with your announcement at Berlin. What you say there will be telegraphed here instantly, – so don't let it come on a Saturday; for a 48 hours' start would make the misrepresentations serious.
>
> I hear that a Jingo meeting is getting up for tomorrow, but I don't think it will do much harm. Our men are generally quite loyal though uneasy. But the air is electrical, and it would not take much to bring about such a movement as that which upset Palmerston in 1858.[72]

Salisbury replied reassuringly from Berlin: 'I am much less apprehensive of what will happen here than I was when I left home.' He thought that W. H. Waddington, the French Foreign Minister and first plenipotentiary, with his 'ganz bürgerlisches Aussehen', was unlikely to 'do anything dangerous' in response to the British move on Cyprus. The domestic situation seemed to hold more perils than the international one. 'How would you wish us to bring out the Convention? Would you prefer to lay it on the table of the House before we bring it out here?' Salisbury asked Northcote: 'If it is possible to keep it dark till Beaconsfield comes home I should prefer it: as the Jingoes require to be calmed in their own language, & he is the only one among us who speaks it fluently.'[73] Northcote agreed, but he felt that if the agreement became known, the government would have to lay the convention before parliament immediately, though it might defer questions until the Prime Minister's return.[74]

At Constantinople and Berlin, knowledge of the secret Anglo-Turkish convention of 4 June 1878 was widespread, and the British ministers feared that premature confirmation of the news in London would prove politically embarrassing. Salisbury telegraphed to Sir Henry Layard on 27 June: 'Do all you can to keep issue of Firman secret. We are very anxious to keep things quiet a few days longer.'[75] By the beginning of July the German, Austrian and Russian delegations at the congress knew of or strongly suspected the British designs on Cyprus. 'Our torpedo must explode in a very few days,' Salisbury informed Northcote on 3 July: 'I trust we may avoid Saturday – in deference to your instructions.'[76] Cross warned Tenterden to be ready to act on the instant to instruct the Admiralty to despatch ships to the island: 'we must lose no time in telegraph Dept of F:O:'.[77] Delays ensued in Constantinople. The publication of the protocol of 30 May had aroused the resentment of the Turks. They suspected, with good reason, that they had sacrificed the pawn of Cyprus, *en passant*, when the British and Russian grandmasters had already agreed to a draw. Although the Turkish Grand Council reluctantly ratified the convention on 4 July, only constant badgering by Layard secured the Sultan's final authorization three days later. Beaconsfield and Salisbury wanted to postpone the public announcement until Tuesday 9 July, but the *Daily Telegraph* published the substance of the convention on the Monday, forcing government spokesman to inform both houses of parliament later in the day.[78]

Most Conservatives greeted the news with enthusiasm. 'The Convention is very well received here, among our own men with the rarest exceptions', Cross assured Salisbury: 'Very well received in the City, & at Liverpool. ...Strongly disapproved by our late Foreign Secretary.' According to both the German and Austrian ambassadors, the Liberals were 'aghast! & will do nothing', and many of them 'highly approved'. According to Cross: 'Batoum had become a pure Shibboleth: no one knew anything about it – so they all cried out the louder. The Convention has now put all that out of sight.'[79] Northcote reported similarly to Beaconsfield: 'The Cyprus arrangement is well received among our own people...and Dyke says it will be accepted by a large number of our opponents. Hartington, he thinks, will not be keen against it; but of course Gladstone and the Radicals will go wild.'[80] The Chief Whip himself had already written to the Prime Minister:

> Gladstone is rabid, and looks as if he must tear something or somebody in pieces or expire with rage. My impression is that they are utterly confounded at present, but the old story will be repeated. Harcourt will frame a Resolution & Gladstone & others will bully Hartington into a contest which he hates. It seems to me that you have placed us in a glorious position & your return will be a triumph.

Dyke asserted that the House of Commons had been more enthusiastic than the country; he had never known a better spirit of cooperation in the Conservative party.[81] Manners described the situation succinctly: 'Gladstone & Co. of course are furious, and an attempt is being made by the Birmingham clique to agitate the country; but it will fail. In the City the feeling is very favourable, and all sorts of honours are proposed wherewith to greet your return.'[82]

The reception which awaited Beaconsfield and Salisbury in London was a political demonstration, carefully prepared in advance. Lord Henry Lennox, who had served a disastrous term as First Commissioner of Works (1874–6) and was obviously trying to regain the Prime Minister's favour,[83] took the lead in 'an extensive organization'. He planned, he had informed Corry on 1 July 1878, 'something which will enable the working men to join in, which shall startle Europe & be the grandest reception ever given to a subject in this Country'. Lennox had the promise of substantial subscriptions, 'and I think I can assure you, that my energy & the promptings of my Heart, will make it something which will reverberate through the Empire from one end to another'. He asked Corry to give him some idea when Beaconsfield would return, and suggested that his arrival at Charing Cross station should be

> at the best Hour for a monster Gathering. Of course, I ask no questions; but I feel, that in either case this great demonstration will do good service to the Conservative cause. If the Result of the Congress should be, what we hope it will be, why a Public reception is a necessity – if on the other hand our Dear Chief has not been able to achieve all, that he & we wish – then the Demonstration will do real service, by covering our retreat and displaying our gratitude & affection for our Illustrious Ruler.[84]

The directors of the South Eastern Railway promised to erect seats for two hundred people at Charing Cross and, together with Lennox, invited Beaconsfield's friends to be present to welcome him. Northcote confirmed this arrangement.[85] He informed Salisbury: 'You will have a very hearty reception at home.[86] Local Conservative associations mustered their followers to form cheering crowds in Dover and London.[87]

The British plenipotentiaries in Berlin 'recoiled' when they learned of the demonstrations which would greet them. They forced Corry to admit that he had received information from Lennox and apparently ordered him to limit or eliminate the ceremonies. To do so at the last minute proved impossible without outraging the organizers, who were staunch party supporters. Corry hurriedly telegraphed to Lord Barrington, a whip and personal friend of Beaconsfield, from Berlin on the last day of the congress, 13 July 1878: 'Chief anxious to do nothing ungracious would not arrest arrangements if gone too far quite ignorant here what they are kindly use your discretion about communicating with Henry.'[88] In a letter, Corry elaborated on these instructions:

> But pray, like a good fellow, see that no 'brusquerie' is committed towards our friends!
> I write you in *confidence*. Dont let Henry feel he is snubbed – and – if it seems right – let the conceived plans be executed.
> It won't do to be rude to zealous friends.
> The *Chief* is ready for anything. Some one else is shy![89]

Despite his shyness, Salisbury endured the welcoming ceremonies by Beaconsfield's side when they arrived in England on Tuesday 16 July.[90] The Dover Working Men's Constitutional Association presented an address to the Prime Minister. His response was significant: 'We have brought a peace, and we trust we have brought a peace with honour, and I trust that will now be followed by the prosperity of the country.'[91] In London the metropolitan police deployed 800 men of all ranks to control the crowds and traffic.[92] The Prime Minister's 'triumphal entry...was a considerable affair – nosegays – a vociferating crowd – carriages – red cloth &c &c', Carnarvon noted with displeasure: 'S. completely effaced by Disraeli & patronised by him – a very curious spectacle & how different in every way from S.'s return from Const[antinople] when Lady Derby drove down to the Station to receive him & he came & dined alone with me in Bruton St. How wonderful all these revolutions of the wheel of Fortune are.'[93] As soon as Beaconsfield reached 10 Downing Street, Corry telegraphed to the Queen: 'There has been a marvellous exhibition of public feeling from Charing Cross to Downing St. and the Street is now filled with a dense crowd singing loyal songs.'[94]

Some manufacturers, traders and financiers, who hoped to do well out of an aggressive imperial policy in Asia Minor, lent their voices to the Conservative chorus lauding the Cyprus convention. On the very day that the news became public, Barrington had informed the Prime Minister: 'The territorial guarantee is naturally more objected to than the occupation of Cyprus.... If John Bull can be made to think that vast fields of enterprise will be opened for the investment of his loose cash, the measure will soon cease to be looked on with jaundiced eye.'[95] Cross welcomed Salisbury home on 16 July 1878 with this announcement: 'I hear from our Lancashire manufacturers that orders are already coming in. And they look forward to Asia Minor. I do hope that you will be able to introduce some Anglo Indian men there: I am sure it would give such confidence if this were done that Capital would soon flow in.'[96] When, the next day, the Duke of Richmond wanted to break an engagement to attend a banquet of the City Carlton Club, Beaconsfield urged him not to miss the function: 'It is of the highest importance, at this moment, to keep the City in good humour.'[97] The occupation of Cyprus raised a fever of speculation in Englishmen interested in the building of railways in Asia Minor; but the government, though it encouraged a scheme under the auspices of the Duke of Sutherland, refused to offer any material guarantee.[98] The political as well as the financial cost of doing so deterred the Prime Minister and his colleagues.

The attitude of the policy-makers of *The Times* reflected a widespread scepticism about Beaconsfield's achievement at Berlin. The manager, MacDonald, wrote that he was not sure 'that I myself as a unit in the mass feel altogether disposed to drift with the tide about this new diplomacy of ours. It looks brilliant — surprizing — Oriental — the appropriate work of a great Adventurer like Beaconsfield — but all the same I am not convinced that it will succeed & I am quite certain that its good fortune will very much depend on the judgment & caution with which we enter on our new Protectorate.'[99] In declining a social invitation from Granville, Thomas Chenery, who had replaced J. T. Delane as editor at the beginning of the year, admitted: 'This has been an anxious and trying time for any one concerned in politics. With respect to the Anglo-Turkish Convention, it is I think an experiment which we must allow the Government to make on its own responsibility.' He could detect little enthusiasm for it but rather 'an expectant acquiescence'.[100] Although Corry offered Chenery intelligence,[101] *The Times* under his direction, as under that of his famous predecessor, avoided a commitment to either of the political parties. Apparently Beaconsfield tempted John Walter III with the bait of a peerage at the end of August 1878, but MacDonald warned the newspaper's owner: 'Certainly nothing could happen more injurious to The Times under present circumstances than your acceptance of a Title. At any time it would be doubtful policy for you to receive such honours, but just now the universal feeling would condemn it.'[102]

The government was weaker in the country than at Westminster. Whereas Gladstone and the Radicals expressed heated dissent over eastern policy, the Whigs and moderate Liberals were lukewarm in their opposition, if they bothered to oppose at all. A division in the House of Commons on foreign affairs on 3 August 1878 had produced a governmental majority of 143.[103] Dyke, the Conservative Chief Whip, knew that many Liberals would welcome such a result, as it removed any excuse for dissolving parliament at a time when their party was deeply divided. Although for his own side he likened a dissolution to 'throwing up a rubber at Whist whilst holding nothing but good cards', he recognized that the Tory hand was in need of improvement. 'You may reduce the Army & especially the

Navy expenditure to a great extent the coming year,' he had advised the Prime Minister as early as 19 July: 'You have forestalled ship-building expenditure for some years & Smith tells me he quite sees his way to a large reduction. This will all help a future budget.'[104]

On 26 August Dyke, repeated his strictures against calling for an election, despite arguments that after five sessions the government should seize upon this moment of triumph in foreign policy to do so. In support of his position he cited three reasons: first, Conservatives in the House of Commons, who had not failed in an important division in five years, would feel disgust at such a move; secondly, Liberals would be able to launch an attack in the areas of trade and taxation, where only time and good administration could provide an effective reply; thirdly, the government had no precedent for a dissolution after enjoying a majority of more than 140, and it would be subject to the charge of not wanting to accept the consequences of its bold policy. Dyke forecast that the deterioration of the Liberal party would continue unabated: 'The Birmingham school led by Mr Chamberlain are promoting daily more & more discord in the ranks of our Opponents, and I hear of Divisions increasing in every Constituency — such Divisions I believe will not be healed for many years.' Although the Conservatives were improving their electoral chances in Ireland, according to the Chief Whip, they would lose seats upon a dissolution now. The economic situation was also bad, he reminded Beaconsfield: 'a popular feeling obtains in many of the manufacturing Towns, that a Conservative Government invariably causes bad trade'. He urged that the ministry had the opportunity of producing two more budgets which might show such a balance sheet in 1880 as to command the support of the country. In that case, he concluded, the government might argue that the success of its foreign policy had achieved this result, for which the Conservative party would gain full credit.[105]

Beaconsfield's diplomacy was partially successful abroad and at home. By setting Austria-Hungary against Russia, it contributed to heightening tensions within the Dreikaiserbund.[106] The subsequent Austro-German alliance of 1879 was the first strand in a network of Continental agreements. Great Britain, excluded from them, did not exercise the commanding role in Europe which had been the Prime Minister's ambition. Nor did she secure definitive safeguards for her imperial commitments. Salisbury soberly assessed the British achievement at the congress of Berlin: 'I think we have got as good a settlement as could fairly be expected — without bloodshed. But we have not settled the Eastern Question. That will not be done for another fifty years to come.'[107] He recognized that the government had no further fund of warlike spirit in the country upon which it could draw to enforce the terms of the treaty of Berlin.[108] Although the government's foreign policy, to Gladstone's dismay, won adherents even in the north of England,[109] its appeal was limited. The general opinion seemed to be one of relief that England had avoided a conflict with Russia, with some approval of the acquisition of Cyprus. Beaconsfield, by including Salisbury in the honours accruing from their Berlin mission, not only expressed his gratitude for his colleague's services, but also tried to strengthen the Tory party by identifying the austere aristocrat with its appeal to the masses. A few days after the Prime Minister and the Foreign Secretary had accepted the garter together, five hundred prominent Tories cheered them at the Duke of Wellington's Riding School in Knightsbridge on 27 July 1878.[110] But Monty Corry, who described the fete at length to the Queen, had to admit that an attempt at a 'political banquet' at Apsley House, composed of people from various strata of society, of whom not a score attended, had been 'a failure'.[111] Salisbury had good reason for hoping that 'we have done with the Eastern Question in English politics'.[112]

The semblance of diplomatic success was no guarantee of electoral victory. Most voters were more concerned with the economic recession than with the eastern question. During the spring of 1878, strikes and lockouts in the Lancashire cotton mills had commanded attention in the north of England, and troops had been called out.[113] The partisan triumph of Beaconsfield's return from Berlin solidified the ranks of the Conservative party and split the Liberal opposition. It diverted attention from, but could not completely mask, the adverse situation at home. The Prime Minister had played the role of diplomatist, but the new electorate was not an entirely appreciative audience. Gladstone's criticism of the performance in 1878 was a preparation for the scathing indictment of the Midlothian campaigns.

5 Popular Politics

After the congress of Berlin, both Lord Beaconsfield, the Prime Minister, and W. E. Gladstone considered their strategies for a general election. The parliament of 1874 was by 1878 in its fifth session, and by law it could live no more than seven. Timing a dissolution was awkward for the government. Difficulties in regard to foreign affairs and, above all, the domestic economy beset it. The Liberals recognized the vulnerability of the Conservatives on these issues, but they had to contend with divisions between Whigs and moderates on the one hand and Radicals on the other. To unify the two factions and rally the electorate to his party, Gladstone attacked the government's foreign policy. He staged his campaigns in Midlothian to attract national attention. He used popular politics to work his will upon his party and to gain victory at the polls in April 1880.

Beaconsfield wanted to husband the credit accruing to his party from the peaceful settlement of the eastern crisis. Unfortunately for him, the European powers had difficulty in enforcing various clauses of the treaty of Berlin, and his government became involved in imperial conflicts in Afghanistan and South Africa.[1] The Prime Minister's remark 'respecting this Afghanh. business' applied as well to the other problems abroad which plagued his ministry after the congress of Berlin:

> So long as the country thought they had obtained 'Peace with honour', the conduct of H.M. Govt. was popular, but if the country finds there is no peace, they will be apt also to conclude there is no honor.
>
> I see strong symptoms of this feeling becoming very prevalent, & by no means confined to one party.[2]

Beaconsfield feared that rumours of war in the Near East and actual battles in central Asia and southern Africa would squander not only Tory political capital but also the pecuniary resources of the

103

Treasury. He deprecated an autumn session of parliament in 1878, 'especially if it involves, thro' the unsatisfactory state of our finances, the necessity of increased taxation, wh., with an Afghan war, would be inevitable'.[3] He and Lord Salisbury, the Foreign Secretary, were wary of enquiries from the Italian government about the British attitude toward its sale of Vatican property, for the Conservatives wanted to keep their 'Orange friends' as well as to increase the 'support of the R. Cath. party in England'.[4] In the autumn of 1879, when he briefly entertained the hope of allying Great Britain with Germany and Austria-Hungary, Beaconsfield commented:

> Notwithstanding the general depression, a fear of Russia, as the Power that will ultimately strike at the root of our Empire, is singularly prevalent....I believe that an alliance between the three powers in question, at this moment, might probably be hailed with something like enthusiasm by the country. It would explain many passages, that are now ambiguous or unsatisfactory. They would, then, be treated as parts of one coherent whole.[5]

Great Britain never joined the dual alliance of Germany and Austria. Even had it done so, Beaconsfield would not have solved his primary problem. Issues of foreign policy could not extricate the Conservative government from the economic morass at home.

Beaconsfield and his colleagues briefly considered action to alleviate the consequences of the depression which was affecting both agriculture and industry. In December 1878 Frederick Greenwood, the editor of the *Pall Mall Gazette*, who three years before had assisted in the British government's purchase of the Suez canal shares, warned the Prime Minister that distress in the north of England was great and increasing. 'The strike riots in Blackburn must not be forgotten, nor the fact that the mining population is prone to turbulence,' he stated. He advised Beaconsfield that the government should organize a national subscription, started by contributions from the royal family and the Cabinet, and ask Liberals of business acumen such as G. J. Goschen and W. E. Forster to join the managing committee — of course, 'emphatically dissociating the plan from the idea of state aid'. He cautioned that if the opposition initiated such a scheme, 'the distress may be used for political or party purposes'.[6] Beaconsfield put the proposal, as his own, to Salisbury and other Cabinet members.[7] He revealed his principal motive to his trusted political adviser, Earl Cairns, the Lord Chancellor: 'I fear much that the enemy contemplate making the public distress a party cry, & the effect of such a step to the country, as well as the Government, might be serious.'[8] Salisbury and Cairns approved of the proposal.[9] To launch it publicly, Beaconsfield desired to have a royal donation, '& that takes time, & damnable cyphered tels., & I have not even a secretary here,' he groused to Salisbury from Hughenden: 'Quite alone: fair dames & roasted Turkeys have seduced all my staff. I suppose, if I got a good warranty from the great Lady it wd. do — & the rest might follow? I want her to give £2,000.'[10] Salisbury replied: 'I think the first announcement should be simply your letter & the Queen's subscription: accompanied perhaps by Prince Hal's — if he can afford it.'[11]

Although the Queen and the Prince of Wales were amenable, the Chancellor of the Exchequer was not. Sir Stafford Northcote, steeped in the economic orthodoxy of *laissez faire*, objected to hoisting 'a flag of distress when there has been no visible calamity to account for it.'[12] Although unconvinced by this argument, the Prime Minister recognized that 'it is ingenious & prudent. We cannot, however, run a-muck against the leader of the H. of C. & the Finance Minister.'[13] Salisbury retaliated: 'Starving is starving all the same — whether it comes from a special or a general cause.' He agreed with Cairns: 'If the distress should go on, & become more acute, it will be very easy for some opposition man — like Harcourt or Gladstone — to come forward with a backing of rich Whig Dukes — & to say that they had waited in the idea that perhaps H.M. Govt. would take the lead, but that as there was no sign of any such action, they thought the time had come &c., &c., &c.'[14] The Home Secretary, R. A. Cross, telegraphed urgent instructions to his Permanent Under Secretary: 'Request Mayors in all great Manufacturing Districts to keep me informed as to the amount of distress & local means of meeting it with expressions of sympathy let Circular go out tomorrow telegraph to Newcastle & Sheffield today.' Returns from eighty-five towns in England, Wales, and Scotland indicated that fifty-five of them (including Birmingham, Cardiff, Leeds, Liverpool, Manchester, Sheffield, Dundee, Edinburgh and Glasgow) had taken special measures of relief.[15] Beaconsfield reported to the Queen on 21 January 1879 that the Cabinet 'considered the question of the alleged General Distress, which seemed however, by official accounts, to be partial, & not to be increasing; & the financial prospect not so black as is supposed'.[16] Greenwood was prepared for this verdict: 'To me too, it seems that the prospects brightened immediately after Christmas, instead of darkening, as so many of us feared: doubtless more harm than good would have been done by the course contemplated.'[17] On 22 January Zulus decimated a British force at Isandhlwana; and once the news reached England, the Cabinet diverted its attention to the war in South Africa, which Cairns declared had 'dealt us the heaviest blow we have sustained since we came into office'.[18] Meanwhile the depression deepened, and unemployment increased sharply in 1879.[19] Mary Derby observed:

> every supporter of the Gov't. feels bound to make little of the general distress. . . . I did not know till this year what distress in Lancashire could be. There is uncomplaining mute suffering. . . the people seem to think that it comes to them as a matter of course. I wonder so much what it means. . . . No signs hereabouts of distress abating. I am getting altogether depressed & out of sorts from hearing of nothing but misery; it is impossible to relieve all, & I shall be quite glad of a change to London.'[20]

By April the Prime Minister admitted to the Queen: 'The rallying in trade which had commenced is arrested by the Collier strike, & the continued gloom of the weather. A nation will not be sanguine without a little sunshine.'[21]

The Conservative Chief Whip, Sir William Hart Dyke, was well aware of the bearing of the economic distress on his party's electoral chances. After a by-election defeat at Newcastle-under-Lyme at the end of August 1878, he had explained to Beaconsfield:

> I hear from those who were engaged in the struggle on our side, that the Irish Vote turned the Election, coupled with the strong feeling as to the badness of trade (all ascribed by agitators to the Government). Sir Charles Russell, whose brother in law was our Candidate, wrote to me that he was quite astounded, how little the Eastern Question influenced the Electors, & that Financial considerations completely swamped it. Cross writes to me today − 'Our future depends upon our Estimates, & I hope the Treasury are alive to it.' I do not think this affects us in the South of England, but in the North to a grave extent.

Dyke opined that Conservative prospects in a general election were good, 'if we devote ourselves to the production of a sound Financial scheme in 1880'.[22] From the north of England, he received accounts of generally favourable feeling toward Conservative policy, especially in foreign affairs, 'but the Rads work the distress cry, without intermission: & we are going to get Lecturers & speakers to go down, and counteract this as much as possible.'[23] In July 1879 he repeated: 'After a most careful review of the Position, by our Political Committee, I have a strong opinion that we need not fear an appeal to the Constituencies.' He remained convinced, nonetheless, that success depended upon the financial question, and suggested that the Cabinet avoid isolating it from general issues, including foreign policy, and that, 'if taxation be inevitable, as little Financial information as possible be given to our opponents before the close of this Session'.[24] He insisted upon delaying a dissolution of parliament until after the new registers came into force in January 1880, 'rather on account of the extraordinary care which, this year, we have given to registration, than on the strength of returns, which can not yet be satisfactorily made'.[25] Dyke apparently hoped that many Liberals in the country would copy the behaviour of the opposition in the House of Commons during the past five sessions, either voting on the government side or abstaining; 'but much', he admitted, 'will depend upon Finance'.[26]

Before they could take full advantage of the electoral opportunity offered by the economic depression, Liberals had to cope with the divisions in their own ranks. By July 1878 their party was demoralized.[27] Frustrated by his failure to form Liberalism into an effective instrument of opposition, Gladstone blamed the parliamentary leaders for their impotence during the eastern crisis:

> I could not undertake to explain the conduct of the Liberals as a party in this great matter or of leading individuals among them, for instance of Mr. Forster in the Autumn of 1876 on his return [from Constantinople]. But my own course was of course made to bend, as far as I possibly could, to their views. I in vain strove to get them to bring on, early in 1877, or to support me in bringing on, the terrible indictment against the Turkish Government on the Bulgarian question established by the Blue Books. Failing in this I had to put it into a pamphlet which drew but moderate attention.

Gladstone was disappointed, too, in his own inability to sway the masses:

> With regard to the early months of the present year I must own that the *people* showed a changeableness between December & March which I have not been able thoroughly to understand. But I think the Liberals of the City were dastardly to the last degree in shrinking from the duty of exposing the organised and paid rowdyism (from the Lord Mayor's part downwards) which was undoubtedly a main agent in the apparent change.[28]

Now Gladstone complained bitterly about the government's acquisition of Cyprus, 'on which the majority of the people are likely to be dazzled. . . . As to the grand scheme of their Protectorate I think it worthy of Bedlam in some respects and of Botany Bay in others, such is my sense of its madness & its duplicity.' He professed to fear 'difficulties in the party' if Lord Hartington did not speak out.[29] 'In truth there is no effective opposition, nor any great disposition to create one,' Lord Cardwell admitted: 'The government has us all at its feet.'[30] This situation incensed Gladstone. After Beaconsfield's apparent triumph at Berlin, a Conservative whip observed: 'Gladstone looks like a caged tiger with his bone taken from him.'[31]

As he had during the past few years, Gladstone continued to advocate the necessity for Liberal organization in the country and staunch criticism of the government's foreign policy. By this dual approach he hoped to avoid divisive domestic issues such as disestablishment, to maintain his personal hold on Nonconformist opinion, and to promote the integration of Radicals into the Liberal party. Speaking at a meeting marking the first anniversary of the Southwark Liberal Association in July 1878, he encouraged the formation of other constituency organizations on the Birmingham pattern. Aware that the Conservatives were adopting this form in many of the large boroughs, he stressed that the Liberals had to do the same.[32] Gladstone knew that the perfervid supporters of the atrocities agitation looked to him for guidance. The Duke of Argyll warned him in September 1878 'to disavow' that his arguments were those of 'the "Peace at any price" party. . . . In this respect I think you have not shaken yourself free from the feelings of a Party Leader − not to say anything to run counter to the tendencies of an important section of the "Liberal Party". But there is a "taint" in this party, on this subject, as well as on others with which I have no sympathy.'[33] Although Argyll was an idiosyncratic politician, 'not disposed to the new Radical school',[34] his tone of moral righteousness echoed that of many Nonconformists to whom Gladstone desired the Liberal party to appeal.

Whigs and moderate Liberals, led by Lords Granville and Hartington, hesitated to attack the government or to welcome the Nonconformists with the vigour demanded by Gladstone and the Radicals. In the autumn of 1878 Hartington reacted negatively to Gladstone's attempts to oppose governmental preparations for war in Afghanistan, where the Indian Viceroy was trying to prevent Russian influence from predominating over British.[35] To Granville, Hartington privately broached the idea of resigning as leader in the House of Commons:

> I tried to believe that the importance of the Eastern Question & the part wh. he had taken in its former stages, explained & justified Mr. Gladstone's taking the lead on every important occasion.
> But it is quite clear that so long as this Govt. is in office, & probably always, it will be the same. In fact he appears to become more excitable & active every day.
> If he takes an active part in Parliament, he must be the real leader. If I thoroughly agreed with him, it might be worth while to act the part of nominal leader, in order to keep the party slightly together. But I very seldom do agree with him altogether, & it becomes a question not merely of sham leadership, but of losing the independence wh. I shd. have if I were a follower instead of a leader.[36]

After Beaconsfield remarked at the Guildhall on 9 November that events in Afghanistan would probably enable the British government to remove 'all anxiety respecting the North-Western frontier of India', Granville managed to dissuade Gladstone from joining an Afghan Committee which demanded the calling of parliament.[37] One of the Whig organizers, Lord Grey, feared that Gladstone's adhesion would cripple his movement and split the Liberal party. He agreed with Granville that to change British policy toward Afghanistan required the defeat of the Tory government: '& this is not likely to be accomplished while so large a number of people believe that a change of Govt at the present moment wd be only "out of the frying pan into the fire" as Gladstone whether in or out of office would in all probability mainly guide any new govt that could be formed. I must confess that I share this apprehension, & I am not therefore very anxious to get rid of these people, even after reading the Guildhall speech.'[38] The meeting of parliament in December demonstrated that 'a large portion of the liberal party are in fact thorough Jingoes'.[39] Divisions in both houses produced large majorities for the government. 'What a beating they gave us!' Lord Halifax exclaimed to Granville: 'I must say that I was astonished by the votes of some of our friends. You have kittle cattle to drive − & it makes me unhappy to see the way in which the old Whig families are degenerating.'[40]

The parliamentary Liberal leaders disliked the National Liberal Federation under the direction of Joseph Chamberlain. Forster, who had met with considerable opposition from his own constituency association in Bradford, charged that the men who elected the local committees were a small minority of 'wire-pullers' or, as in Bradford, agitators for disestablishment or some other special interest.[41] When, in December 1878, Chamberlain pressed him to attend a meeting of the National Liberal Federation in Leeds the next month, Hartington was apprehensive. Although 'sincerely anxious to unite at all events for the present all sections of the party', he recognized that only criticism of the government's foreign policy united Whigs and Radicals: 'I do not know how long it may be possible for us to act together, for when the country is again able to attend to domestic politics, it is possible that the advanced section may require a policy, which the more moderate section, wh. I may be supposed more directly to represent will be unable to support.'[42] To Granville, Hartington declared: 'The mischievous fact of the Association is one for wh. Chamberlain is himself greatly responsible ...I mean the dictation from Birmingham.'[43] In contention with Sir William Harcourt, he argued: 'Whatever may be the merits of the plan for local purposes, there can be no doubt that a great deal more has been aimed at than the local management of elections, and that an attempt has been made to influence the policy of the party, through the means of a central organization. ...it would have been a mistake to identify myself with these Associations in any way, until they have formally renounced any pretensions of this kind.' Hartington also thought 'that the assault upon the Govt. foreign policy may easily be over-done'.[44] Granville, although admitting that the NLF was probably beneficial in large towns, saw 'no advantage in making it our master'. He approved of Hartington's decision not to go to Leeds, as did Forster.[45] Harcourt did not, 'as I fear it may have serious consequences. I confess I do not share your reluctance to attack the foreign policy of the Govt.'[46] The Liberal Chief Whip, W. P. Adam, was of the opinion that the Birmingham model was 'not applicable to small boroughs or to counties but it operates well I think in large towns and tends to prevent that division of the party at elections which is the bane of the Liberal Party'. He had advised Hartington to speak at Leeds to keep the Radicals in 'good humour', throwing 'cold water' as he thought necessary but without greatly chilling them. But he assured Hartington, after he had decided not to attend: 'It is quite a mistake to say that there is no organization in the Party except through Birmingham. *We do not make a fuss about it* but we have now a very extensive organization in communication with almost every place in England and our organization in Scotland is complete.'[47]

After the parliamentary session of 1879, both parties prepared in earnest for an electoral campaign in which, despite the expanded electorate and the ballot, influence and money counted for much. 'The Opposition is entirely indifferent to the opinion of the present House of Commons', Beaconsfield sniped: 'They will speak & act only with a view to the General Election.'[48] Lord Derby observed: 'Forty years ago, & even to some extent within my recollection, it would have been reckoned indecorous for leading ministers to pass most of the recess in going from one town to another, haranguing from platforms in praise of their own party.'[49] The voters, whether in great industrial towns or rural counties, seemingly loved a lord. A. J. Mundella, Radical MP for Sheffield, complained: 'We are surrounded with Tory noblemen who know that Sheffield is the key to at least six seats. Our only Liberals are the Fitzwilliams and the Earl has done us more harm of late years than our open foes.' To redress the balance, Mundella asked Lord Rosebery, a fine orator, to practise his art in the town.[50] Salisbury spoke at Manchester in October 1879, and Hartington followed him a week later.[51] John Bright assured the latter: 'Our friends are not so "mobbish" as our opponents. They drink less & think more.'[52] Ten thousand pounds, nonetheless, were necessary for the Liberal effort in Manchester: 'but it draws all the ready money of the working Liberals,' explained an organizer, 'so that I must have men who will pay for the county. ...I have been trying everywhere for a good men [sic] with

£5000.'[53] This plaint took an echo throughout the land. This general election was even more expensive than the two which had immediately preceded it.[54]

The cockpit of the electoral contest, as it had been in 1874, was Lancashire. This time the Liberals fought more effectively than the Conservatives. Encouraged by local politicians and coached by his private secretary and Granville, Hartington stood in north-east Lancashire and gamely overcame his deep aversion to public-speaking.[55] The influence of the house of Derby was split. The Secretary for War, F. A. Stanley, did battle for the government.[56] Derby himself refused either to assist his brother or to oppose him and other of his former colleagues. Otherwise, he promised to 'let it be known that his wishes are with the liberal candidates, if they are not objectionable'.[57] He was cautious in doing so, explaining to Hartington: 'Farmers and others who have not followed recent public events, and who have always voted Conservative under the lead of my family, are puzzled by a change of front, and I can't press them to go against what they may suppose to be their convictions.'[58] Without declaring openly for Liberalism until mid-March 1880, Derby, under constant exhortation from his wife and Lord Sefton, ostentatiously offered the hospitality of Knowsley to Liberal speakers who visited Lancashire.[59] Although Liberal leaders disagreed on the importance of Derby's influence, they were pleased to have it working for their party rather than against it.[60]

The campaign which drew the most public attention was that in Edinburghshire, or Midlothian, where the contest took on a national as well as local significance because of Gladstone's involvement. Whigs and moderate Liberals from in and around Edinburgh, under the guidance of Adam, who was a Scottish MP as well as Chief Whip, had formed the East and North of Scotland Liberal Association in February 1877. Rosebery, the owner of Dalmeny House and more than 15,000 acres in Midlothian, was its chairman. Hartington, who persistently refused to appear at gatherings of the National Liberal Federation, attended the inaugural meeting of the ENLA. That body rebuffed Radical attempts to promulgate a programme advocating land reform and the disestablishment of the Church of Scotland and competed for influence with the Glasgow Liberal Association, organized with Chamberlain's blessing in 1879.[61] Adam was anxious to win the Midlothian seat, which, after a Liberal victory in 1868, the Earl of Dalkeith, eldest son of the Duke of Buccleuch, had captured for the Conservatives in 1874. After asking Gladstone to stand, Adam reported to Rosebery: 'He is not so hot on Midlothian as you and I are.'[62]

The old man had more than Scottish considerations in mind. Although he had the guarantee of a safe seat at Leeds, Gladstone recognized that by fighting a closely contested constituency he might attract the national interest which he had tried to arouse for the past three years. Perhaps, too, he felt a sense of rivalry with Hartington, who had not shrunk from the challenge of a county constituency which had returned Conservatives in both 1868 and 1874. But Gladstone feared the personal and political consequences of defeat. He insisted initially upon having proof of a Liberal majority in Midlothian before becoming the candidate there. On the advice of his close political associate, Lord Wolverton, the former Chief Whip, he settled for a strong requisition from the county and for a return indicating that, in effect, unless dead men could vote, he would have a majority of the electors.[63] Gladstone officially accepted the candidature in January 1879. Hartington wrote to him: 'I hear however that the contest will be severe, & I admire & wonder at your accepting it, when so many safe seats would have been at your disposal.'[64] Granville knew better: 'I feel sure that Adam & Wolverton would not have allowed you to embark in it − unless with a certainty of success.'[65] For Gladstone in Midlothian, the appearance of risk was greater than the reality. During the next fifteen months, Rosebery, John Reid, the secretary of the ENLA, and Ralph Richardson, the secretary of the Midlothian Liberal Association, worked assiduously to ensure his election.[66]

With similar care Rosebery and Reid planned Gladstone's first tour of his new constituency at the end of November 1879. The candidate was 'most docile and complying', concerned only that 'our friends will be no less careful to make security doubly sure'.[67] Reid arranged Gladstone's railway journey from Liverpool to Edinburgh so as to give Liberals at various places en route an opportunity to cheer him and present addresses.[68] He scheduled the major speeches five weeks in advance, 'because this will much simplify the Midlothian arrangements in which otherwise there will be much confusion caused by the selfassertion of non-electors. We propose for the Midlothian meetings to issue tickets to every elector to admit ½ an hour before any of the public.'[69] By the end of October, Rosebery had sent Gladstone a detailed itinerary of his trip, beginning with the time of his departure from Liverpool at 9.20 a.m. on Monday 24 November. It included information on train stops, addresses for presentation, halls and dinners.[70] Gladstone, in turn, made an outline of the topics which he wished to discuss, in order to achieve completeness not in any one speech but 'in the operation as a whole', and submitted it to Rosebery:

> In brief I may put the heads of subjects as follows
> 1. County & Scotch matters
> 2. What concerns the Liberal party
> 3. Indictment agt. the Govt.
>   a. abroad — everywhere!
>   b. at home — Finance
>   c. compared with Feb. 1874
> 4. General subjects: such as
>   Ireland
>   Free Trade & Protection
>   Economy
>   Public Distress.

Gladstone desired to concentrate upon criticizing the government: 'Plainly No 3 is overmuch for one speech.'[71] He deliberately avoided local and particular questions: 'Nothing would be more absurd than for me to make the discussion of them the aim of my mission in Midlothian.'[72] Gladstone's was a national 'mission'. For him, the constituency was a stage, upon which Rosebery and Reid had arranged the props and extras. Here, the aging political actor gave one of the greatest performances of his distinguished career: an heroic battler of three-score years and ten condemning the forces of evil to the rapturous applause of an adoring populace.

In Midlothian Gladstone concentrated on his 'indictment' of the government's foreign policy. He condemned the government for not cooperating with the Continental powers to coerce Turkey. He blamed it for the fighting in South Africa and Afghanistan. He attacked it for making the Salisbury–Shuvalov agreements and the Cyprus convention with Turkey. He argued for the preservation of peace, the maintenance of the concert of Europe, and the avoidance of needless entanglements. He looked forward to self-determination for the people of the Balkans. He complained of the neglect of domestic affairs.[73] The power of his oratory, the extensive reportage and commentary in the press, ensured that Gladstone's tour was a national as well as a local phenomenon. The reviews, in a press which outside London was predominantly Liberal, were favourable.

The event of the week, Lord Derby observed on 30 November, was Gladstone's Midlothian campaign, 'making a deep impression not only on the local public, but throughout the country', although 'his arguments & conclusions have been those of a decided, but not violent, Liberal'.[74]

Gladstone had intended that his attack on the Conservative government should serve to unify Liberals on a policy of his choosing. His object, as it had been since the autumn of 1876, was to integrate the Radicals into the party without endangering its role as a defender of such traditional societal interests as land, property and the established Church. In aiming at this goal, he paid almost as little heed to the susceptibilities of the Whigs as to those of the Tories. With the vindictiveness of a man of repressed passions, he remembered slights — real and imagined — which he had suffered from his colleagues during the past decade and a half. Gladstone had known when he accepted the candidacy for Midlothian 'that the contest would place him in a very prominent position at the general election'; but for the benefit of Granville and Hartington, as well as for the sake of his own conscience, he represented that his duty was 'to do his utmost to obtain the condemnation of the policy of the Government, and that he can then retire into the back ground'.[75] He understood, however, that the apparent acceptance of his views by the party and public would make the position of the two Whigs untenable. His attitude toward resuming the leadership Granville interpreted in October 1879 as '*Alors comme alors*'.[76] A month later, during his triumphant tour of Midlothian, Gladstone began to consider the question seriously, though he gave expression to his thoughts in a typically circuitous manner. After his speech at West Calder, in a long letter to John Bright, he justified his refusal to assume his old place at the head of the party. His most important reason was 'that a liberal government under me would be the object from the first of an amount and kind of hostility, such as materially to prejudice its acts and weaken or, in given circumstances, neutralise its power for good'. Gladstone apparently had in mind fractious Liberal opposition which would prevent, as it had during the latter half of his first administration, his devising and implementing of legislation. 'The more I think about the matter,' he asserted now that he had again sipped the heady wine of mass adulation, 'the more strange and mysterious does it seem to me that any party in this free nation should be found to sanction and uphold policy and proceedings like those of the last two years in particular.'[77] For

Gladstone the Midlothian campaign vindicated his conduct during the eastern crisis; at least by implication, it also cast aspersions upon Liberals who had opposed him. From the hustings of Scotland he now called upon the country not only to chastise the Tories, but also to compel his own party to follow him. His success was apparent. 'The Liberal party *must* unite under *Gladstone*,' declared Lord Bath: 'no other name will go down, and an attempt to form a Government under another leader must end in failure.'[78]

Many Liberals, and the Queen as well, disliked this lesson in popular politics and the teacher who recited it. Henry Ponsonby, Queen Victoria's private secretary, had already told Granville in October 1879 that his mistress wanted a pledge from the leaders of the opposition not to disestablish the Scottish Church or to reverse the foreign policy of the present government. He thought that she would object to having Gladstone, Robert Lowe or Sir Charles Dilke as ministers.[79] In the midst of the Midlothian campaign, Lord Barrington wrote to Beaconsfield: 'That Whigs shd. be in dismay over Gladstone's discourses is natural enough, but how about some of my friends who have always been considered rather extreme Radicals?' Francis Knollys, the Prince of Wales's private secretary, Barrington continued, 'went so far as to say that he was once more ruining the Liberal party, that it wd. give so much more strength to yr. Govnt., that if you paid him for it, he could not do more'; and Granville's brother, Frederick Leveson Gower, who had in the past praised Gladstone, protested against what he conceived to be his attack on landed property at West Calder.[80] According to Bath's shrewd assessment, the style of the campaigner had roused more suspicions than the content of his programme:

> Gladstone's Scottish pilgrimage has been certainly a great success there...and politically in England the effect cannot fail to be great, and he has been in general moderate and will have raised no alarms among timid people; that he has society as strongly as ever against him cannot be doubted, and I rather dread the evil that will result from society being found almost en masse on the defeated side.[81]

The political as well as the social ramifications of Midlothian dismayed Whigs. 'What a progress has been Gladstones!!' exclaimed Lord Spencer: 'It will be wonderful if such a man is not again in office, but what trouble [?] if he thinks [?] of it!'[82]

After Gladstone's display of energy and power in Midlothian, Hartington asked 'why should he not come back?'.[83] Considering 'the Scotch campaign, & the effect it has had in the country & on the party', he again contemplated resigning the Liberal leadership in the House of Commons.[84] Forster, a supporter of Hartington, seemed inclined to force Gladstone to state his intentions.[85] According to the editor of the *Daily News*, Frank Hill, Gladstone was offended at the idea of his serving as Chancellor of the Exchequer under Granville or Hartington, and 'only wants a little squeezing to declare himself as Liberal leader once more'.[86] Hill thought that this course would be injurious to the party and that it found no favour even with such Radicals as Dilke and Henry Fawcett. He explained cynically to Forster's private secretary: 'If Mr. G. were Premier... he must collect as many dukes & great people as he can to his Cabinet to show that he is not a revolutionist. On the other hand Lord G & Lord H to prove their radicalism must appoint many of the extreme people, & so these men hope that something may fall to them.' So as to disappoint neither Whigs nor Radicals, Hill advised the Liberal leaders to make no changes at present.[87] In this opinion they concurred, Granville 'evidently having real fears that many of our weak-kneed ones would feel some alarm if Hartington went from the front *now*, and that the tories would intensify this to the uttermost'.[88]

Although electoral considerations prevented his immediate assumption of the title, Gladstone was, after his tour of Midlothian, the effective leader of the Liberal party. Whigs and Radicals co-operated in preparation for a general election. 'We ourselves may be well aware that, though differences do & always will exist, yet they won't prevent cordial union for common objects', Chamberlain had assured Harcourt when asking him to speak at the opening of the Birmingham Liberal Club; and the latter's appearance in January 1880 apparently created the desired impression.[89] Yet many Whigs resented the growing strength of Radicalism, and they vented their anger on Gladstone. 'It is extraordinary how hateful Gladstone is to some otherwise Liberal minds... although I do not myself think that it will be to the advantage of the Party if he returns to the lead,' declared Spencer.[90] However embittered their feelings about Gladstone, the Whigs needed him. Upon receiving a report that in some constituencies 'nobody wd. have a chance who stood as an avowed supporter of Gladstone's, Lord Halifax commented: 'On the other hand we depend a good deal on popular feeling & there is no enthusiasm for H.'[91] In February 1880 the Liberals failed to win a seat at Liverpool and lost one in Southwark, where, Gladstone complained, 'a counterfeit of the Birmingham organisation' proved ineffective.[92] These results heartened the Conservatives. 'Southwark after Liverpool is good: − Is it not?' Cross enquired of Salisbury, who replied: 'Southwark really is a considerable achievement.'[93] The government announced on 8 March its decision to dissolve parliament in a fortnight's time. The next week Gladstone began his second tour of Midlothian.[94] He won his contest and the Liberals the election, with a majority of about fifty seats over Conservatives and Irish home rulers. Exultantly, Gladstone wrote to Bright:

> It is a great and wonderful time. Toryism or Conservatism will rise again from its ashes, but I hope upon different lines, the lines of Party not the lines of Beaconsfield. You and I probably both think we see the hand of God manifest in what has been going on. For my own part, I seem to have had a thousand signs of it, from day to day. I rejoice in it from the bottom of my soul. But I am against all outward signs of exultation or crowing over the fallen.[95]

After a conversation with Gladstone at Hawarden on 16 April, Bright came away convinced that 'the power and success of the new Government will be greater in his hands than in any other'.[96] Lord Ripon admitted: 'He is undoubtedly a great power in the country.'[97] Although the Queen sent for Hartington, he had to defer to Gladstone, who on 23 April 1880 became First Lord of the Treasury for the second and Chancellor of the Exchequer for the fourth time.[98]

In forming his administration, Gladstone paid as little heed as he could to the Radicals, seeming to believe that he rather than they truly represented the electorate to which he had appealed from Midlothian. Socially conservative, he preferred experienced ministers, who were of necessity Whigs and moderate Liberals, and they were dominant in the Cabinet. He immediately asked Derby to join. The former Conservative Foreign Secretary refused, but he pledged that 'the support which I shall endeavour to give to your government, however little it may be worth, will be cordial and sincere as well as independent'.[99] When the Prime Minister appointed Radicals, he expected them, as new men, to be obedient.

He insisted upon economy when naming Mundella as Vice President of the Committee of Council on Education, and the latter promised to 'deem it my duty to exercise the utmost care and vigilance to secure the highest educational results at the lowest possible charge to the country'.[100] Chamberlain, as President of the Board of Trade, was the only Radical, or 'representative of the Extreme Left',[101] in the Cabinet, and he had made 'a forced entry' in alliance with Dilke, the new Parliamentary Under Secretary at the Foreign Office.[102] Lord Bath criticized the new Prime Minister's party tactics, stating that if 'a few extreme men are admitted into the Cabinet they will be held in check by their colleagues, the Cabinet will be more powerful in the House & the unity and the solidity of the advanced party broken up'. Relieved of the responsibility of power, the Radicals would, he feared, eventually dictate their own terms and 'Democratise' every governmental proposal. For this reason, he asserted, 'Gladstone's Cabinet strikes me as weak and too Conservative even for Conservative interests'.[103]

The magnitude of their losses dismayed Conservatives. Lord Cranbrook had never imagined that 'such a complete crumbling away of our position was possible'.[104] The Duke of Richmond, who had not expected 'so disastrous a state of affairs', keened: 'What a fearful collapse. I had not the slightest idea we should be so completely annihilated.'[105] Salisbury viewed the result as 'a perfect catastrophe — & may I fear break up the party altogether'.[106] Beaconsfield and his colleagues generally blamed 'Hard Times' for their defeat.[107] 'I suppose bad harvests and bad trade have done the most,' lamented Salisbury: 'A sick man who makes no progress is apt to change his doctor, though the doctor may not be in fault: & the mass of borough voters know that they are pinched, and nothing more.'[108] Robert Bourke, the Parliamentary Under Secretary for Foreign Affairs, who had voted in Midlothian, attributed the Liberal victory there and 'throughout the Country' to 'bad harvests and depression in trade. . . . I do not believe that the Foreign policy has had anything to say to it.'[109] Many Conservatives held their party managers responsible for the failure at the polls. Lady Salisbury declared: 'I feel sure that the madness of the people will soon subside — but I do not think our side has talked enough & by all accounts the organization has been deplorable. We must have "caucuses".'[110] Beaconsfield also had complaints about the managing of the Tory side in the House of Commons: 'But what are we doing about the Whip? I heard much murmuring, when in town, on that head: that there was no one to guide, inform, & instruct, those, who wanted a pair, or to dine at Grenwich [sic], or go up in a balloon for an hour or two's relaxation.'[111] The Tory leaders set about improving their organization. They reinstated J. E. Gorst as agent, and dismissed Dyke from his post as Chief Whip.[112] At a meeting of Conservative peers and MPs at Bridgewater House on 19 May 1880, Beaconsfield agreed to continue as head of the party.[113] He recognized that the situation required 'youth & energy. When they are found, & they will be found, I shall make my bow. In the meantime, I must act as if I were still young & vigorous, & take all steps in my power to sustain the spirit, & restore the discipline of the Tory party. . . .they must not be snuffed out.'[114]

The Conservative strategy now was to rely on the possibility 'that the House of Lords may be able to keep the House of Commons in check'.[115] Beaconsfield had refused to meet parliament after the election. Its discussions, he explained to Salisbury's nephew, A. J. Balfour, would not convert the country to a Conservative policy: 'Such an opinion is all d——d nonsense. The beaten party is always in the wrong.' Divisions in both houses would follow any debate, he stated, with a majority of one hundred for the government in the Lords and of one hundred against in the Commons. The result, he predicted, would be that 'the new régime' would begin 'with a conflict between the two Houses, in which the House of Lords would have ignominiously to give way. The H. of L. would "ask to be kicked".'[116] Salisbury agreed that a 'Confidence division. . .would only have the effect of making our defeat seem larger than it is − for several members whom we may find on our side in future struggles would think it prudent to establish their Liberal orthodoxy by voting against us. . . .Our great hope is in Gladstone's arrogance: & late events are of a nature to feed it.'[117] Until the old man blundered, Salisbury admitted: 'An impatient & tyrannical majority would not allow a debate over the merits of their idol.'[118]

Although the rhetoric of Midlothian had aroused Conservative fears, the election of 1880 was less a democratic triumph than a demonstration that the balance of political power was shifting away from the aristocracy and in favour of the upper middle class. Lord Derby, when still a member of the Conservative government, had judged that the reputation of the House of Commons was declining for a variety of reasons: 'but a more permanent influence is exerted by the marked preference of constituencies for local candidates, generally middle-aged men who have made money, & want a seat for social rather than political reasons. The parliaments of 1868 & 1874, whatever else they were or are, have been certainly the most plutocratic that we have yet had.'[119] The deterioration in the political position of the aristocracy affected the Whigs more than the Tories, although it concerned both groups. When Derby contemplated announcing his conversion to Liberalism, Lord Carnarvon, who remained a Conservative, advised him that, 'in a public aspect', the change would be satisfactory:

> Looking beyond the mere tactics & requirements of Parties, I have − as I think I have more than once said to you − feared the passing over of the great body of land and wealth to the Tory side, and have desired to see a full representation of those two elements on the Liberal side of the House. Toryism will always enlist an ample supply of wealthy supporters: the danger is that Liberal doctrines may not be sufficiently ballasted by men of property[,] rank & political ability combined. I cannot conceive a greater misfortune than a repetition of what occurred in Pitt's day.[120]

The trend toward plutocratic participation persisted in the parliament of 1880. The corrupt and illegal practices act of 1883 failed to stem the rising economic tide which deposited a flotsam of wealthy MPs upon the political shores of Westminster.[121] As Gladstone deliberately recruited bourgeois Nonconformists into the Liberal party, Whigs watched with misgivings the erosion of their supremacy. Outraged by his appeals to the masses, they did not always perceive that the substance of his politics was as socially conservative as Beaconsfield's.

Issues of foreign policy, upon which Gladstone had largely waged his Midlothian campaign, were probably not of primary interest to the majority of the electorate, nor had they determined the verdict at the polls. John Morley had gauged the old man's appeal when he predicted 'that there will soon be a great call for Gladstone: he has always been associated with prosperity, and people will begin to miss their prosperity before long, unless I am mistaken'.[122] He was not. The enfranchised working class was chiefly concerned about the economic depression, of which low wages and unemployment were consequences. For this problem neither Liberals nor Conservatives had a solution. Landed aristocrats among them were puzzled as to how to manage their own estates in a period of grave agricultural difficulties.[123] Politicians of both parties were generally agreed on not attempting to interfere with the economy. When a railway strike in the United States had necessitated the calling in of troops, Derby condemned 'the distinctively socialistic idea that it is the business of the State to provide employment for the laborer'. He feared that workers elsewhere would make similar demands: 'All over the world, the masses will ask, "Where is the good of having votes, if we are not to use them for the advantage of our class?" & it is on the cards that we may see a social war of strikes & locks out [sic] such as England has not yet witnessed.'[124] The doctrine of *laissez faire* precluded political interference with the economy; hence Gladstone's concentration on foreign policy. The Midlothian campaign, with its large public meetings, wide newspaper coverage and national appeal, was a logical consequence of the reform act of 1867. The concentration on foreign affairs was the culmination of the eastern crisis. Whether the Liberals could retain the favour of a majority of the electorate and pursue their own policies abroad remained to be seen.

6 Imperialism in Egypt

For the first three-quarters of the nineteenth century, Great Britain had defended Egypt by shoring up its suzerain, the Sultan of Turkey. From the mid-1870s the rivalry of France and the erosion of Ottoman authority by a rising tide of nationalism rendered this approach increasingly untenable. When the Conservative Prime Minister, Benjamin Disraeli, purchased the largest single shareholding in the Suez canal company in 1875, he provoked little domestic opposition. In terms of strategy, investment and trade, British policy-makers were convinced that they could not afford to allow any other power to control the canal or Egypt. So far as the diplomatic situation permitted, Disraeli and Lord Salisbury, the Foreign Secretary after March 1878, struggled to establish British paramountcy there. They had largely succeeded when, in 1880, the Liberals, under W. E. Gladstone, again took office. The new Prime Minister failed to form the concert of Europe which he had proposed in his Midlothian speeches. At home, controversy over Ireland divided his party and threatened to force Whigs to join with Tories in opposition to his legislation. In the midst of his Irish difficulties in the summer of 1882, Gladstone was aware that he could rally Liberals and disarm Conservatives by taking a bellicose stand against an Egyptian nationalist movement, and he sanctioned the invasion of Egypt.

From its opening in 1869 the Suez canal was of vital concern to the makers of British foreign policy. For the rulers of a nation dependent upon seaborne commerce and naval power, with an empire in India and trading interests and possessions in the Far East, the narrow isthmus between the Mediterranean and the Red Seas was a crucial crossroads. The Liberal government took steps to protect shipowners against steep rises in users' rates which the canal company, headed by Ferdinand de Lesseps, tried to impose in the first half of the 1870s.[1] For diplomatic and political reasons, however, Gladstone was reluctant to adopt an assertive policy in Egypt. 'The French Foreign Office has always had an unaccountable suspicion that we want them to commit themselves on the Egyptian Reforms and that when they have done so, we shall leave them in the lurch,' explained Lord Lyons, the British ambassador in Paris.[2] The Prime Minister had no desire to exacerbate this feeling of distrust, although he admitted that the 'basis of the old *entente*...is gone'.[3] Gladstone also wanted to economize on expenditure and to avoid outraging his Nonconformist supporters by embarking on foreign adventures. His Chancellor of the Exchequer, Robert Lowe, in 1870 found nearly a dozen objections to purchasing the Suez canal for four million pounds. Among them was a fear that a considerable military force would be necessary to protect it. He warned his colleagues that the British government would 'be involved more deeply than at present in the politics of Egypt and might very probably' be 'driven to an occupation'. He did not consider that India was 'worth the sacrifice implied in a permanent occupation of the Canal with its jealousies and risks. ...It would stir up anew the Eastern Question which now France is weakened I greatly dread.' Lowe preferred to rely upon the Cape route for Indian communications.[4]

By the time that Disraeli came to power in 1874, shipping through the Suez canal had increased in volume, and three-quarters of it was British. He proposed, through Baron Lionel de Rothschild, that the government buy out the company's shareholders, but Lesseps refused to negotiate.[5] In November 1875 the Prime Minister succeeded in purchasing more than 40 per cent of the shares from Ismail, the Khedive of Egypt. 'In truth, the act on our part was sudden,' he later admitted, 'tho' my mind had long been brooding over the subject. ...I never dreamed our object would have been obtained in the quarter in wh. it was accomplished.'[6] The Cabinet, 'by a sort of whirlwind of agreement', decided on 17 November to attempt to purchase the shares.[7] The Chancellor of the Exchequer, Sir Stafford Northcote, cited its reasons for doing so in a letter to the Foreign Secretary, Lord Derby, the next day:

> I suppose that our objects in purchasing the Khedive's shares would be these: − 1. to prevent their falling into the hands of those who might use them to our prejudice: 2. to obtain for ourselves some power over the actual management of the Canal affairs: 3. to obtain a position which would give us rights under certain contingencies to interpose in arrangements that might be proposed by others: 4. to help Egyptian finance.[8]

On 22 November the Cabinet 'Virtually agreed to leave the question in Disraeli's hands – to buy the shares if he gets the chance'. Three days later it approved of paying four million pounds for them.[9] The Rothschilds lent the money, providing half of it on 1 December.[10] Northcote arranged, with the Baron's approval, that the shares 'should be deposited in the Bank of England, in the joint names of the Govt. and yourselves'.[11] Disraeli's feat testified not only to his bold imagination but also to his political shrewdness. After the reform legislation of 1875, he had no substantial domestic proposals to offer for the coming parliamentary session, and he hoped that issues of foreign policy might prove an adequate substitute. He also wanted to divert attention from various embarrassments at the Admiralty which had prompted him to try to remove the First Lord.[12] Politically, the purchase of the shares was 'an immense success'.[13] Most Liberals as well as Conservatives approved of it.

The reaction of J. T. Delane to the news was significant. By furnishing the editor of *The Times* with advance intelligence on the purchase, Disraeli had made a clever bid for his backing.[14] Delane enthusiastically communicated the story to his assistant editor:

> I send you one of the most extraordinary bits of news which have ever happened in our time. It is of the highest importance and I think reflects the highest credit on Disraeli for one sees that it is all his work.
>
> It is a peaceable declaration to Europe that we mean to keep the Canal open. Gladstone would never have dared to do such a thing. He would have talked about consulting Parliament and the chance would have been lost. Disraeli has now gone down to Windsor to tell the Queen though I suppose he 'took her pleasure' yesterday. I feel an inch taller since we have a Minister capable of such a resolution.... And yet it is not an act to which any other Power can object. It is not like the seizure of the Spanish frigates, or the Danish fleet, we simply embark our capital in an enterprise whose success is of imperial moment to ourselves.

Delane's instructions ensured that the columns of *The Times* mirrored his own approval of Disraeli's policy: 'I have told Chenery, but shall be glad if you will further "insense" him on the great political import of the step and beg him to treat it as an act worthy alike of the nation and the Minister. I would also tell Macdonnell [sic] so that he might adapt his article to the Event.'[15] Delane's

personal proclivities reflected, and reinforced, the imperial sentiments of the readers of *The Times*.

Liberal leaders were unwilling to criticize the shares purchase
because many of them approved of it and all of them acknowledged
its popularity both in the country and in their own party. Lord
Carlingford slyly wrote to Lord Hartington: 'I have amused myself
by thinking what sort of a Cabinet *we* should have had on the
question of buying the shares!' The government's action had, he
stated, given England the 'g[rea]test lift in European opinion, &
with my Board of Trade recollections of Lesseps manoeuvres, I am
not sorry to be inside the Company, instead of only pressing it from
without. But the exaggerations & brag of the press have been
offensive.'[16] W. E. Forster was 'rather taken with the purchase of
the shares'.[17] Lord Kimberley was 'inclined on the whole to think
that the Govt. have acted rightly' and perhaps should announce to
Europe that 'we are resolved at all hazards to prevent Egypt & the
canal from falling under the control of any Power but ourselves'.[18]
Lord Halifax concurred: 'we shd. be prepared in the *ultimate*
necessity to go to war & even to annex Egypt in order to insure
that...the Canal shd. be open to us at all times & for all purposes'.[19] Hartington, although ever anxious lest he appear 'too civil
to Dizzy about foreign affairs', recognized that the Prime Minister's
move was 'well received in the country, & I shd. think may turn out
to be a most successful coup'.[20] His co-leader, Lord Granville,
according to Lord Barrington, a Tory whip, 'cd. not see how the
purchase of the Khedive's shares in the Suez Canal wd. improve the
position of England in case of further complications arising out of
the Eastern question, as the Govnt. wd. anyhow, under such circumstances, make a "coup d'état" by an armed intervention'.[21]
Granville nonetheless advised his colleagues 'to be merely oracular,
till we have an opportunity of consultation'.[22]

Gladstone was bitter about his rival's apparent triumph. He was
'totally unable to take any view of it in which the reasons against do
not immensely preponderate'.[23] Persuaded by his colleagues 'not to
run his head against the national feeling about the Canal',[24] he
tempered his language, 'out of respect, such respect as is due, to the
sense of what seems an overwhelming majority'.[25] Only a minority
of Liberals, among them John Bright and Charles Bradlaugh,
openly condemned the transaction.[26] When parliament met in
February 1876, Gladstone searched for means of turning this discontent to advantage; but he declined to play a political Canute

against the rising tide of popular opinion. As he 'did not yet see signs that the people were escaping from their gross delusion', he merely placed his opposition 'quietly upon record'.[27] Hartington informed Disraeli 'that, notwithstanding all the rumours about a combined attack on the Govnt. from Lowe & Gladstone, *re Suez Canal*, he knew nothing of it at present, & did not in consequence anticipate a lengthened debate on the Address'.[28] The Liberal Chief Whip, W. P. Adam, told Hartington that the canal purchase was popular in the constituencies and few MPs wanted to speak against it. 'I find that it is quite impossible to make a two nights debate on the Suez question', Hartington cautioned Gladstone, who, under the circumstances, was unable to challenge the Conservative government.[29]

Condemnation of Disraeli's action was politically unfeasible because Great Britain had interests not only in the Suez canal but also in Egypt itself. One-third of Egypt's total debt of about ninety million pounds was in the hands of British bondholders. They had influential backers, including G. J. Goschen, who through his family firm of Fruhling and Goschen had helped to float large Egyptian loans in the 1860s, and the house of Rothschild, which was deeply involved in Egyptian finance.[30] Although they produced less than 4 per cent of Great Britain's total earnings from overseas investment, Egyptian bonds together with Turkish had accounted for nearly 25 per cent of all foreign securities issued in London during the twelve years prior to 1875.[31] When, at the end of that year, Turkey defaulted on its debts, the continuation of Egypt's payments seemed particularly important. In Egypt British contractors participated in spending the money which the Khedive Ismail had borrowed. Expenditure on railways there between 1863 and 1879, for example, was greater than that in Ireland, and the chief engineers of the Railway Administration were British subjects; and British companies undertook the reconstruction of the harbour at Alexandria. Such projects served British merchants and shippers by opening the interior of Egypt to exploitation and improving the port facilities through which almost all Egyptian foreign trade passed.[32] By 1880, Great Britain took 80 per cent of Egypt's exports and supplied 44 per cent of her imports. In this exchange, the industry which was the largest contributor to British overseas trade had a disproportionate share. The restriction of cotton imports from the southern United States during that nation's civil war had stimulated the development of Egypt as an alternative source. Approximately

15 per cent by value of the raw cotton imported into the United Kingdom came from Egypt, and 5 per cent of exported cotton manufactures went there in the mid-1870s.[33] When, in 1874, Manchester industrialists, through their MPs, complained to Lord Derby about the quality of Egyptian cotton, their petition earned serious attention.[34] Trade, as well as investment, was a factor in the government's adoption of an interventionist policy in Egypt. In March 1875 the Board of Trade sent two officers to act as heads of department in the new Egyptian Ministry of Commerce. One of them, E. A. R. Acton, tried to promote trade between Egypt and the British dominions, with some assistance from Derby. Both the Foreign Office and the Board of Trade displayed concern for his career in the valley of the Nile.[35] This involvement with the khedival economy and with the Suez route to the East augmented traditional strategic considerations. Downing Street found support not only in the City but also in the industrial areas of Manchester and the dockyards of Liverpool.

The maintenance, and if possible the strengthening, of British influence in Egypt became the object of governmental policy after 1875. 'It seems to me impossible to rate too highly the importance of that decision, as a declaration of policy,' Lord Salisbury, the Secretary of State for India, perceptively remarked about the purchase of the shares in the canal company.[36] That act precipitated a debate in the Cabinet as to whether further intervention in Egypt was necessary. Northcote considered that he and his colleagues ought not 'to mix ourselves up more than is inevitable with the maintenance of Egypt or of Turkey, or to make ourselves responsible for their proceedings'.[37] Derby moralized: 'The canal is one of the great highways of the earth, and ought not, in the common interest, to be in the hands of any one Power. . . .even in the days of Bismarck I believe in justice.'[38] The Colonial Secretary, Lord Carnarvon, on the contrary, asserted that the country would not welcome such notions: 'The common idea, I think, is that Egypt, quite as much as the Canal, is the thing that ultimately interests us, that the control of the Canal is valuable as a step to the control of Egypt and that it is no special object to us to be mixed up with many other nations who may have very different interests to serve in keeping the Gate of the Eastern Empire.'[39] Disraeli sympathized with Carnarvon's argument, 'the vein of wh in my mind is correct',[40] but was unable immediately to act upon it. During 1876, when he was trying to break up the Dreikaiserbund and to outmanoeuvre

Russia in the Near East, he desired cordial relations with France. He continued to rely upon defending Egypt through the authority of the Sultan. 'Constantinople is the key of India, and not Egypt and the Suez Canal,' he insisted in October 1876. Any other idea he derided as 'moonshine'.[41] But he, like the German Chancellor, Otto von Bismarck, qualified the adoption of any political or diplomatic policy with an unspoken reservation: *rebus sic stantibus*. The atrocities agitation and the failure of the Constantinople conference caused him to reconsider his attitude toward the Ottoman empire in general and the Egyptian khedivate in particular.

After the outbreak of the Russo-Turkish war in April 1877, the Cabinet began to contemplate active intervention in Egypt. Even Northcote asserted that, if either belligerent attempted to prevent the passage of British warships through it, 'I would lose no time in taking the Canal'.[42] Salisbury apparently suggested seizing Egypt.[43] Derby's fear that his colleagues were inclined to do so was one motive behind his circular despatch of 6 May 1877, warning Russia of British concern for the Suez canal, as well as for the Straits and the Persian Gulf.[44] On 6 March 1878 the Cabinet, as part of its consideration of a peace settlement, discussed 'the whole of our situation with respect to Egypt, both political & financial'.[45] When Derby voiced his opposition to any separate British action there, Salisbury snapped: 'Don't pledge yourself to that for the future.'[46] Within a month Salisbury replaced Derby at the Foreign Office. He understood that finance, as much as military or naval power, was an element of modern diplomacy. Although he never assumed that the two were identical, he wanted to use the interests of the bond-holders to further those of Great Britain in Egypt. Such a policy had strong domestic backing at a time when the Cabinet was anxious to avoid adverse political repercussions after the defeat of Turkey and the resignation of Derby. A Conservative member of the Liverpool town council had advised that 'no stroke of foreign policy would be more popular' then the annexation of Egypt: 'The Egyptian bond-holders are very numerous and these to a man irrespective of political feeling would go in favour of some such scheme.'[47] In cooperating with France to improve the finances of Egypt, Salisbury hoped to 'increase British influence' and perhaps to initiate 'English predominance'.[48] Salisbury's plans, as Northcote reminded him, went 'far beyond' simply restoring Egypt's financial position.[49]

An opportunity to assert British authority in Egypt came in the spring of 1879. In April Ismail rejected a plan of financial reform drawn up by a commission of enquiry, and dismissed an English and a French minister whom he had taken into his service some months before. Salisbury acknowledged that his government was involved financially and diplomatically in Egypt, '& our capitalists have an interest in Alexandria harbour which we could scarcely afford to disregard. But above all these "entanglements" is the apprehension, which forced us to accept them, that if we stand aside France will become as dominant there as she is in Tunis. . . . The position is an anxious one − because it is ambiguous, & hard to explain publicly. But the Khedive is going straight on to ruin: & we cannot afford to be out of the way when the crash comes.'[50] Northcote agreed: 'Nothing can deprive us of our right to act in whatever manner we think best if the National interests in the Canal, or the Harbour, or the Railways, should be threatened.' The Anglo-French entente he treated brusquely: 'We dont want to separate from France; but I dont think it is just now our cue to be too demonstrative towards her. We should let her see that we are aware that we have interests not wholly identical with hers, and that we mean to look after them.'[51] Involvement in the Zulu war prevented the British government from crushing Ismail's display of independence by force. 'If it were not for the South African affair, we shd. prepare for the eventuality of a military occupation of Egypt,' Beaconsfield declared: 'Let us hope it may not be necessary, or may be postponed.'[52] Salisbury explained to Northcote:

> I feel no doubt that we must come to a deposition: but the apprehension which fills my thoughts is lest any resistance (which is very probable) should give to the French an opportunity of interfering alone by force. If we were in a position to interfere too, I should mind the danger less: because then the French would not do it.
>
> But all our force is locked up − Oh! that Bartle Frere! I should like to construct for him a gibbet twice the height of Haman's.[53]

As the Conservative leader in the House of Commons, Northcote prepared his own rationalization of British interference in Egypt: 'we had to protect our own special interests in the country: to make sure of our highway not being stopped: and therefore to prevent any other country from gaining a dangerously preponderating influence, or Egypt itself from falling into a state of anarchy.'[54] At the end of June the French and British governments, supported by Bismarck, bullied the Sultan into deposing Ismail and replacing him with his son Tewfik.[55]

During the next year, although the two European powers co-operated to order the political and financial affairs of Egypt, Salisbury had no intention of abandoning past arrangements that 'gave England a vantage ground from which we ought not to descend'.[56] A khedival decree of 15 November 1879 acknowledged the Anglo-French dual control. A law of liquidation of 17 July 1880 placed Egyptian finances into international receivership; a commission on which Great Britain and France had two representatives each, and Austria-Hungary, Germany and Italy one, regulated the debt. Within the framework of the dual control, British influence rapidly outstripped that of France in administration and commerce.[57] Exclusive reliance upon one section of a multifarious society, the bondholders, weakened the French thrust into Egypt. Beaconsfield had been at pains to demonstrate that his was not 'a mere bondholders' policy'.[58] In England other powerful interest groups, among them manufacturers, shippers, traders and contractors, supported the government. Having for many years suspected that the French would use their financial interests in Egypt as a means 'to covertly assume the lead',[59] the British government had finally forged ahead.

Liberals were prepared to maintain Great Britain's imperial commitment in general and her paramountcy in Egypt in particular. Mindful of Tory representations to the contrary, Hartington had warned Granville in November 1878: 'I think that we have rather suffered from a mistaken idea of our Colonial policy.... You are the leader of the party; & you are the greatest sinner in the public opinion, on Colonial matters & most in need of absolution.'[60] The apparent success of Beaconsfield's foreign policy had convinced Joseph Chamberlain, the Radical MP for Birmingham, of the political virtues of imperialism:

> The fact is great harm has been done to the Liberal Party by its connection with those who are in favour of peace at any price, and others who measure everything by a pecuniary standard. It is our business to show that we are as keenly alive to the responsibilities and duties of a great nation as our opponents; that we also have 'Imperial instincts'; but that we desire that these should be directed to worthy objects, and not used, as the Prime Minister is doing, for ignoble party purposes.[61]

Thus Chamberlain was in 'no particular hurry' to criticize the government over the Zulu war, but regarded the issue with the eye of a political opportunist: 'It is sure to cost a lot of money & cannot be a popular war.'[62] Although Derby objected 'to squeezing the fellahs in the interest of the French or English bondholders', most Liberals approved of the Conservative policy in Egypt.[63] Although afraid that it 'would divide the Liberal party', Chamberlain agreed with W. T. Stead that a British occupation of Egypt would be popular in the country. He opposed the idea, at the end of 1877, as inexpedient: 'We take Egypt to protect the canal; we should have to occupy Syria to protect Egypt: what we should have to take to protect Syria I do not know.' He had information, too, 'that France would resent the occupation of Egypt by England more than any other possible act of ours'.[64] In respect to Egypt, Liberals generally accepted the advice which Captain Evelyn Baring, after his appointment as British controller general in 1879, gave to his cousin, Lord Northbrook. 'He thinks', the latter informed Hartington, 'that if there was a change of Government the Liberal Party would find it quite impossible to do otherwise than continue the French partnership, and that it would be very desirable, if they came into office, that they should be unshackled by any previous utterances.'[65]

Difficulties abroad and at home, for which Gladstone bore a heavy responsibility, hampered the Liberals in their attempts to maintain the *status quo* in Egypt after they came to power in April 1880. The new Prime Minister's conception of a concert of Europe betrayed his age. It was an anachronism, more appropriate to the period following the congress of Vienna than of Berlin. Gladstone desired to meet Great Britain's continental commitment at a minimum of cost. But the bayonets of armies rather than the platitudes of politicians impressed European statesmen. In Berlin, Vienna, Paris and Constantinople they viewed Gladstone's accession to power with apprehension.[66] Even in St Petersburg, where Liberal opposition to Turkey over the eastern question had won appreciation, the Assistant Minister for Foreign Affairs harboured no illusions. He expected 'that probably there will not be much change in the attitude of England towards this country'.[67] Mutual suspicion, not trust, caused the powers to cooperate, and diverging interests put strict limits to cooperation. During a 'stormy' first session of parliament one of Gladstone's private secretaries opined that foreign affairs, though 'somewhat ticklish, promise fairly well'.[68] Sir William Harcourt, the Home Secretary, reportedly asserted in July

1880 'that, conscious of a considerable failure in Home Affairs, H.M.'s Ministers find full compensation in the success which an obedient Turkey is about to give to their Foreign Policy!'.[69] In attempting to force Turkey to cede Dulcigno to Montenegro, Gladstone in October 1880 resolved to send British warships to Smyrna, although Austria-Hungary, France and Germany refused to participate in such a demonstration.[70] When the Porte surrendered, Harcourt wrote to Gladstone: 'I congratulate you & Granville most heartily on the final success of the "European Concert" which has put its enemies to shame.'[71] The Prime Minister himself was under no misapprehension. He remarked to Granville that 'out of the old Jade "Concert" we must still get what good we can'.[72] He later admitted: 'In 1880 we tried hard to work the concert of Europe but finding that Three of the Powers were bent on making it an imposture we parted company[,] pursued our own end and gained our end.'[73]

Gladstone's abortive attempt at a concert of Europe ultimately affected the dual control in Egypt. His active policy in the Near East had awakened doubts in Germany 'as to the maintenance of the "entente" between the Powers', according to Bismarck's banker, Gerson von Bleichröder: 'People are not slow to perceive that Mr. G. regards Smyrna as an "etappe" and we know that England is endeavouring to bring about an understanding with Russia and proceed hand in hand with that power. It is however by no means certain that Russia will accept the offer.'[74] Bismarck now increased his efforts to reach an agreement with Germany's eastern neighbour. In June 1881, Austria-Hungary, Germany and Russia signed the secret three emperors' alliance.[75] When Beaconsfield had left office he feared 'the revival of the Kaiser-Bund', the dissolving of which he considered the 'paramount feat' of the Berlin congress: 'one of those vast results, that do not appear in treaties or protocols, & can, perhaps, never be publickly mentioned, but which are more important than all that is signed or sealed'.[76] Probably no British government could have prevented Bismarck's negotiations from reaching fruition; but Gladstone's certainly accelerated the process. Now that he no longer feared Russia's allying with either Great Britain or France, the German Chancellor had less reason than in the past to worry about the consequences of their rivalry in the Mediterranean. Although he did not encourage conflict between them, he avoided direct intervention, such as he had practised in 1879, to prevent it. In the context of European diplomacy in the summer of 1882, the fate of Egypt rested with the two liberal powers.

From September 1881 until the end of the summer of 1882 Gladstone had to deal with a nationalist movement in Egypt. Precipitated by the bondholders' exactions and directed by disgruntled army officers under Arabi Bey, it appeared to threaten the dual control.[77] Gladstone refused to permit any loosening of the Anglo-French stranglehold on the khedival regime, particularly as Great Britain had the stronger grip. As early as the beginning of August 1881, the British consul, Edward Malet, had conceived that unrest in Egypt might afford the opportunity of diminishing, or perhaps eliminating, the French share in the European hegemony there:

> I think that the time has come when we should give the French a hint that the alliance in Egypt can only be maintained on the condition of a more scrupulous and loyal adherence to the balance of interests as it existed when the entente was entered upon and that if they pursue the policy of encroachment, we have another string to our bow — ready & strong. For I think that our position as the defender of Egypt with the sanction and conjunction of the Porte and without any annexationist policy is the platform which we may be forced to run up before very long.[78]

The Prime Minister had no intention of allowing Turkey to wield influence over the Khedive, except at the behest of the British government. 'The Sultan has been cherishing notions of getting back his power in Egypt,' he wrote in September 1881, 'but I do not think he will kick over the traces.'[79] In the 1850s and 1860s Gladstone had been an advocate of European nationalisms. Between 1876 and 1880 he had raged against Turkish suppression of native uprisings in the Balkans. Now, in 1882, forced to choose between British interests for which the Liberal government was responsible and the principle of nationalism, he sacrificed the latter — or rather, he tried to deny that Arabi represented Egyptian nationalism at all.[80] He seemed to share Chamberlain's opinion that if Arabi's movement were 'the legitimate expression of discontent and of resistance to oppression...it ought to be guided but not repressed'.[81] When the nationalists chafed at guidance, Gladstone denied their legitimacy and applied repression. His methods were similar to those which he adopted in regard to Ireland and South Africa.[82] There the Prime

Minister, so long as he possessed the ultimate authority, could afford an appearance of compromise. In Egypt, because of French rivalry, nominal Turkish suzerainty, and the uncertainties of European diplomacy, that authority itself appeared to be at risk when Arabi challenged the rule of Tewfik. Bluff failed the dual control: a joint note of 8 January 1882 and a naval demonstration in mid-May did not cow the Egyptian nationalists; indeed, it stiffened their resistance.[83] By 2 June Hartington acknowledged that the situation made the 'use of some force almost inevitable';[84] and Gladstone studiously ignored hints as to 'the *national* character of the movement in Egypt'.[85]

The Cabinet initially did not favour intervention either by Great Britain alone or in partnership with France. The first alternative carried a risk of French opposition and perhaps that of other powers; the second, the erosion of British paramountcy within the dual control. Gladstone preferred to have the Porte intervene to restore the *status quo ante* Arabi, but he so distrusted the Sultan as to fear that he might attempt to restore his own rule.[86] The French knew 'that Turkish intervention at the request of Engld. & Fr. is not "Turkish intervention" at all', and rejected the idea.[87] They proposed a conference of the ambassadors of the great powers at Constantinople. 'Much discussion' in the Cabinet resulted in British agreement.[88] On 21 June, Gladstone expressed the hope of using the conference to sanction the Sultan's despatch of troops or 'a military intervention other than Turkish under their authority'. At the same time the Cabinet consented to reinforce the British garrison in the Mediterranean.[89]

A riot in Alexandria ten days earlier, in which some Europeans had been killed, gave the proponents of military intervention an excuse for propounding their views to their more recalcitrant colleagues – and the latter an excuse for heeding them. The First Lord of the Admiralty, Northbrook, and the Colonial Secretary, Kimberley, as well as Hartington, insisted upon action. They thought 'that we should tell the French that our honour and our interests prevent us from accepting the present condition of things in Egypt'. They were ready to accept a joint intervention with France, but 'early rather than late or the opportunity may be lost'.[90] Chamberlain agreed, as did his fellow Radical Dilke, who reckoned that 'there is an overwhelming public opinion here for very strong measures' and 'that the great majority of the Cabinet share that view'. He wanted to demand 'a startling reparation' for the consequences of the riot of

11 June.[91] He originally called for execution of the guilty parties; a salute to the British fleet at Alexandria and Cairo; an award of £10,000 to the relatives of each of the eight British subjects killed; and payments to the men injured, for destruction of property, and possibly for loss of business.[92] Should the nationalists meet this exaggerated ultimatum and come to an agreement with the Khedive, Gladstone asked: 'If neither Sultan, nor Conference, nor France will act...are we then, on our sole account, to undertake a military intervention to put Arabi down?'[93] That Gladstone put this question indicated his willingness to entertain an affirmative answer. He refused to reply to a conciliatory enquiry from Arabi on 2 July.[94] Of his ministers only John Bright, the Chancellor of the Duchy of Lancaster, stood staunchly against intervention.

During the first week in July the Cabinet decided on violent action against the nationalists, with the object less of protecting the Suez canal than of asserting British dominance over Egypt. In mid-June the Admiralty had drawn up a plan which stressed the necessity of silencing by naval fire all batteries bearing on the harbour at Alexandria and clearing troops from all buildings overlooking the beach, in order to prepare for the landing of an expeditionary force.[95] Now the Cabinet agreed to instruct the commander of the British warships there, Admiral Sir Beauchamp Seymour, to bombard the fortifications.[96] Hartington, Northbrook and the Secretary for War, Hugh Childers, supported by Chamberlain and other ministers, urged sending troops at once to the Suez canal. Gladstone hesitated to take this step. He had hitherto regarded the canal *as a part of Egyptian territory*', but not as a separate issue.[97] As such, it served as an additional rationalization for aggression.[98] Childers cheerfully acknowledged as much:

> the road to Cairo will be, I think, via the Canal rather than via Alexandria. Of course there may be a blow struck at Alexia. if the fleet is in any danger, but our first interest is the Canal, and if it is in danger we shall I hope send a strong force to protect it. (I can send 15 to 20m men from this side & 6 to 18m from India *at once*, & nearly as many more in a month.) All the details of supply have been worked out & much has actually been done.[99]

Childers felt that the shelling of Alexandria 'means war with Arabi, & that at once we should protect our Canal interests. I hope the Cabinet will see this.' Apparently it did, for it sent two batallions from Malta to Cyprus and two others from home to Gibraltar in advance of despatching fifteen more 'when the actual blow is struck'.[100]

After considering the political implications of this aggressive policy, Gladstone endorsed it. At the end of June, according to one rumour, he was 'convinced that he has settled the Egyptian business very cleverly & has been successful in tiding Ireland over a Social Revolution'. He had, in fact, done neither, and was in parliamentary difficulties. 'The Extremists who in 1880 looked on Gladstone as a Deity are now beginning to perceive the cracks in their Idol & to confess that he had been a bad & foolish leader,' a Whig MP, Albert Grey, observed: 'The Liberal members are either disgusted or dispirited & in all cases displeased.'[101] The Prime Minister had initially hoped to postpone the 'Egyptian Question'[102] in order to deal with that of Ireland. In a memorandum of 5 July 1882 he complained:

If ever there was a time when unless with a real necessity Parliament ought not to be called upon by us to discuss peace & war & make provision for military measures, it is the present moment when for the next three or four weeks Parliament should direct an undivided attention to matters immediately connected with the establishment of peace and order in Ireland.

Concerned not to set precedents in regard to the Suez canal which might prove detrimental to British interests elsewhere, Gladstone argued: 'England has no separate rights which justify the adoption of military measures in respect to this international water-passage by her own sole authority without reference to Europe.' Yet he acknowledged that 'our practical interest in the common right seems to me so great' as to warrant separate action in an emergency.[103]

That emergency was now upon Gladstone not only in Egypt but also in Ireland. The government was having trouble with its arrears of rent bill in the House of Commons, and on 7 July suffered a defeat on the prevention of crimes bill. In so far as it threatened to distract parliamentary attention and disrupt the government, the Egyptian complication was an obstacle to the expeditious passage of this Irish legislation. Whigs who had voted for coercion on crime found conciliation on rent distasteful. They were particularly insistent upon the use of force in Egypt, to which Radicals were not uniformly opposed. 'I am not a "Peace at any price" man, & have no sympathy with the views of the Manchester school on this subject,' Chamberlain declared.[104] Gladstone's private secretary, Edward Hamilton, had asserted: 'The south-east corner of the Mediterranean is the one point of all others where our interests have always been admitted and rightly admitted to be really material even by the most fanatical of anti-Jingoes....Probably a Jingo policy would temporarily be popular.'[105] Drawing the sword in Alexandria might hold Liberals together on Irish legislation at Westminster and deflect Conservative criticisms. In this sense Egypt was a weapon which Gladstone could wield to maintain the unity of his party – or surrender into the hands of his opponents. Over such a choice the old political warrior did not long brood. Seymour's ships opened fire on the forts of Alexandria on 11 July. Albert Grey wondered why Gladstone and Dilke told the House of Commons 'that the bombardt. was caused by the fact of the arming of the forts' in the harbour: 'It was evident that the nominal reason was not the real reason.'[106] The shelling accomplished a domestic purpose. 'The bombardment of Alexandria, like all butchery,' Dilke commented, 'is popular.'[107] For the Prime Minister and his entourage 'the catastrophe' was not the death and destruction but the resignation of Bright, which all Gladstone's casuistry was unable to prevent.[108]

The Cabinet now made preparations for a military invasion of Egypt. Gladstone and Granville assented on 15 July 1882 to Seymour's use of two battalions of British soldiers 'as a police force' in Alexandria. At the same time Northbrook and Childers were arguing as to whether some detachments of marines or a large military expedition would be necessary to suppress Arabi. 'On the 14th the Admiralty & the war office fell out, & they have been fighting more or less ever since,' Dilke informed Lord Ripon, the Viceroy in India, on 20 July.[109] That morning Gladstone called in both ministers, to talk 'about the finances which must I conceive be involved in any large proceedings'.[110] In the afternoon the Cabinet decided to send an army under Sir Garnet Wolseley to Cyprus and Malta to be prepared 'for operations in any part of Egypt'.[111] As an excuse for such a move, Gladstone asked Granville 'whether we ought not to press very gravely on the Khedive the necessity of his immediately denouncing Arabi as a rebel'.[112] Tewfik duly complied, and Gladstone was able to develop his sense of moral outrage in time to request a vote of credit from the House of Commons on 24 July.[113] The Cabinet that day ordered Indian troops to Egypt, and on the next British soldiers from the Mediterranean garrisons began to land.[114] On 27 July, it 'decided to bombard the forts at Aboukir on intervention grounds'.[115]

No meddling by the other powers hampered Great Britain. Gladstone had not welcomed the prospect of French participation in 'the settlement of the interior question of Egypt'.[116] By the end of July the possibility of France's assisting merely 'in the protection of the Suez Canal' disappeared when the Chamber of Deputies refused to appropriate funds for such an enterprise.[117] The Italian government, which had contemplated sharing in the potential glory of an Egyptian adventure, then withdrew. Germany, Austria-Hungary and Russia had no reason to interfere.[118] Turkey did. At the end of June Gladstone had rejected an offer from the Porte to appoint Great Britain as its administrative agent in Egypt.[119] He, instead, wanted Turkey to bear the burden of fighting Arabi – for the sake of reestablishing British, not Turkish, control. The Sultan naturally balked at playing so ignominious a role. Granville had hoped that 'we shall be at Cairo before the Turks & the Italians have made up their minds to move'. He was now 'glad to think there seems little chance of the Turk sending his troops'.[120] When, once the British government had decided upon a military invasion of its own, the Sultan expressed an intention of intervening, Hartington declared:

It seems to me however that we have gone too far to draw back, and that we cannot now leave the Khedive to the mercies of the Sultan, or let the latter do what he likes in Egypt with no control except the very unsubstantial one which the discordant Concert of Europe can furnish. I believe that Parliament and the country will support us now, if we go straight on, although our position will perhaps not be a very consistent one.[121]

On 3 August the Cabinet instructed Seymour 'not to let the Turks land unless under our command'.[122] Hartington the next day proclaimed that 'it looks very much as if we should have to prevent their landing by force'.[123] A week later he admitted that the government had hurried its military measures in order either to force Turkish action or to render it unnecessary. The Sultan, although he had reluctantly agreed to proclaim Arabi a rebel, had failed to meet a second British demand for a military convention which would confine his intervention, in Hartington's words, 'within the most harmless limits'.[124] With brutal determination, the British government prevented the suzerain of Egypt from exercising his discretion or authority. On 19 August Wolseley landed at Port Said. After leisurely preparation, he crushed the nationalist forces at Tel-el-Kebir on 13 September. Great Britain was the *de facto* ruler of Egypt.

Gladstone's aggressive policy in Egypt left the Conservatives little excuse for criticism, and prevented them from mounting a successful attack on his Irish legislation. On 19 July 1882 the Tory leaders had resolved to amend the arrears bill, and they 'also agreed to a vote of censure about Egypt – but...that came to nothing, owing to the announcement of the Vote of Credit'.[125] When in early August opposition to the arrears bill by Tory peers made imminent 'the prospect of a collision between the two houses of Parliament', Lord George Hamilton, a shrewd judge of the mood of the House of Commons, wrote to caution Salisbury. Having consulted Lord Crichton, an MP for Fermanagh and a whip concerned with Irish affairs, he warned the leader of the Conservative party in the House of Lords that Rowland Winn, the Chief Whip, had misjudged his followers:

> From what has reached my ears during the last few days I am pretty confident that the members of the late Cabinet in the House of Commons have been misled as to the feeling of the men behind them, & they may have conveyed to you their erroneous impressions. There is no doubt that the great mass of Conservative M.P.[s] regard with misgiving a political crisis at this moment. The certainty of the Government obtaining in the constituencies a solid Irish vote, & the national feeling, upon which we mainly rely, being at this moment attracted towards the Government by their temporary resolute attitude in Egypt combines against us two elements that we cannot successfully withstand. Winn has told Northcote that our men want to fight now. Crichton who is a far shrewder man told me last night he is confident from his enquiries that Winn is entirely wrong. Crichton says that whereas six weeks ago our agents gave a favourable account of our prospects in many constituencies those reports related to things as they then existed, & not to the issue which might now be raised.[126]

Salisbury replied: 'From a tactical point of view the question – the only question – is whether a dissolution at this time on this bill would be advantageous. Everything else is of secondary importance.' He explained why he was adamant in his opposition to the arrears bill:

> If Gladstone floats anyhow through this Irish & Egyptian affair: & can pass his procedure resolution, he will unquestionably proceed to a County Franchise Bill, which must involve a redistribution of seats. With his present majority which on such a question will be intact, he can easily so manipulate these arrangements as to efface our party for a generation: & the House of Lords will have to submit to the result, or to appeal to the country on the Reform Bill — a very dangerous cry for such an operation. If a dissolution happens *now*, he must lose considerably — & we shall be in a position to make our influence really felt in the discussions on the Reform Bill.[127]

According to Dilke, Gladstone had 'agreed to a scheme of mine for forcing County franchise on the Lords, if they brave us'.[128] The old man was, however, basically conservative on issues of reform. When the House of Commons met on 8 August 1882, Hamilton reported: 'As regards to-night Gladstone in manner & tone was very conciliatory & I think went to the full tether of the concessions he could, without provoking dissent from the Radicals.' On their only challenge the Conservatives had a bad division, Hamilton continued: 'There is evidently little fight amongst our people.'[129] Two days later, the arrears bill passed the House of Commons. Nor were Tory peers favourable to their leader's political bellicosity. 'I am sure Salisbury is wrong,' grumbled the Duke of Richmond: 'In the present state of things both at home and abroad we ought to do all in our power to avert a crisis instead of producing one.'[130] Salisbury complained about the Tory MPs: 'I did not expect them to desert in batallions. ...A golden opportunity for breaking Gladstone's dictatorship has been lost. When shall we have another?'[131] The crisis in Egypt contributed to postponing one over reform and Ireland for at least two years.

The invasion of Egypt caused Gladstone more trouble with his own followers than with the Conservatives. 'Let me congratulate you on having got through the worst of the Egyptian difficulty,' Derby wrote to Granville after Wolseley's victory at Tel-el-Kebir: 'If the war had gone on it would have divided the party. Now, there is an end of that risk.'[132] Derby was mistaken. In July Sir Wilfrid

Lawson, the Radical MP for Carlisle, had denounced the 'Cotton Jingoes' in the House of Commons. He had challenged Gladstone to 'make a campaign of the large towns of England, and call upon the working men to fight...and he would find that the working men were not in favour of this policy of gunpowder'.[133] Lawson and other Radicals continued to have strong reservations about the British occupation of Egypt. In mid-October 1882 Lord Randolph Churchill informed Northcote:

> the Radicals in the H of C are bitterly hostile to Gladstone on the Egyptian question & are willing to go to any lengths to emphasize their disagreement with him. They are quite prepared to risk the chance of a Tory Govt. I believe Bright to be at the bottom of it, but there have been meetings of the Radicals lately in London & the accusation they mean to develope is that Mr. Gladstone has abandoned the Liberal Foreign Policy, & has spent the money of the taxpayers in the interests of the bondholders. This is a very healthy state of things if true.[134]

Although Churchill exaggerated Liberal discord in order to embolden Northcote, the Radicals were discontented.[135] They focused their attention on the fate of Arabi. Gladstone, perhaps searching for a sin-offering to expiate a sense of his own guilt, chose the Egyptian patriot as a scapegoat. Although admitting that he had no evidence to support his opinion, the Prime Minister asserted, 'beyond doubt', that Arabi was 'a criminal' who 'should be hanged'.[136] Bright and other Liberals protested, to Gladstone's annoyance.[137] The proceedings against the accused were a contemptible farce. When the prosecution could substantiate no other charge, Arabi pleaded guilty to rebellion and was exiled to Ceylon.[138] Chamberlain later admitted the possibility that 'we have done a great wrong by throwing our weight into the scale against him'; and on the subject of Egypt, the younger MP for Birmingham eventually confessed to Bright: 'I am afraid you were right & we were wrong.'[139]

During 1882 the question of money more than morality vexed the Liberals in their handling of the Egyptian involvement. To meet the military costs Gladstone had announced a rise of three halfpennies in income tax: for 1883 the rate was 6½d, the highest for nearly two decades.[140] The government proposed partially to shelter the British voter from the fiscal storm behind the Indian taxpayer. When, in mid-March 1882, Hartington had first alerted Ripon to the possible need to despatch some of his forces to Egypt, the Viceroy had warned him: 'I ought to say that we should be strongly opposed to sending these troops to Egypt if the cost were in any degree to fall upon the revenues of India – the consent given in my telegram is entirely dependent upon our being put to no expense.'[141] The government ignored this caveat when it required Indian participation in the invasion of Egypt. 'Nothing has caused me greater regret since I came out here', Ripon stated to Hartington on 26 July, 'than the receipt yesterday morning of your telegram informing me that the Government at home proposed, subject to a final decision on any representation which we may desire to make, that all expenses of the Indian Contingent for service in Egypt shall be borne by the Indian Revenue.' Ripon reminded Hartington that the poverty of the subcontinent, where the average annual income was £2/14s, prevented the Indian government from dealing adequately with such necessities as primary education, sanitation, and famine relief.[142] These pleas from Calcutta or Simla found little echo in Whitehall. The home government insisted upon making India pay.[143] Hartington, who Ripon had hoped would 'defend us firmly against any attempts of the English Treasury',[144] proved a weak protector. He wrote to the Viceroy from Newmarket on 28 September that he remembered a discussion of the Indian payment a fortnight earlier 'because it was the battle of Tel el Kebir and the Leger'.[145] Obstinate political opposition, especially on the part of the Radical Postmaster General, Henry Fawcett, eventually obliged the ministry to lower the levy on India for the Egyptian war to about 15 per cent of the total expenditure. To stop the cavilling of Ripon, Dilke cautioned him that 'the cabinet are unanimous upon the point of not paying more'.[146] The home government obviously intended that India should make contributions in men and money toward imperialist ventures.

Despite the disapproval of some Radicals, most politicians of both parties approved of the attack on Egypt. Among Liberals, not only Whigs were favourable. Gladstone himself was elated at Wolseley's easy military victory and exhibited signs of feeling, like one of his secretaries, 'quite Jingoish'.[147] Chamberlain, the foremost representative of Radicalism in the Cabinet, reacted similarly. He publicly denounced 'the policy of non-intervention or peace at any price, which I have believed to be an unworthy and ignoble doctrine for any great nation to hold'.[148] Although these words chagrined

Bright, he and other dissenters over the intervention in Egypt represented a dwindling minority even of bourgeois Nonconformists.[149] Granville was not worried about international complications: 'The French are sure to be sore, whatever we do, but they are helpless and we must endeavour to make it as little disagreeable to them as we can consistently with our pledges, our interests, and the goodwill as well [as] prosperity of Egypt.'[150] Conservative leaders found little of importance to complain about in the conduct of the Liberal ministers. 'We must admit that in the end they acted as we should have wished; & according to the traditions of English policy', confessed Salisbury; 'but,' he managed to grumble, 'for the sake of humouring weak brethren inside & outside the Cabinet, they deferred doing so for so long, that they inflicted on Egypt needless war & havoc, & on us needless waste of blood & treasure.'[151] Northcote felt unable 'to carp at our success', and settled for asking 'how the Govt. mean to turn it to account'.[152] In a speech at Glasgow early in October 1882 he said 'nothing...to which an opponent could take exception'.[153] The expressions of satisfaction at Westminster echoed the political opinion of the country, though perhaps not popular opinion.[154]

Politics, as the expression of societal forces, had thrust the British government into Egypt. Behind the reasons of strategy, diplomacy, finance and commerce lay the interests of influential sections of the aristocracy and middle class. Shippers and manufacturers, importers and exporters, bankers and bondholders – who on many other issues were competitors – favoured intervention. Their preoccupations reinforced the traditional concern to maintain British control over the Suez route to the East. Nonconformists, who increasingly approved of state action as they gained a voice in the councils of state, joined with Anglicans in lending a guise of morality to military aggression. In order to unite his party and to pass his Irish legislation, Gladstone acquiesced. Although Arabi's nationalist movement and the rivalry with France spurred the Liberal government to immediate action in the summer of 1882, the coalescence of British opinion made the invasion politically acceptable.

Conclusion

After 1882 domestic developments strengthened Great Britain's imperial commitment. While aristocrats dominated Gladstone's Cabinet and the franchise was expanded, the increasing influence of the middle class affected the making of foreign policy. Finance and trade reinforced the strategic considerations of the Foreign Office as the expansionism of the other great powers challenged the British empire. The work of the Colonial Office grew heavier, and the chartered company became a means of supporting overseas ventures at minimal cost. Egypt remained the government's primary foreign problem.

When Lord Derby joined the Cabinet in 1882 he surveyed the social standing of his colleagues with satisfaction. Almost all of them, he remarked, were '*Large*' or '*Moderate-sized landowners*' or '*connected with the Whig aristocracy*, or with *the landowning class*'. He classified Sir Charles Dilke and Joseph Chamberlain as 'Of the middle or trading class.... And of these two last, one is a baronet, & the other they say not far from a millionaire. It would be difficult to find a Cabinet with less admixture of anything that in France would be called democracy in its composition.'[1] This fact Derby considered important 'since the social position which a man holds is apt to affect his conduct more than the opinions he supposes himself to hold'.[2] He judged the Cabinet to be 'as little democratic as any we have had in the present century'.[3]

Gladstone tried to hold the Liberal party together. Derby, with the biased insight of a landowning patrician, had observed 'that the masses having strong likings but few opinions of their own, take as their representative some well known name, & leave all in his hands'. As men of the middle class became more numerous in the House of Commons, he commented, the constituent had little respect for 'the politician who is socially his equal, & politically his servant.... And the marked tendency among the masses is to choose a dictator – to take some one leading man, Gladstone, Gambetta, whoever he may be, & insist on his being followed blindly by all who are elected as his supporters.'[4] Gladstone hoped that the impression of mass support created by the Midlothian campaigns would enable him to unite Radicals and Whigs.

After three years in office, the Prime Minister's chances of success were dwindling. He had increasing difficulty in controlling his Cabinet. The longevity which increased the popular glamour of the Grand Old Man loosened his grip on colleagues who anxiously contemplated the consequences of his political demise. Chamberlain's object was to snatch the mantle of Gladstone's popular reputation, but the former screw manufacturer was so impatient that he seemed to grab at his presumed inheritance whilst the body was still warm, indeed ambulatory. Hartington had no use for the legacy, hoping to transform it into a shroud for the fallen hero rather than see it upon Chamberlain's shoulders. Gladstone slyly made play with the apprehensions of both Radicals and Whigs, pleasing neither faction. Toward them he acted as a crotchety schoolmaster dealing with unruly fourth-form boys. He maintained a 'Good Conduct List', showing the participation of ministers in parliamentary divisions: it proved in 1881, alas, that the master himself had the worst record.[5] His egocentricity increased with age. He was obsessed with measuring his achievements, particularly the length of his service in parliament and in office, against those of statesmen ranging from Newcastle and Pitt to Beaconsfield and Granville.[6] The exertions of the sessions of 1881 and 1882 told on his health, which nonetheless was remarkably good for a septuagenarian. His omnivorous reading was a sign of his inability to concentrate regularly on governmental business. He admitted that he usually limited his work to three hours a day, or in exceptional circumstances to five, but that anything more exhausted him.[7] Perhaps few of his peers laboured harder, and Gladstone's great abilities probably enabled him to do much in a short time. Yet the sensible waning of his powers and the rebellion against his authority in the Cabinet and the House of Commons often turned his thoughts toward retirement after 1881, more seriously at some times than at others. Many of his colleagues both welcomed and dreaded the prospect of his disappearance from the political stage, but the aged actor talked so frequently of his proposed exit that he exasperated his audience. As for 'Mr. Gladstone's proposed retirement,' Dilke groused, 'I never know what to make of that'.[8]

Worse than old age for Gladstone was the apparent staleness of his politics. Having concentrated upon Irish and Egyptian affairs, he had few legislative achievements to his credit, and the session of 1883 proved as disappointing as the previous three. After a defeat in the House of Commons in May, Edward Hamilton remarked: 'There is a slackness and discouragement on the Government side which must be remedied.'[9] By October, anticipating a conference at Leeds of the National Liberal Federation, Gladstone decided on franchise reform as the issue for 1884. He wanted the government rather than the constituencies to have the initiative on this question. Herbert Gladstone explained his father's motives to John Bright on 15 October:

> As in the case of the Irish Church Act & the Land Act of 1870 the impetus given by the passing of a great popular measure would carry in all probability those that are less popular but scarcely less necessary. He would therefore give priority to the Reform Bill not only becasue it is the most important measure but because such priority would facilitate the passage of the other great measures.[10]

Two days later the Leeds meeting voiced its approval of these tactics.[11] Gladstone's aim was to unite his party on the issue of franchise extension and then to attempt certain administrative changes, an approach reminiscent of that of the late 1860s.

The reforms of 1884/5 were conservative measures. Gladstone was no believer in 'manhood suffrage'.[12] 'The safe working of the household franchise in Boroughs', he argued, 'has removed...all, even the most shadowy grounds for apprehension from the enfranchisement of what may be considered as even a safer class of the population.'[13] The franchise act of December 1884 extended the borough qualification of 1867 to the counties. It did not abolish plural voting. Forty-shilling freeholders, borough freemen and university graduates retained the suffrage. Women did not gain it. About two million more men received the right to vote, raising the total electorate to five million, although the system of registration prevented many of them from casting a ballot.[14] The seats bill, which passed into law in June 1885, rearranged the electoral map of the United Kingdom largely into single-member constituencies, most of which contained approximately 50,000 inhabitants. Boroughs with a population of between 50,000 and 165,000 remained two member constituencies, as did the universities. Rural areas retained their character so far as possible.[15] These arrangements made the assertion of individual influence possible within the new electoral boundaries and weakened the power of the caucus so far as it rested upon the wholesale organization of large urban districts. By allowing increased participation to their supporters in the provinces, the parties ultimately strengthened their central headquarters, which were the sole centres of national coordination.

By 1885 four-fifths of Liberal and two-thirds of Conservative MPs were of middle-class origins. Accompanying this trend toward bourgeois domination of the House of Commons was a growth in the number of MPs concerned with imperial affairs.[16] Perhaps partly in reaction against this shift in the balance of power away from the aristocracy, many members of the Foreign Office and the diplomatic corps adopted a disdainful attitude toward trade and finance. When Louis Mallet left the Board of Trade in 1872, he had railed against 'the narrow & illiberal spirit' in which the Foreign Office and the revenue departments dealt with commercial matters.[17] Six years later, he complained to Salisbury in a similar vein, concluding: 'The old tradition that there is something vulgar in trade, still lingers, as if, without it, we should not still be eating acorns.' The Foreign Secretary concurred, 'I have a general feeling that we don't get anything like our money's worth out of F.O.: but I am not satisfied as to the fitting remedy.'[18] C. M. Kennedy, the head of the Commercial Department of the Foreign Office, laboured assiduously to obtain 'fair satisfaction for our Export and Shipping Trades'; but he protested in 1879 that 'the Commercial Dept. remains in a position inadequate...for the proper discharge of its functions, & for the due maintenance of our Commercial Interests abroad.'[19] Despite the lingering distaste of permanent officials, governmental departments were gradually adjusting to the requirements of a capitalist economy. When Francis Rowsell retired from the Contract Department of the Admiralty at the end of 1878, he tendered some advice to the First Lord about choosing his successor:

> The head of the office must be in intelligent sympathy with the official & the commercial worlds & try to reconcile them....The head of a large house in Birmingham wrote last week 'I know that business now with the Admiralty is valued & sought after; whereas in former days it was avoided by leading firms, fair play being despaired of. A feeling of confidence has been established which must prove advantageous to the Government, & which I hope will long continue.'
> It is of first necessity to secure this aim.[20]

The Foreign Office, however reluctantly, also adopted this view, and it intervened to secure opportunities for British businessmen to compete with their foreign rivals.[21]

Finance and particularly trade reinforced the strategic considerations of the Foreign and Colonial Offices. By 1885 Africa south of the Sahara, Asia, including India, and Australia and New Zealand accounted for 55 per cent of total British exports.[22] Ministers were able to assert Great Britain's imperial commitment and to fend off foreign rivals with the backing of influential sections of the middle class. British expansion accelerated from the 1870s. When Lord Kimberley returned to the Colonial Office in 1880 after an absence of six years, he complained, before the transfer of Cyprus to his jurisdiction, that the work had 'increased about 1/3rd. since I was there before'.[23] The chartered company was one means by which the government tried, at minimal cost, to accommodate the expansive drive of capitalist enterprise. In December 1878 a British company operating in north Borneo applied for a royal charter. A Foreign Office memorandum of the next year called attention to 'the political, strategical, and commercial advantages to Great Britain of the northern part of Borneo' as well as to 'the extraordinary thirst for colonial power in the Eastern Archipelago manifested by Spain and Holland'. With the cooperation of Germany, Great Britain had tried to halt the 'immense acquisitions' and 'incessant aggressions' of these two small monarchies. Its action was 'a matter of policy', and had no legal justification in the opinion of the Law Officers. As Foreign Secretary, Lord Granville approved of the request for a royal charter, which was granted in 1881, in order to keep north Borneo out of the clutches of Spain without establishing a British protectorate. Within a short time, when the French seemed bent upon annexations in Indochina, the strategic and commercial significance of north Borneo appeared greater than before, especially as British trade with China, according to the inflated estimate of the minister at Peking, amounted to at least fifty million pounds annually.[24] 'North Borneo lies in the fair way of an immense British maritime trade between China, Australia, India, and the United Kingdom,' Granville explained to his minister at Madrid: 'Its occupation by a foreign Power would be a source of disquietude to this country.'[25] Gladstone defended the granting of the north Borneo charter in the House of Commons.[26] It later furnished a model for similar charters in Africa.[27] Derby, no advocate of an aggressive policy in foreign affairs, considered that the government's decision regarding Borneo had been reasonable: 'it is wise to give free vent to the colonising & conquering tendencies of the English race, where it can be done with little risk of international complications.'[28]

That risk increased markedly after 1880, as domestic pressures and diplomatic rivalries drove the other major European powers as well as Great Britain to seek colonial acquisitions. During the 1880s, Russia extended her boundaries in central Asia and the Far East; Austria-Hungary, by political and economic methods, exploited the Balkans; Germany gained colonies in the Pacific and in east and west Africa, and influence in Turkey; France grasped for territory in northern, western and central Africa and in south-east Asia; Italy searched for recompense on the northern and eastern coasts of Africa. Already the most advanced capitalist state and in possession of a worldwide empire, Great Britain came into conflict with these other powers. The Foreign Office official who during this period acted as Granville's private secretary later likened the British empire to 'a huge giant sprawling over the globe, with gouty fingers and toes stretching in every direction, which cannot be approached without eliciting a scream'.[29]

Egypt was a focal point of the political and imperial difficulties of the Liberal administration of 1880–5. From the letters received by the Prime Minister, Edward Hamilton inferred 'that the country at large does not really care about Egypt. The London papers, headed by the *Times*, who are always dinning into the ears of the Government to rise to a better sense of their responsibilities and are urging a protectorate, do not apparently represent public opinion. These papers represent the Bondholder class.'[30] Yet politicians of both parties generally shared Lord Salisbury's view that Great Britain 'must not allow Egypt to fall back into chaos... & as some other nation would certainly seize the post we are abandoning, we should be sacrificing all the objects for which we have hitherto fought'.[31] Lord Rosebery declared that Gladstone's vacillating Egyptian policy was 'a great obstacle' to his joining the Cabinet:[32] 'In a country like Egypt, where we have acquired supremacy at so much cost, we cannot permit even the possibility of interference with our constructive work.' Nor did he change his mind after becoming a minister.[33] The Radicals, Dilke, Chamberlain and Henry Labouchere talked of handing 'Egypt over to the Egyptians', with a caveat: 'namely, that we should warn off other Powers,' and 'establishing our own influence over the Canal, remain masters of the position so far as we needed to do so'.[34] G. J. Goschen, whose recipe for patriotism included a large measure of self-interest, was so discontented with the government's lack of assertiveness abroad that W. H. Smith offered to retire to the Tory back benches 'to make room for him in the Cabinet'.[35] Governmental officials added the weight of their influence to that of journalists, politicians, bondholders, entrepreneurs and traders. Prominent among them, in addition to Sir Evelyn Baring, the British agent and consul general in Egypt, were Sir Lintorn Simmons, the governor of Malta, and Sir Julian Pauncefote, the Permanent Under Secretary of State at the Foreign Office.[36] In mid-January 1884 the First Sea Lord cautioned that, although the temporary use of marines on land was beneficial, in Egypt 'their employment cannot be looked on as a purely temporary measure. The period is *necessarily indefinite*, and will probably extend to some years.'[37]

That combination of political considerations, based upon diplomatic rivalry, strategy, trade and finance, which had thrust Great Britain into Egypt kept her there. Although 'convinced of the inexpediency of our entangling ourselves more lastingly in Egypt', particularly because of the expenditure involved,[38] Gladstone was unable to abandon the commitment. He dared not, in foreign policy, alienate the constituencies he was trying to reconcile in domestic politics. He knew that 'others than "Jingos" proper' shared the fear of weakening British control in Egypt and that, regarding his 'Indisposition to extend the responsibilities of this country', he was 'a vanishing quantity'.[39] After one Radical MP had spoken against 'scuttling out of Egypt', the Prime Minister lamented that this 'good & honest fellow', who had denounced the invasion of 1882 as a crime, now, in May 1884, warned against compromising the advantages gained from it.[40] At a conference in London during the summer of 1884 the other states involved in Egyptian financial arrangements refused to allow Great Britain to enjoy the fruits of the Nile valley without paying for them. 'What the Powers would agree to, Parliament would not look at; and what Parliament would agree to, the Powers would disavow': here, in essence, was the government's dilemma.[41] 'Would, indeed, that we were well out of Egypt!' Gladstone declared.[42] His aim by the beginning of 1885 was 'to steer a middle course between annexation and scuttling out'. He accepted that Great Britain could quit only 'providing that no one else should take the position we now hold there'.[43] The criticism of the government occasioned by the fall of Khartoum finally forced from him an admission which he had hesitated to make for the past two years and a half. Although Great Britain's work in Egypt 'ran counter to my strongest convictions', he confessed to Rosebery early in February, 'I did not mean that I thought the time was close at hand when the question of evacuation would come up.'[44]

The continuation of the occupation of Egypt entailed diplomatic complications. Gladstone's government was isolated, and suffered the full impact of imperial collisions with the other European states.[45] It had, by smashing the dual control, ended the entente with France. The German Chancellor, Otto von Bismarck, who had already formed the triple alliance and the three emperors' league, cooperated with the French to force Great Britain to display solicitude for Germany's colonial ambitions. The presence of Derby at the Colonial Office after December 1882 contributed to the worsening of Anglo-German relations, for he was as lethargic in the execution of policy and as distrustful of Bismarck as he had been six years before. He and Granville were unable to fashion an appropriate response to the Chancellor's demands. Gladstone grumbled: 'I think we are all too much afraid of Bismarck'; but Granville recognized that the German held the whip hand in European diplomacy.[46] His influence extended to Egypt, where British financial arrangements were subject to international approval. The khedival government was dependent upon a monthly loan of £1,200,000, which the house of Rothschild advanced on the strength of a letter from the British Foreign Secretary, though without legal security. By early in 1885 Gladstone faced the prospect of Egyptian bankruptcy within six months.[47] When Bismarck's son, Herbert, told him that 'there is and can be no quarrel about Egypt if colonial matters are amicably settled', the Prime Minister urged Granville to press forward the 'settlement for the North Coast of New Guinea which seems to me the main or only point remaining. It is really impossible to exaggerate the importance of getting out of the way the bar to the Egyptian settlement.'[48] Shortly afterward, Bismarck agreed that Germany would participate in an internationally guaranteed loan to Egypt of nine million pounds.[49] Rosebery, who had entered the Cabinet as First Commissioner of Works and Lord Privy Seal in February 1885, regretted 'the apparent want of harmony with Berlin'. He soon ascertained that minor colonial concessions would mollify Bismarck, who made Zanzibar 'the touchstone' of Anglo-German amity.[50]

When the Conservatives replaced the Liberals in office in June 1885, they continued the negotiations, and by mid-August received 'the very best thanks of the Imperial Government for...cooperation in Zanzibar'.[51] Sir Stafford Northcote, now Earl of Iddesleigh and First Lord of the Treasury, asked Salisbury, who was Prime Minister and Foreign Secretary,

> do you think you could do anything to induce your friends the Germans to make us some return in the way of trade facilities for our good nature in encouraging them to develope their colonial system?
>
> I am quite in favour of encouraging them to take an interest in Asia and Africa, so that they may be induced to keep back Russia from swamping us in the former Continent. But if we support them in their colonising policy, it should be not by simply sitting still with our hands folded, and seeing them help themselves; but by making terms for our own advantage as well as theirs.[52]

Salisbury replied: 'I am quite alive to the point you mention.' He hoped to exchange British cooperation in regard to Zanzibar and the Caroline Islands for German help in Egypt and Asia.[53] By September 1885, when the union of Bulgaria and eastern Rumelia seemed to endanger peace in the Balkans, the Parliamentary Under Secretary of State at the Foreign Office exclaimed: 'What a mercy it is that we are on good terms with Bismarck.'[54] The new state of Anglo-German relations was a triumph for the diplomacy of the German Chancellor and a recognition of Great Britain's altered international status.

Meanwhile, regarding Egypt, Bismarck remained willing to support British policy, at a price. He had informed Salisbury early in July:

> Our colonial questions are to to my great satisfaction nearly regulated and their final settlement is close at hand.
>
> I hope I shall be able to comply in some way or other with your wish concerning the bringing out of the Egyptian loan. You may rest assured that I shall do my best to promote any arrangements that may be satisfactory to you.

The Chancellor, nonetheless, refrained from submitting to the Reichstag for ratification the guarantee which the powers had approved in March.[55] He apparently wanted the British government first to agree to allow German bankers to float part of the loan; and the French, in that case, would also take a share. This procedure involved problems for the Chancellor of the Exchequer, Sir Michael Hicks Beach. His predecessor had committed the loan to the Bank of England. If London was to manage two-thirds of the nine million pounds and Berlin and Paris the rest, coordination of the three operations was essential. Salisbury and Beach decided to remove the Egyptian loan from the Bank of England, to the fury of its directors, and to place it with the house of Rothschild, which of course dealt at London and Paris, and was 'in intimate relations with the house of Bleichröder in Berlin'.[56] Bismarck shortly afterward designated that German firm, the head of which was his private banker, to handle the loan in the Prussian capital.[57] In Egypt the alliance between statesmen and capitalists was particularly close.

By 1885 British foreign policy had to cope with conditions different from those of twenty years earlier. On the Continent the strength of the new German state and the formation of the Bismarckian alliance systems seemed to threaten the balance of power. The expansionist drive of the other great powers posed a challenge to the British empire. At home, although the aristocracy still dominated the higher governmental positions, the widened franchise lent added significance to public opinion. The middle class, which manned the party machinery, owned newspapers and carried on the trade and finance of the nation, increased its political influence. The importance of trade and commerce overseas, the role of Lord Derby, the organizing of atrocitarian or pro-Turk demonstrations, the attempt to turn diplomatic success at the congress of Berlin to political account, the rousing of opinion for a forward policy in Egypt: all were examples of the way in which the strands of domestic politics and foreign policy were intertwined. Sustained interest in foreign affairs ran deepest in the ranks of the aristocracy and middle class. The new voters of the lower classes were more likely to be swayed by issues, such as the economic recession of the late 1870s, which touched them personally. Yet emotive appeals to Britain's continental or imperial commitment might, at least temporarily, affect all classes and make foreign policy the centre of political attention. So far as they championed the aristocracy and assumed the inviolability of Britain's international position, Disraeli and Gladstone carried on the traditions of the past. In enfranchising the lower classes, broadening the role of the middle class, and recognizing the need to meet new challenges abroad, they laid the groundwork for the future.

Appendix A

Thursday Night. 12.30
Ap. 19. 77

I find the House fully alive to the importance of the Salford victory; – our men elate, – almost dismay in the camp of the enemy!. I have taken some pains to ascertain the 'raison' of the result, and have data for a decided opinion that the election turned on the Foreign question, mainly.

Up to Saturday night Hardcastle and Charley were for treating it, and did treat it, as a local affair. – On Saturday night Grantham went there, and, at the fag end of a meeting, after the Candidate and Hardcastle had *left the room*, made a speech on the great question.

I hear that he was enthusiastically received.

That night, he made a second speech, elsewhere in Salford, and then returned to London. On Monday he received an urgent telegram, begging him to return to Salford and '*repeat his Eastern Speech*'. He did so. David Plunket also went on that day, and tells me he addressed three crowded meetings.

Between them, they afforded the only external aid to our Candidate.

I have crossexamined each, closely, as to the matter. Grantham maintains that *his* success (which was undoubted, and which I hear generally acknowledged) arose from his putting the Eastern question before them from the English point of view, which, he argued, affords a full justification for all the Government have done.

Plunket tells me that three things were his strong points, and, in his mind, were the considerations which swayed the vote.

1. *Cross*: – your selection of him, and, thereby, proved confi-

dence in Lancashire, − and his legislative successes, especially in the interest of the people.

2. The increasing evil odour of Home Rule.

3. Your Foreign Policy.

He (Plunket) cannot say whether 2 or 3 was the most weighty; on each he was very outspoken.

Both he and Grantham agree that the feeling of the working class is neither for Russia, nor for Turkey, but thoroughly excited at the prospect of the interests or honour of England being touched.

I sounded both as to whether they, or any one else, had touched on this point and its future aspect *in its details* − the freedom of the Straits, or otherwise. 'Not at all,' they say, 'the subject is not within the present comprehension of the working classes.[']

It is evident that, in *particulars*, some education will be needed: in *general*, I feel assured that Lancashire is determined that England shall not kiss the feet of Russia.

I consider what I have heard about this election tonight, from many people, to be eminently satisfactory.

M.C.

Appendix B

Dear Lord Beaconsfield

You have always dealt leniently with any opinions I have expressed upon Public Affairs, and I cannot resist therefore placing before you my views upon the present Crisis.

Of two alternatives — 'that of taking immediate action possibly resulting in War' — and 'that of allowing Russia to advance to a position from whence she can dictate her terms regardless of those Interests which the Cabinet has pledged itself to preserve' — In my opinion if the first be adopted 'that of taking immediate action' You will find you have in the House of Commons with a few exceptions a united Party at your back — also a very considerable support from our opponents, resulting in a majority I believe more than double the actual number upon which we usually rely. We shall have some agitation & meetings & much obstruction, but we have passed through such difficulties before, & gathered strength rather than weakness from them. The following I quote from much information I have gathered of a like nature —

Mr Cowen MP for Newcastle states that he knows well none of the meetings lately held express Public opinion — they are got up by nonconformists chiefly & others entirely to embarrass the Government, & he says openly they are unworthy of any attention.

Mr Mundella lately held a meeting in Sheffield & he did not even dare summon it by Ticket, but was obliged to pack it, by personal canvass carried on by his Political friends.

Much more evidence I have from Sir Charles Dilke & others.

Should however the second alternative be adopted I can see nothing but disaster in the Future — A Divided Party in the House of Commons — hostile motions from members sitting behind Ministers & a feeling of disgust amongst our supporters in the country generally, which must prove disastrous at every Election.

The honest and abiding opinion of this country apart from agitation and the only opinion worth estimating at such a time as this is always some months in process of formation & we must not be deceived because we hear little today of bitter feeling or out-spoken complaint. The feeling in the House of Commons amongst our supporters is intense & is largely shared by all the younger members of your Government. This is the tenth year since I first became connected with the management of your Party & I claim a right to speak plainly — although the position is a grave one and even perilous — one thing only can injure the Tory Party of the future — namely if it ever can be hinted either in Public or Private that in a great historical emergency, of two courses open, it's Leaders forsook the brave one & preferred the timid. I remain

always faithfully Yrs

W. Hart Dyke

Appendix C

The manager of *The Times*, John Cameron MacDonald, informed
his foreign correspondents of the state of public opinion in Great
Britain during the eastern crisis and of the reaction to it in Printing
House Square. Although suspicious of Russia, MacDonald person-
ally was averse to British participation in the Russo-Turkish war.
During the first week of hostilities, he wrote to the correspondent in
Austria-Hungary, Ferdinand Eber:

> If Russia makes the running chiefly in Asia Minor as some
> people anticipate there will be a great effort made here to drag
> England into the war; & it might be successful. Russia will be able
> to seize the Euphrates Valley, the most direct route to India; &
> this Country is already too jealous to see that happen with com-
> posure. Ever since the declaration of war we have been trying to
> keep cool but I am not sure that the attempt is very successful −
> & the disgust is very general at the bare faced way in which
> diplomacy was used to play with the other Great Powers & gain
> time.[1]

Five months later, MacDonald believed that Russia 'must succeed,
& that the Turkish Power in Europe is doomed'.[2]

In March 1878, MacDonald provided Eber with a description of
the course of events in England, 'for the drift of public feeling is not
to be entirely gathered from what you read in the Paper'. By this
time, Russia had defeated Turkey and forced it to sign the treaty of
San Stefano. 'As long as the Turks had a chance of saving any
considerable part of their power in Europe there was a Party in this
Country quite able & quite determined to keep us out of the
fighting,' MacDonald explained: 'It was a minority but wielded
influences which could not be set aside.' The destruction of Turkish

power in Europe had altered the British view of the eastern question, he continued:

> Practically we all begin to see it from the same standpoint − & we are becoming daily & hourly more united & I fear more warlike. We do not so much feel our interests threatened, but we see that Russia is tearing up the treaty of Paris & flinging the pieces in our faces. There is a sense of being challenged, if not of positive affront offered & we firmly believe that even single-handed we could 'crumple up' Russia. Our volunteer movement has made the well to do classes exceedingly pugnacious & the upper ten who officer the Army & the residuum [?] who supply us with soldiers are all red hot for war. The movement is so strong that I feel very doubtful whether it can be successfully withstood; yet it must be a very anxious time for all Public Men who retain their calmness & moderation of mind. I cannot myself see why we should lavish blood & treasure for objects which only individually concern us; but we seem bent on fighting Russia & nothing short of a doubled income tax & a heavy butchers bill, with perhaps reverses, will bring us back to reason.

Since Austria was unreliable, Great Britain faced war with Russia without an ally, a 'rather wild policy for a prudent Nation like this to face', confessed MacDonald. Yet he suspected that success in such an undertaking was not beyond reach:

> You can hardly realize the intense desire felt not only by soldiers & Sailors but by the community at large once for all to test on a practical scale what all the modern warlike appliances which we have been so many years elaborating are worth. If the fighting comes off, some very curious operations will undoubtedly be tried, & tho we may fail at the very outset to get the full use of our weapons I have no doubt that in a remarkably short time the Russians will find ample occupation for all their Armies.

Although fascinated by the technical details, MacDonald, who was *The Times*'s engineer as well as manager, found the prospect of war 'profoundly disgusting & painful'.[3]

A day later, MacDonald elaborated on his theme to Donald Mackenzie Wallace, the correspondent in St Petersburg. He insisted that the group, 'not very numerous but exceedingly influential', which had sided with Russia out of hatred of Turkey, could not now resist the warlike spirit infecting 'the People...who are only too prone to respond when appeals are made to their pride, their passions, their pugnacity & their extreme readiness to take up a challenge from an old Foe'. No special British interests were in danger, according to MacDonald:

> But the Court, Society, the military & Naval Classes, the volunteers, & the belongings of all these powerful interests are keen for a fight & the feeling is fast becoming uncontrollable....It is strongest in the South especially about London but it spreads everywhere even into our own Scottish land....Among the many powerful influences to which the war fever may be ascribed I place volunteering in the front rank. It has undoubtedly developed in this manufacturing & trading nation a spirit so full of martial ardour that nothing short of the full experience as to what a great war really means will bring us back to our senses. Tho Dizzy & other members of the Cabinet have appeared to go with the stream I doubt whether au fond they seek to embroil matters, & I am quite certain that men like Northcote & Derby & Salisbury must desire & hope intensely that peace may be preserved.[4]

Before Wallace read this letter, the terms of the treaty of San Stefano were known in London, and Derby had resigned from the Foreign Office.

As opinion became increasingly bellicose during the spring of 1878, *The Times* was unable to resist it. MacDonald wrote at length to Eber in mid-May:

> After a long struggle the conflict of opinion here seems approaching a close. There is still great reluctance to engage in war: and possibly the present position of armed preparation will be adhered to until some act of the Russian army precipitates matters, but it is now pretty clear that even if we have to go into it single handed we are quite ready to face the Czars power & you will not fail to have observed that the Paper has at last firmly taken ground consistent with that state of public feeling. Bright calls us a 'Great but cowardly paper' and it must be admitted that the current of public feeling has to a certain extent swept us beyond our own estimate of what the national policy ought to be. But perhaps Russia may not be so strong south of the Balkans as

she pretends to be. Perhaps her past sacrifices in men & money may make her pause.

MacDonald did not mention that war was likely to increase the circulation of *The Times*. He provided other rationalizations for the change of front at Printing House Square:

> I have put to you the views of the problem which prevail in this Square but which do not always crop up to the surface in the Paper. There many other things have to be considered. Allowance has to be made for many considerations which belong to the domain of sentiment rather than of reason & judgment. The Court, Society, the Army & Navy, the volunteers, & many powerful interests such as war would enrich all these are eager to fight: there is a wide spread sense that Russia measures her strength against ours in a way which sooner or later we must meet. We are not satisfied with the way in which operations in the Crimea illustrated our real prowess & there is a decided national wish to prove should a proper opportunity present itself that without help from France or Austria we can to use Cobden's words 'crumple up' Russia. A small but influential body still retain a feeling of genuine sympathy for the Turk & would wish & will strive hard in some form or other to get his power reconstituted. When the Russians took Plevna & advanced to Constantinople their case seemed hopeless & it was said & believed that whatever happened the Turkish Empire in Europe was gone. That utterance is still maintained because it shuts up the opposition of the Humanitarians & atrocity mongers when a Russian war is advocated. But if that war comes & we are again victorious I expect to see the Philo Turks again pretty urgent & very difficult to ignore.

The Times obviously was preparing for that possibility. In the meantime, its manager assured Eber: 'Like all the rest of the world we feel to some extent the depression of trade but it is quite surprizing how little in comparison with former similar periods we are now affected.'[5]

By the beginning of June 1878, MacDonald thought that the threat of war had passed, and that the '"jingo" party' would not be able to do much harm. With a sense of relief he stated to Wallace:

While Russia held out for her own treaty, bought cruisers in America, & made torpedo preparations in the Marmora our fire eaters were dangerous, but her moderation since Count Schouva- loff's visit strengthens enormously the hands of the sensible classes whom The Times aspires to lead & upon whose support its influence depends. When all is said & done we feel oppressed by the apparently insoluble difficulties of the Great Eastern puzzle; but whatever helps towards leaving that solution to time & re- flection rather than the sword is still keenly watched for and welcomed, while we stand prepared for the worst.[6]

MacDonald assigned both Eber and Wallace, as well as Carl Abel, the Berlin correspondent, to assist Henri Blowitz of the Paris office in reporting on the congress of Berlin. He was 'well satisfied' with their work there.[7]

From the summer of 1878, *The Times* lent its approval to Beaconsfield's foreign policy. MacDonald toward the end of the year gave Eber its ostensible reason for doing so: 'Up to the moment at which the real drift of the San Stefano treaty became understood here, there was a disposition in P.H.S. to withstand the popular jealousy towards Russia, but since then so much has happened to prove the grasping & unscrupulous character of that Power that we have been as you are aware steadily increasing our support of the Beaconsfield Govt in every phaze of the Eastern question.' He believed that Russia would duly execute the clauses of the Berlin treaty because, among other factors, 'the result of the Debates now in progress here will have put it beyond question that the active Eastern Policy of our Government has the emphatic approval of Parliament & the People'.[8] Here was the real reason for *The Times*'s change of its own policy in the spring of 1878: to prosper as a business enterprise and to appear to influence the public, a newspaper must print what its readers find congenial. Once the owner, John Walter III, the editor, Thomas Chenery, and MacDonald were convinced that the government had the general backing of the readership of *The Times*, they ensured that their newspaper followed suit. In doing so, it provided another proof of the political success of Beaconsfield's foreign policy.

Archival Sources

I Official Documents in the Public Record Office (London)
Board of Trade, Colonial Office, Foreign Office, Home Office,
  Metropolitan Police, and Treasury files
Cabinet reports

II Private Papers
In the Manuscript Collection of the British Library (British
Museum, London)
  A. J. Balfour Papers
  John Bright Papers
  Carnarvon Diary and Papers
  R. A. Cross Papers
  Sir Charles W. Dilke Papers
  Benjamin Disraeli Papers
  T. H. S. Escott Papers
  W. E. Gladstone Papers
  E. W. Hamilton Papers
  Iddesleigh (Sir Stafford Northcote) Papers
  Ripon Papers
  Stanmore (Sir Arthur Gordon) Papers

In the Public Record Office
  Cairns Papers
  Edward Cardwell Papers
  Carnarvon Papers
  Granville Papers
  Tenterden Papers
  F. O. private collections: Clarendon (361), Hammond (391),
    C. M. Kennedy (800/4−5), F. Lascelles (800/6−20), E. Malet
    (343), H. Ponsonby (800/3), P. Sanderson (800/21),
    T. H. Sanderson (800/1), W. A. White (364)

In the National Library of Scotland (Edinburgh)
  Rosebery Papers

In other record offices
  Cranbrook (G. Gathorne Hardy) Papers (Suffolk RO, Ipswich)
  Derby Papers (Liverpool City Libraries)
  Goodwood (Richmond) Ms. (West Sussex RO, Chichester)
  Sir Michael Hicks Beach Papers. D2455 (Gloucestershire RO, Gloucester)
  George Ward Hunt Papers (Northamptonshire RO, Delapre Abbey, Northampton)
  Lytton (E. R. B.) Papers (Hertfordshire RO, Hertford)

At Windsor Castle
  Royal Archives (Victorian)

In the Bodleian Library, Oxford
  Clarendon Papers
  Sir William V. Harcourt Papers
  Hughenden (Benjamin Disraeli, Philip Rose) Papers (formerly at Hughenden Manor)

In the University Library, Cambridge
  Hickleton (Halifax) Papers (microfilm)
  Jardine Matheson & Co. Ltd Archives

In the Birmingham University Library
  Joseph Chamberlain Papers

In the Library of the University of Newcastle
  C. E. and G. O. Trevelyan Papers

In the Archives of *The Times* (London)
  J. T. Delane Correspondence and Papers
  Printing House Square (*The Times*) Papers
  John Walter III Papers

In the Archives of W. H. Smith & Son (London)
  Hambleden (W. H. Smith) Papers

In private possession
  Derby Cabinet Minutes and Diary (Earl of Derby, Knowsley Hall)
  Devonshire Mss., Chatsworth., 2nd Series: 340 and uncalendared (Duke of Devonshire and Trustees of the Chatsworth Settle-

ment, Chatsworth House)
Salisbury (3rd Marquis) Papers (Marquis of Salisbury, Hatfield House) (formerly at Christ Church, Oxford)

Notes

Notes to Introduction

1. Charles Webster, *The Foreign Policy of Castlereagh* (London, 1931; 1963 edn, 2 vols) vol. I, pp. 351, 490.
2. Harold Temperley and Lillian M. Penson (eds) *Foundations of British Foreign Policy from Pitt (1792) to Salisbury (1902)* (London, 1938; 1966 edn) pp. 28, 47–8ff.
3. Harold Temperley, *The Foreign Policy of Canning 1822–1827* (London, 1925; 1966 edn).
4. Ibid., pp. 459–60.
5. See Charles Webster, *The Foreign Policy of Palmerston 1830–1841* (New York, 1951; 1969 edn, 2 vols), especially vol. I, chs 1 and 2; vol. II, ch. 9; Kingsley Martin, *The Triumph of Lord Palmerston* (London, new and rev. edn, 1963).
6. Gladstone to Robert Phillimore, 13 Feb. 1865: Morley, *Gladstone*, vol. I, pp. 775–6.
7. Gladstone to W. H. Gladstone, 16 Apr. 1865: ibid., p. 793.
8. Ibid., p. 837.
9. Ibid., p. 812.
10. Disraeli to Derby, 24 Nov. 1865: in Maurice Cowling, *1867 Disraeli, Gladstone and Revolution* (Cambridge, 1967) p. 83.
11. H. C. G. Matthew, R. I. McKibbin and J. A. Kay, 'The Franchise Factor in the Rise of the Labour Party', *English Historical Review*, 361 (Oct. 1976) 726, 735.
12. S. Northcote to Disraeli, 23 Sept. 1872: Idd. P. 50016.
13. Carn. D., 17 July 1870. In general see W. H. G. Armytage, *A. J. Mundella 1825–1897: The Liberal Background to the Labour Movement* (London, 1951).
14. See, for example, the files on charges of conspiracy against the gas stokers, including L.O.O. 274 (1873): H.O. 45/9326/18243; and on the conspiracy and protection of property bill, including L.O.O. 377 concerning Robert Lowe's amendment (1875): ibid/9384/45462. Also Paul Smith, *Disraelian Conservatism and Social Reform* (London, 1967) pp. 171, 215–18, 257–8. For a summary account of 'Trade Unions and the Law' see W. Hamish Fraser, *Trade Unions and Society: The Struggle for Acceptance 1850–1880* (Totowa, N.J., 1974) ch. 8; and, in general, Henry Pelling, *A History of British Trade Unionism* (Harmondsworth, 1963; 1965 edn) ch. 4, especially pp. 75–6. On a strike and lockout in the Merthyr Tydfil collieries in 1875 see (26 Jan.–20 Mar. 1875): H.O. 45/9377/41103.
15. See Charles Seymour, *Electoral Reform in England and Wales* (Newton Abbot, Devon, 1915; 1970 edn) apps. 3, 4.
16. See W. E. Williams, *The Rise of Gladstone to the Leadership of the Liberal Party 1859 to 1868* (Cambridge, 1934) ch. 9; Henry Jephson, *The Platform: Its Rise and Progress* (London, 1892; 1968 edn, 2 vols) vol. II, p. 473; and especially

H. J. Hanham, *Elections and Party Management Politics in the Time of Disraeli and Gladstone* (London, 1959; 1969 edn) ch. 14.

17. J. E. Gorst to Gerard Noel, 22 Sept. (enclosed with Noel to Disraeli, 24 Sept. 1870): H.P. B/XXI/N/120a.
18. T. E. Kebbel (ed.), *Selected Speeches of the Late Right Honourable the Earl of Beaconsfield* (London, 1882, 2 vols) vol. ii, pp. 517–22, 529–30.
19. Carlton J. H. Hayes, *A Generation of Materialism 1871–1900* (New York, 1941) ch. 6.

Notes to Chapter 1: Imperial and Continental Commitments

1. Philip Rose to Disraeli (Private), 11 July 1868: H.P. B/XX/R/28. In the mid-1860s, Disraeli had also invested in an Italian State Domain Loan (G. D. Wilkins to Disraeli, 19 May; P. Rose to Disraeli, 20 May 1865; ibid./25).
2. G. W. Sandford to Salisbury (Very Private); Salisbury to Sandford (Private), July 1871; S.P.; ibid. D/68/7. Gladstone, who inherited about £120,000, was not an incompetent man of business, although he did lose a considerable amount on his shares in the Metropolitan District Railway. See S. G. Checkland, *The Gladstones: A Family Biography 1764–1851* (Cambridge, 1971), especially pt 5 and app. 2; and H. C. G. Matthew (ed.), *The Gladstone Diaries*, vol. vii *January 1869–June 1871* (Oxford, 1982) pp. cviii–cx.
3. Manchester to Charles Montague-Lisson, 30 May 1877, 15 July 1878: Dev. P. (unc.). For general background see Howard L. Malchow, *Population Pressures: Emigration and Government in Late Nineteenth-Century Britain* (Palo Alto, Cal., 1979) ch. 2.
4. F. Young to Manchester, 5 Jan. 1882: Dev. P. (unc.).
5. W. E. Forster to Duchess of Manchester, 23 Mar. 1884: ibid.
6. Northcote to W. H. Smith, to Carnarvon, 15 Oct.; Northcote to W. R. Callender, 9 Nov. 1874: Idd. P. 50052.
7. Northcote to Derby (Private), 12, 15 Apr.; Derby to Northcote (Private, Copy), 13 Apr. 1876: D.P. 16/2/6; 17/2/6. Derby eventually saw a deputation which told him that investments in Peruvian bonds were worth thirty million pounds – 'a vast sum to be invested in a country which is ill governed, thinly peopled, & really poor', he observed (D.D. 4 July 1877). Two years later, Salisbury informed the Prime Minister: 'Great complaints are being made by the trading world about this Peruvian war. I have asked Munster to ascertain whether his Govt, which is suffering in the same way, would look favourably upon the idea of a joint diplomatic intervention for the purpose of procuring an armistice. The people are fighting about nothing at all – not coming to blows but only destroying English & German property.' (Salisbury to [Beaconsfield], n.d. [29 May 1879]: H.P. B/XX/Ce/119.) On the attitude of the British government toward Peruvian bondholders see D. C. M. Platt, *Finance, Trade, and Politics in British Foreign Policy 1815–1914* (Oxford, 1968) pp. 336–9; and on the background to the guano trade, W. M. Mathew, 'Antony Gibbs & Sons, the Guano Trade and the Peruvian Government, 1842–1861', in D. C. M. Platt (ed.), *Business Imperialism 1840–1930 An Inquiry Based on British Experience in Latin America* (Oxford, 1977).
8. Cranborne to Stanley, 1 Feb. 1867: S.P. D/72/28.
9. Salisbury to Lytton (Private), 22 Mar. 1877: ibid./40/93. Salisbury was also

worried about the world price of silver, which was the basis of the Indian currency. See his private correspondence with Lytton between April and October 1876, especially 21 Apr. and 16 June: ibid./17, 35.

10. Salisbury to General R. Strachey, 21 Feb. 1878: ibid. C/4. Salisbury feared 'such an *imperium in imperio* as an independent Company wielding so vast a power in India' (Salisbury to Lytton, 11 Jan. 1878: ibid.). The government of India purchased the East India Railway Company the next year: Horace Bell, *Railway Policy in India* (London, 1894) pp. 78—9.

11. See Harold Perkin, *The Origins of Modern English Society 1780—1880* (London, 1969; 1976 edn) pp. 221—30.

12. Disraeli to G. W. Hunt, 27 Aug. 1867: Hunt P. W.H. 220; Hunt to Disraeli, 17 Aug., 17 Sept. 1867: Letter Book, pp. 249—50, 254: ibid. 297.

13. Disraeli to M. Corry, 4 Sept. 1866: H.P. B/XX/D/10.

14. C. M. Kennedy, Memorandum *Confidential* (4779) 'Printed for the use of the Foreign Office. April 11, 1883' (30 Mar. 1883): F.O. 800/4.

15. C. M. Kennedy, 'Memorandum. For Mr Bourke, in reply to his request for further information in regard to Memm. of Novr. 20. 1877', 10 Mar. 1879: ibid.

16. How to achieve that end remained a matter of considerable debate. See Bernard Mallet, *Sir Louis Mallet A Record of Public Service and Political Ideals* (London, 1905) ch. 2.

17. For a brief contemporary account of income tax from its reimposition by Sir Robert Peel see Stephen Dowell, *A History of Taxation and Taxes in England* (London, 1884, 4 vols) vol. iii, pp. 119ff.; also J. H. Clapham, *An Economic History of Modern Britain Free Trade and Steel 1850—1886* (Cambridge, 1932) pp. 398—406. On taxes generally in the 1870s and early 1880s, see Dowell, *Taxation*, vol. ii, pp. 363—94; and in earlier years, H. C. G. Matthew, 'Disraeli, Gladstone and the Politics of mid-Victorian Budgets', *Historical Journal*, 22, 3 (1979).

18. See D. C. Gordon, *The Dominion Partnership in Imperial Defense, 1870—1914* (Baltimore, 1965) ch. 2; Paul Knaplund, *The British Empire 1815—1939* (New York, 1941; 1969 edn) pp. 198—9, 204—5, 213—15, and *Gladstone and Britain's Imperial Policy* (London, 1927; 1966 edn) pp. 125—8; Peter J. Durrans, 'The House of Commons and the British Empire 1868—1880', *Canadian Journal of History*, 9, 1 (Apr. 1974) 42—3.

19. From Cardwell's estimates furnished to Granville on 'Proposed Distribution of Regimental Establishments in the Colonies for 1869—70' (Jan. 1869); Cardwell to Gladstone, Memorandum, 24 July 1870; Cardwell, Memorandum (Confidential), printed circular, 29 Dec. 1870: Glad. P. 44119. (The figure of about 21,000 men in Morley, *Gladstone*, vol. i, p. 994. n.1, was based on an early proposal in Cardwell to Gladstone, 9 Jan. 1869: Glad. P. 44119.) On 'the withdrawal of the imperial garrisons', see R. L. Schuyler, *The Fall of the Old Colonial System A Study in British Free Trade* (London, 1945) pp. 225—33; also C. P. Stacey, *Canada and the British Army 1846—1871* (London, 1936) ch. 9.

20. D.D. 21 Mar. 1876.

21. Northcote to G. Hardy (Private), 29 Jan. 1875: Cran. P. T501/271.

22. Northcote to Sir John A. Macdonald (Private), 25 May 1878: Idd. P. 50053. At about the same time the naval commander-in-chief in the Pacific was pressing the Admiralty to fortify Esquimault on Vancouver Island and not to rely upon Canada for its defence. Algernon de Horsey to W. H. Smith (Confidential), 29 June 1878: Hamb. P. PS6/119.

23. Carnarvon to Disraeli (Private), 17 Oct., 27 Oct. (7 p.m.) 1874: H.P. B/XX/He/ 109, 111; Carn. D. 17 Oct. 1874. See generally E. Drus, 'The Colonial Office and the Annexation of Fiji', *Transactions of the Royal Historical Society*, 4th series, 32 (1950); and W. David McIntyre, *The Imperial Frontier in the Tropics, 1865–75* (London, 1967) ch. 11.

24. Carnarvon to A. Gordon (Private & Confidential), 23 Oct. 1864: Stanmore P. 49199.

25. R. G. W. Herbert to A. Gordon (Private), 20 Oct. 1875: ibid. Herbert suggested that one possible solution to the problem of colonial governance was 'a strong Chartered Company, under & in aid of the High Commissioner. . . . Many think that by throwing the trade of the Islands into responsible hands, such as those of the Directors of a big Company with Capital, many abuses wd be obviated.'

26. Disraeli to the Queen, 12 Nov. 1874: RA A47/74 [CAB 41/6/16]. The Cabinet appropriated more than £100,000 for the expedition: Carn. D., 12 Nov. 1874.

27. Clarendon to Granville, 4 June 1870: Gran. P. PRO 30/29/55.

28. John D. Hargreaves, *Prelude to the Partition of West Africa* (London, 1963) pp. 151–65; McIntyre, *Imperial Frontier*, pp. 107–8.

29. Carn. D., 15 May 1874.

30. Derby to Carnarvon (Private), 16 Dec. 1874: Carn. P. PRO 30/6/8. See also Arthur Hardinge, *The Life of Henry Howard Molyneux Herbert, Fourth Earl of Carnarvon 1831–1890* (London, 1925, 3 vols) vol. II, pp. 141–5.

31. See Hargreaves, *West Africa*, pp. 174–95, and McIntyre, *Imperial Frontier*, pp. 285–9; D.D., 3 Feb. 1876. In general, see Memoranda and Minutes on the Gambia in Connection with Proposal for the Cession of the Gambia to France, 1873–1937: C.O. 967/1.

32. *Report from the Select Committee on Africa* (West Coast) [House of Commons, 412], 26 June 1865, p. iii.

33. Clarendon to Granville (Private), 5 Oct. 1869: Gran. P. PRO 30/29/55. See in general J. D. Fage, *An Introduction to the History of West Africa* (Cambridge, 3rd edn, 1962) pp. 131–40; also Colin W. Newbury, 'Trade and Authority in West Africa from 1850 to 1880', in L. H. Gann and Peter Duignan (eds), *Colonialism in Africa 1870–1960* (Cambridge, 1969).

34. Granville to Clarendon (Private, Copy), 16 Oct.; (Copy) 1 Dec. 1869: Gran. P. PRO 30/29/55.

35. Clarendon to Granville, 30 Nov. 1869: ibid.

36. Kimberley to Gladstone, 14 Oct. 1870: Glad. P. 44224; also Granville to Gladstone (Copy), 8 Oct. 1870: Ramm, *Corr.*, vol. I, no. 326. In general see McIntyre, *Imperial Frontier*, pp. 121–6. On the Dutch cession of the Gold Coast see Douglas Coombs, *The Gold Coast, Britain and the Netherlands 1850–1874* (London, 1963) chs 4, 5.

37. Kimberley to Halifax (Private), 24 Dec. 1873: Hick. P. A4/151.

38. Carnarvon to Derby (Private), 14 Apr. 1874: D.P. 16/2/4.

39. J. T. Delane to Carnarvon, 4 Apr.; Derby to Carnarvon, 15 Apr. 1874: Carn. P. PRO 30/6/8.

40. See McIntyre, *Imperial Frontier*, pp. 278–81; Hardinge, *Carnarvon*, vol. II, pp. 146–8; Hargreaves, *West Africa*, pp. 170–1. When colonists in Sierra Leone pressed him to annex some seaboard territory in 1877, Carnarvon admitted to Derby, '*I am very much disinclined to this*. I do not want more territory on that coast: it is almost useless, & dangerous as well as inconvenient.

...The whole question of these settlements is a disagreeable and difficult one and always will be — and the best conclusion will be the one to which there are fewest objections.' Derby replied, 'I dislike West African annexations: and especially where they are, in effect, proposed with a view to restrain instead of developing trade.' Carnarvon to Derby (Private), 21 Aug.; Derby to Carnarvon (Private, Copy), 22 Aug. 1877: D.P. 16/2/4; 17/2/5.

41. Kimberley to Granville (Private), 2 Sept. 1873: Bright P. 43387.
42. Kimberley to Ripon, 3 Sept. 1873: Ripon P. 43522.
43. Derby [to Disraeli], '*China*', 7 Nov. (1875): H.P. B/XX/S/976.
44. Derby to Salisbury, 6 Oct. 1875: S.P.
45. Harry S. Parkes to Tenterden (Private), 3 Jan. 1876: Tent. P. F.O. 363/2, ff. 473–4.
46. F. R. Plunkett to Tenterden (Private), 9 Mar. 1876: ibid./3.
47. Carnarvon to Granville (Private, Copy), 21 Oct.; Granville to Carnarvon, 24 Oct. 1880: Carn. P. PRO 30/6/52, ff. 128–32; Stephen Gwynn and G. M. Tuckwell, *The Life of the Rt Hon. Sir Charles W. Dilke* (London, 1917, 2 vols) vol. I, p. 123.
48. Cairns to Disraeli (Private), 26 Sept. 1873; also 29 Jan. 1874: H.P. B/XX/Ca/105; 108.
49. Carnarvon to Derby (Private), 22 July 1874: D.P. 16/2/4.
50. See Ethel Drus (ed.), *A Journal of Events during the Gladstone Ministry 1868–1874* by John, First Earl Kimberley, Camden Miscellany, vol. 21 (London, 1958) pp. xix–xx; C. D. Cowan, *Nineteenth-Century Malaya The Origins of British Political Control* (London, 1961), especially pp. 166–75, 264–70; McIntyre, *Imperial Frontier*, pp. 199–206, ch. 10.
51. Derby to Carnarvon (Private), 19 July 1875: Carn. P. PRO 30/6/8; Carnarvon to Derby, 22 July 1875: D.P. 16/2/4. On New Guinea see W. P. Morrell, *Britain in the Pacific Islands* (Oxford, 1960) pp. 241ff., and McIntyre, *Imperial Frontier*, pp. 341–50.
52. M. Corry to Disraeli, 27 Nov. [1866]: H.P. B/XX/Co/18, 18a.
53. Carnarvon added that he viewed Sarawak as a quicksand which would swallow up money and which crawled with as many ruffians as reptiles, a place which he hoped Brooke would not leave to the Queen. Carnarvon to H. Ponsonby, 15 June 1876: F.O. 800/3, ff. 501–3.
54. In general see Steven Runciman, *The White Rajahs A History of Sarawak from 1841 to 1946* (Cambridge, 1960) especially pp. 174–92.
55. Derby to O. Russell (Draft), 26 Apr. 1877: F.O. 64/874, no. 153.
56. Salisbury to Cranbrook (Private), 3 Sept. 1879: Cran. P. T501/269.
57. See G. F. Hudson, *The Far East in World Politics A Study in Recent History* (London, 2nd edn, 1939, 1945) pp. 68–9. For a graphic picture of the various developments in the Far East see H. C. Darby and Harold Fullard (eds.), *The New Cambridge Modern History*, vol. 14, *Atlas* (Cambridge, 1970) p. 264.
58. See A. K. Cairncross, *Home and Foreign Investment 1870–1913: Studies in Capital Accumulation* (Cambridge, 1953) tables 41–3, pp. 183, 185, 189; S. B. Saul, *Studies in British Overseas Trade* (Liverpool, 1960) pp. 62–3, ch. 8. Also Peter Harnetty, *Imperialism and Free Trade: Lancashire and India in the Mid-Nineteenth Century* (Manchester, 1972), especially ch. 2.
59. Northbrook to Hartington (Private), 8 Mar. 1875: Dev. P. 340.616.
60. Lytton to Salisbury (Private), 15 Feb. 1878: S.P.

61. Louis Mallet to Salisbury (Private), 25 June 1875: ibid.
62. Cardwell to Gladstone (Copy), 13 Nov. 1873: Card. P. PRO 30/48/2/10.
63. Argyll, Cabinet memorandum (Confidential), 23 Jan. 1871: Gran. P. PRO 30/29/68. For another commentary on the relations between the home government and India by a former Indian Secretary see Halifax to Argyll (Copy), 14 Oct. 1871: Hick. P. A4/82.
64. Salisbury to Northbrook, 26 Aug. 1874: S.P. C/2, f. 48.
65. Salisbury to Disraeli (Private), 16 July 1875: H.P. B/XX/Ce/52.
66. Salisbury to Sir B. Frere (Copy by H. Walpole), 10 Dec. 1875: S.P. Draft C/2/181.
67. Salisbury to Disraeli (Confidential), 19 Oct. 1875: H.P. B/XX/Ce/60.
68. Salisbury to Disraeli (Most Confidential), 10 Oct. 1875: ibid./59.
69. Salisbury to Disraeli (Most Confidential, Draft), 10 Oct. 1875: S.P. On the tariff problem see S. Gopal, *British Policy in India 1858–1905* (Cambridge, 1965) pp. 109–13; and on the tension between Salisbury and Northbrook see Argyll to Halifax, 8 Jan. 1876: Hick. P. A4/82.
70. Argyll to Halifax (Private), 26 Feb. 1876: ibid.
71. Lytton to Disraeli (Private), 30 Apr. 1876: H.P. B/XX/Ly/231. Lytton added that he would not inform his Council in India until he received approval from home: 'You doubtless know that my Councillors are all Liberals – that is to say narrowminded persons; and also practical men, or, in other words, men incapable of giving practical effect to an idea.'
72. Salisbury to Disraeli (Confidential), 7 June 1876: ibid./Ce/77.
73. In general see Gopal, *India*, pp. 113–16, Anil Seal, *The Emergence of Indian Nationalism Competition and Collaboration in the Later Nineteenth Century* (Cambridge, 1971) pp. 132–6; also L. A. Knight, 'The Royal Titles Act and India', *Historical Journal*, 11, 3 (1968) 498–507.
74. Hugh Childers to Gladstone, 22 Jan. 1869: Glad. P. 44128. Some years later, the Treasury, after consultation with the Foreign and Colonial Offices, devised a scheme whereby India would contribute to subsidizing steamship service between Aden and the Cape. One of its objects was to help eliminate slavery 'by the increase of Commerce & spread of Civilization' and thus render unnecessary the maintenance of a squadron on the east coast of Africa – or at least British payments towards it. Note by W. B. Gurdon, initialled by Gladstone, 24 Sept. [1872]: ibid. 44182.
75. Gladstone to Granville, and Memorandum by Gladstone for Granville (Copy), 17 Oct. 1873: Ramm, *Corr.*, vol. II, nos 909–10.
76. Argyll to Granville, 29 Oct. 1873: Gran. P. PRO 30/29/51.
77. Argyll to Gladstone, 30 Oct. 1873: Glad. P. 44103. Argyll was also fighting a battle for departmental jurisdiction with Granville: 'Our relations with Arabian Chiefs have hitherto been all conducted by the Indian Govt. – not the F.O.' Gladstone did not disapprove of this truculent stand. Gladstone to Argyll, 1 Nov. 1873: H. C. G. Matthew (ed.), *The Gladstone Diaries*, vol. VIII *July 1871–December 1874* (Oxford, 1982).
78. Salisbury to Northbrook, 1 May 1874: S.P. C/2, f. 15.
79. Carnarvon to Lytton (Private), 25 July 1875: Lyt. P. D/EK/030.
80. Carnarvon to Lytton (Private & Confidential), 27 Oct. 1875: ibid.
81. Carnarvon to Derby (Private), 27 Oct.; Derby to Carnarvon (Private, Copy), 28 Oct. 1875: D.P. 16/2/4; 17/2/5.

82. Carnarvon to Hardy (Private & Confidential), 11 Dec. 1875: Cran. P. T501/262. On the importance attached to the Cape, see Ronald Robinson and John Gallagher, *Africa and the Victorians* (London, 1961), especially pp. 59—60.
83. Carnarvon to Beaconsfield, 6 July 1877: H.P. B/XX/He/82; also in Hardinge, *Carnarvon*, vol. II, p. 99.
84. Stanley to Disraeli (Private), 1 Oct. 1868: H.P. B/XX/S/826. On the Belgian railway question see Richard Millman, *British Foreign Policy and the Coming of the Franco—Prussian War* (Oxford, 1965) pp. 123—44.
85. Gladstone to Clarendon (Private), 18 Feb. 1869: Clar. P. c.497.
86. Gladstone to Clarendon, 9 Mar. 1869: ibid.; also in *Gladstone Diaries*, vol. VII.
87. Gladstone to Grey, 17 Apr. 1869: Morley, *Gladstone*, vol. I, p. 951.
88. Gladstone to the Queen, 16 July 1870: *QVL*, vol. II, p. 38.
89. Richmond to Cairns, 27 July 1870: Cairns P. PRO 30/51/2.
90. *Hansard* 203, cols 1286—1300 (Disraeli), 1 Aug. 1870; M & B, vol. V, pp. 126—8.
91. Millman, *British Foreign Policy*, pp. 203—6.
92. Morley, *Gladstone*, vol. I, pp. 973—5.
93. Gladstone to Halifax, 29 July 1870: Hick. P. A4/88; also in *Gladstone Diaries*, vol. VII.
94. See A. J. P. Taylor, *The Struggle for Mastery in Europe, 1856—1918* (Oxford, 1954) p. 210. On the balance of power generally in this period, see F. H. Hinsley, *Power and the Pursuit of Peace* (Cambridge, 1963) pp. 247—53.
95. Alfred Austin to Disraeli, 13 Sept. 1870: H.P. B/XXI/A/248. Austin, at the headquarters of the King of Prussia at Rheims, quoted Bismarck as remarking on Jules Favre's attempt to discover through Granville's good offices whether the Germans would negotiate on the basis of the territorial integrity of France: 'I wonder that M. Favre did not ask if Germany would pay the expenses of the war.'
96. Disraeli to M. Corry, 26 Sept. 1870: ibid./XX/D/138.
97. Hardy to Cairns, 8 Sept. 1970: Cairns P. PRO 30/51/7.
98. Granville to Gladstone, 7 Oct., 3 Nov. 1870: Ramm, *Corr.*, vol. I, nos 323, 352.
99. Salisbury to G. W. Sandford, 24 Sept., 26 Oct. 1870: S.P. D/68/4, 5.
100. R. Anderson, 'Summary of Police reports, registered in the Home Office, with reference to *Political* meetings held in the Metropolis during the years 1867 to 1870 inclusive', 31 Aug. 1871: Glad. P. 44617.
101. Derby to Lytton (Private), 15 Oct. 1874: Lyt. P. D/EK/030.
102. In general see A. L. Dunham, *The Anglo—French Treaty of Commerce of 1860 and the Progress of the Industrial Revolution in France* (Ann Arbor, Mich., 1930) chs 15, 16; 'Commercial Diplomacy, 1860—1902', 25 Sept. 1903: T. 172/945.
103. Carnarvon to Salisbury (Private), 27 Jan. 1871: S.P.
104. See Deryck Schreuder, 'Gladstone as "Troublemaker": Liberal Foreign Policy and the German Annexation of Alsace-Lorraine, 1870—1871', *Journal of British Studies*, 17, 2 (1978) 119.
105. Granville to J. T. Delane (Private), 30 Oct. 1870: Delane P. (1).
106. Granville to Gladstone (Private), 25 Sept. 1870: Ramm, *Corr.*, vol. I, no. 309.
107. Gladstone to Granville, 8 Oct. 1870: ibid., no. 324 and n.4.
108. See Raymond J. Sontag, *Germany and England   Background of Conflict*

1848—1894 (New York, 1938) pp. 79—87.

109. E. Hammond to E. R. B. Lytton (Private), 30 Nov. 1870: Lyt. P. D/EK/030.

110. Hammond to Lytton (Private), 2 Apr., also 20 Feb., 1872: ibid.

111. C. S. A. Bille to Salisbury, 4 Dec. 1870, quoted in Bille to Salisbury, 5 June 1878: S.P. G.

112. Salisbury to Bille, 18 Apr. 1871, quoted ibid.

113. See James Joll's provocative and important inaugural lecture, '1914: The Unspoken Assumptions' (London, 1968).

114. Granville to Gladstone, 8 Dec. 1870: Ramm, *Corr.*, vol. I, no. 394.

115. Gladstone to Granville, 23 Nov. 1870: ibid., no. 375. For Aberdeen's influence on Gladstone see Paul Knaplund, *Gladstone's Foreign Policy* (London, 1935; 1970 edn) pp. 3—5.

116. J. Bright to Gladstone, 17 Nov. 1870: G. M. Trevelyan, *The Life of John Bright* (London, new edn, 1925) p. 418. Also Bright to Halifax, 9 Jan. 1878: Hick. P. A4/159.

117. Gladstone to Granville, 22 Nov. 1870: Ramm, *Corr.*, vol. I, no. 374; see also the Queen to Granville, 20 Nov. 1870: *QVL*, vol. II, p. 85; Granville to the Queen, 12 Nov. 1870: ibid., p. 83.

118. Hartington to Devonshire, 11 Nov. 1870: Dev. P. 340.439.

119. Granville to Arthur Otway (Confidential, Copy), 20 Nov.; Otway to Granville, 19 Nov. 1870: Gran. P. PRO 30/29/107.

120. Granville to Delane (Private, 'à la Macaulay'), 27 Nov. 1870: Delane Corr. 19/89.

121. M. Corry to Disraeli (Confidential), 17 Feb. 1871: H.P. B/XX/Co/73.

122. Cairns to G. Hardy, 20 Oct. 1870: Cran. P. T501/262.

123. Carnarvon to Salisbury (Private), 4 Jan. 1871: S.P.

124. Manners to Disraeli, 21 Oct. 1870: H.P. B/XX/M/160.

125. G. Noel to Disraeli, 20 Jan. [1871]: ibid./XXI/N/123.

126. Derby to Disraeli, 22 Jan. 1871: ibid./XX/S/866. See also the Queen to Granville, 20 Jan. 1871: *QVL*, vol. II, p. 112.

127. Disraeli to Derby, 25 Jan. 1871: M & B, vol. V, pp. 132—3.

128. 'Note handed to me in Cabinet, D[erby]', 25 Jan. 1876: D.P. 16/2/2.

Notes to Chapter 2: Party Politics in the Eastern Question

1. Disraeli to Michael Hicks Beach (Confidential), 17 Dec. 1874: H.B. P. PCC/75.

2. Disraeli to Richmond (Private), 7 Apr. 1877: Goodwood Ms. 865. The Cabinet had under discussion continuing the Scottish board of education for another year: 'I doubt not the Board is a job,' Disraeli admitted, 'but it is a very popular one.' Also D.D., 11 Apr. 1877.

3. A. J. Balfour, Memorandum on the Conservative government's foreign policy, 8 May 1880: Balfour P. 49688.

4. D.D., 9 July 1877.

5. Disraeli to Lady Bradford, 4 Nov. 1875: M & B, vol. VI, p. 15.

6. Disraeli to Salisbury, 23 July 1876: S.P.

7. Disraeli to Derby (Confidential), 24 Apr. 1875, 15 Aug. 1876: D.P. 16/2/1, 2; the latter also in M & B, vol. VI, p. 49.

8. H. M. Swartz and M. Swartz (eds), *Disraeli's Reminiscences* (London, 1975)

p. 69. Beaconsfield to the Queen (Confidential), 10 Sept. 1876: RA H9/112; also in *QVL*, vol. II, p. 478. Beaconsfield to Derby, 4 Nov. 1876: D.P. 16/2/2; also in M & B, vol. VI, p. 89.

9. Salisbury to Beaconsfield (Private), 29 Aug. 1876: H.P. B/XX/Ce/82.
10. Disraeli to Derby, 18 May, (Confidential) 17 Oct. 1876: D.P. 16/2/2; also in M & B, vol. VI, pp. 27–8, 81. Cf. R. W. Seton-Watson, *Disraeli, Gladstone and the Eastern Question* (London, 1935; 1969 edn) pp. 44–6.
11. D.D., 9 Aug. 1876.
12. Ibid., 9 Jan. 1876.
13. Ibid., 1 Feb. 1876; Derby to Granville (Private), 7 June 1876: Gran. P. PRO 30/29/26A/1, bundle VIII.
14. D.D., 9 Jan. 1876.
15. Ibid., 12 Jan. 1876.
16. For example Minute by Derby, n.d., on W. A. White to Tenterden (Private), 24 July; Tenterden to White (Private, Copy), 2 Aug. 1876: Tent. P. F.O. 363/4. White was an active private correspondent. See his letters to A. H. Layard, from Belgrade and Bucharest, 29 May 1877–5 Apr. 1880: F.O. 364/10.
17. Malmesbury to Disraeli (Private), 14 May 1874: H.P. B/XVIII/C/39. Also Malmesbury to Derby (Private), 13, 26 May 1874: D.P. 16/2/5.
18. Salisbury to Lytton (Private), 15 June 1877: S.P. D/40/107.
19. For example Alfred de Rothschild to Beaconsfield, 13 Sept. 1877: H.P. B/XXI/R/208; Bleichröder to Beaconsfield, 24 Oct. 1878: ibid./B/548; and Beaconsfield to Salisbury, 28 Oct. 1878: S.P. See also Fritz Stern, *Gold and Iron Bismarck, Bleichröder, and the Building of the German Empire* (London, 1977).
20. When trying to enforce the treaty of Berlin in 1878, the Prime Minister wrote to the Austrian Foreign Minister, Count Julius Andrassy: 'I have seen my friend. His manner, at first, was not encouraging. Foreign loans are not in favour in England and to float the Egyptian successfully, he had to exert all his vast resources, and was supported by the sympathy of two Governments. I told him, then, that next to my own Government, there was none which I wished so much to serve and strengthen as your own, and that I was deeply interested in your personal success.' Andrassy replied that he was grateful for the Prime Minister's personal intervention with the Rothschilds and asked him to continue his efforts, assuring him: 'la politique de l'Autriche Hongrie, independamment des ministres qui la dirigent, aura toujours en vue, avant tout la pursuite de *l'exécution integrale* en commun avec l'Angleterre, du traité de Berlin'. Beaconsfield to Andrassy (Confidential, Copy), 24 Nov., Andrassy to Beaconsfield (Confidential), 22 Dec. 1878: H.P. B/XVI/B/52, /C/1; also [Andrassy to Deym, Dec. 1878]: ibid./XXI/A/179.
21. Disraeli to Derby, 18 May 1876: D.P. 16/2/2. For British diplomacy generally during this period see Richard Millman, *Britain and the Eastern Question 1875–1878* (Oxford, 1979).
22. Disraeli to the Queen (Confidential), 29 May 1876: RA H7/198; also in *QVL*, vol. II, p. 455.
23. Disraeli to Derby, 25 May 1876: D.P. 16/2/2; also in M & B, vol. VI, p. 29.
24. Derby to Disraeli, 4 June 1876: H.P. B/XX/S/1131.
25. D.D., 9 June 1876.
26. Elliot to Tenterden (Private), 9 June 1876: Tent. P. F.O. 363/1, pt 2, f. 323.

27. 'But it is unmistakably the Policy of the Prime Minister, not of the Secretary for F.A.', Lytton added, 'and I anxiously hope it will continue to be so, and that Ld. D. will not be allowed to jib half way up the Hill.' Lytton to Corry (Private), 10 July 1876: H.P. B/XX/Ly/232.
28. Disraeli to the Queen, 2 June 1876: RA H7/221; part in *QVL*, vol. II, p. 456.
29. Ponsonby to the Queen, 3 June 1876: RA H7/222.
30. D.D., 25 Jan., 23 Mar. 1876.
31. Ibid., 6 Mar. 1876.
32. Disraeli to Barrington (Confidential), 10 Aug. 1876: Disraeli P. 58210.
33. Malmesbury to Richmond (Confidential), 5 Aug. 1876: Goodwood Ms. 868. Malmesbury observed: 'As to Dizzy he is immortal. He looked 10 years younger yesterday than when Part. met.'
34. Barrington to Disraeli [Draft copy], 11 Aug. 1876: Disraeli P. 58210: 'owing to many circumstances, the difficulty of selecting a successor to yourself is very great indeed'.
35. Mary Derby to Disraeli, 10 July 1876: H.P. B/XX/S/1457. Lady Derby raised 'another reflection & doubt − will the party consent to have a leader in the H. of C. chosen for them? Will it not say the Liberals as a party chose their leader − we will choose ours?'
36. Mary Derby to Disraeli, 15 July 1876: ibid./1458.
37. Disraeli to Hardy (Confidential, Copy) 2 Aug. 1876: ibid/XIII/124; Hardy to Disraeli (Confidential), 2 Aug. 1876: ibid./XX/Ha/84; Northcote to Disraeli (Confidential), 2 Aug. 1876: ibid./A/VIII/B/5. See A. E. Gathorne-Hardy, *Gathorne Hardy, First Earl of Cranbrook: A Memoir with Extracts from His Diary and Correspondence* (London, 1910, 2 vols) vol. II, pp. 1−11; M & B, vol. v, pp. 525−7; Nancy E. Johnson (ed.), *The Diary of Gathorne Hardy, later Lord Cranbrook, 1866−1892: Political Selections* (Oxford, 1981) pp. xx−xxi, 12 and 16 July, 3 Aug. 1876.
38. On the Queen's advice, Disraeli wrote to his principal colleagues. She particularly insisted that the Duke of Richmond, the Conservative leader in the House of Lords, 'shd. be *one* of the *1st to hear it*, as it changes his position'. H. F. Ponsonby to the Queen, 22 July 1876: RA A50/39; the Queen to Disraeli (Confidential), 22, 28 July 1876: H.P. B/XIX/B/567, 571. For much of the correspondence, see M & B, vol. v, ch. 13.
39. D.D., 12 Aug. 1876.
40. Disraeli to Derby (Confidential), 14 July 1876: D.P. 16/2/2; also in M & B, vol. VI, pp. 44−5.
41. D.D., 13 Feb. 1876; Derby to Disraeli (Private), 15 Feb. 1876: H.P. B/XX/S/ 1002; Tenterden to Disraeli (Private), 19 July 1876: ibid./XXI/T/99. One of Disraeli's closest political advisers had warned him: 'I have no confidence in Tenterden's discretion.' Cairns to Disraeli (Confidential), 18 July 1876: ibid./XX/Ca/182. In later years Lord Lytton briefly characterized Tenterden: 'An industrious but, I think, overrated man. Certainly no statesman.' (Comment on a sheet of paper prefacing letters from Tenterden: Lyt P. D/EK/030.) For a criticism of Tenterden's work see Harold Temperley and Lillian M. Penson (eds), *A Century of Diplomatic Blue Books 1814−1914* (London, 1938; 1966 edn) pp. 251−4.
42. Derby to Disraeli (Private), enclosing Minute by Tenterden, 14 July 1876: H.P. B/XX/S/1139. Here was the origin of the phrase 'coffee-house babble',

which Disraeli used in the debate of 31 July 1876 (*Hansard* 231, col. 203). Derby believed that Disraeli had spoken lightly of the atrocities and then laid the blame on his informants for his own careless talk. He hinted to the Prime Minister that he had done Tenterden, in particular, a 'great injustice'. D.D., 8, 11 Aug. 1876.

43. Tenterden to Disraeli (Private), 14 July 1876: H.P. B/XXI/T/96. Disraeli heavily underscored the italicized words.

44. Disraeli to [A. Turnor ?], 14 July 1876: ibid./96a.

45. W. T. Stead to Gladstone, 26 Aug. 1876: Glad. P. 44303. Stead wrote flattering letters to Gladstone throughout the autumn. On the agitation see especially R. T. Shannon, *Gladstone and the Bulgarian Agitation 1876* (London, 1963). Also David Harris, *Britain and the Bulgarian Horrors of 1876* (Chicago, 1939), and Seton-Watson, *Eastern Question*, ch. 3.

46. Halifax to Granville, 7 Sept. 1876: Gran. P. PRO 30/29/26A/1, bundle VIII.

47. Gladstone to Granville, 7 Aug. 1876: Ramm, *Corr.*, vol. II, no. 1050.

48. Gladstone to Granville, 20 Aug. 1876: Ramm, *Corr.*, vol. I, no. 1.

49. Argyll to Gladstone, 11 Aug. 1876: Glad. P. 44103.

50. Morley, *Gladstone*, vol. II, pp. 160, 162; Shannon, *Bulgarian Agitation*, pp. 114–17.

51. Gladstone to Granville, 7 Sept., (Private) 14 Sept. 1876: Ramm, *Corr.*, vol. I, nos 7, 10. Ironically, Gladstone had a few years earlier considered elevating Sir Thomas Fremantle, father of the Conservative candidate in the by-election, to the peerage. W. B. Gurdon, Memoranda, 17, 19 Dec. [1873]: Glad. P. 44182.

52. Beaconsfield to Cairns (Confidential), 23 Sept. 1876: Cairns P. PRO 30/51/1, and W. Hart Dyke to Beaconsfield, 25 Sept. 1876: H.P. B/XXI/D/468; Spencer to Granville, 24 Sept. 1876: Gran. P. PRO 30/29/29A. In 1879 the Liberal agents in Buckinghamshire were 'strongly of opinion it would be unwise' to run a second candidate in a general election (C. Carington to Rosebery, 8 July 1879: R.P. 10008). Rupert Carington was returned with two Conservatives the next year.

53. Gladstone to W. P. Adam (Copy), 4 Oct. 1876: Glad. P. 44095.

54. Kimberley to Ripon, 23 Sept. 1876: Ripon P. 43522.

55. He added: 'I suspect however that Dissenters are Gladstonian & hate the Turk.' Spencer to Granville (Confidential), 12 Nov. 1876: Gran. P. PRO 30/29/29A. Also Spencer to Hartington, 29 Oct. 1876: Dev. P. 340.682.

56. Harcourt to Granville, 10 Oct. 1876: Gran. P. PRO 30/29/29A.

57. Carington to Granville, 22, 24, 25 Aug. 1876: ibid./26A/1, bundle v. Harcourt to Granville, 12 Oct. 1876: ibid./29A. Even before the by-election, Lionel de Rothschild expressed to Beaconsfield the hope that Russia and England 'will now work well together, and that you will be able to carry out your plan, to your own satisfaction, & to that of the Turks, who at all these public meetings have not been spared. ...Some of our friends think the terms too hard for the Turks.' L. Rothschild to Beaconsfield, 19 Sept. 1876: H.P. B/XXI/R/221.

58. Grenfell to Granville, 23 Sept. 1876: Gran. P. PRO 30/29/26A/1, bundle v, on 'the conservative reaction...among the goers and comers into London' from Maidenhead and Slough.

59. J. C. MacDonald to John Walter, 3 Oct. 1876: Walter P. 453; *The History of 'The Times'* (London, 1935–52, 4 vols in 5) vol. II, pp. 506–8.

60. Shannon, *Bulgarian Agitation*, pp. 153–4, 241–2. One Conservative asserted: 'The Press as a whole supports us.' Hardy to Carnarvon (Private), 25 Sept. 1876: Carn. P. PRO 30/6/12.

61. H. Reeve to Granville, 9 Sept. 1876: Gran. P. PRO 30/29/26A/1, bundle VIII.

62. Granville to Devonshire, 16 Oct. 1876: Dev. P. 340.677.

63. Hartington to Harcourt, Constantinople, 2 Oct. 1876: Harcourt P. 78.

64. Granville to Gladstone, 4 [sic: 5] Oct. 1876: Ramm, *Corr.*, vol. I, no. 17.

65. Argyll to Granville, 26 Sept., 25 Oct. 1876: Gran. P. PRO 30/29/29A; Argyll to Gladstone, 12 Sept. 1876: Glad. P. 44103; Gladstone to Granville, 7 Oct. 1876: Ramm, *Corr.*, vol. I, no. 18; Harcourt to Granville, 10 Oct. 1876: Gran. P. PRO 30/29/29A. Cf. W. P. Adam to Gladstone, 2 Oct. 1876: Glad. P. 44095. Gladstone did not think an early readjournment of parliament desirable, although he calculated that the threat of one might be a useful goad to governmental action. Gladstone to John Bright, 27 Sept. 1876: Bright P. 43385.

66. Granville to Devonshire, 5 Oct. 1876: Dev. P. 340.675; Shannon, *Bulgarian Agitation*, pp. 241–3.

67. Barrington, Memorandum, 23 Oct. 1876: Disraeli P. 58210.

68. Hartington to Gladstone, 27 Oct. 1876: Glad. P. 44144. Also Hartington to Devonshire, 8 Oct. 1876: Dev. P. 340.676; F. Cavendish to Hartington, 20 Oct. 1876: in Bernard Holland, *The Life of Spencer Compton Eighth Duke of Devonshire* (London, 1911, 2 vols.) vol. I, pp. 181–2.

69. Shannon, *Bulgarian Agitation*, pp. 249–50.

70. Granville to Devonshire, 16 Oct. 1876: Dev. P. 340.677.

71. Dilke to Chamberlain, 5 Oct. 1876: JC 5/24/11.

72. Chamberlain to Dilke, 10 Oct. 1876: Dilke P. 43885; also, with omissions, in Stephen Gwynn and G. M. Tuckwell, *The Life of the Rt Hon. Sir Charles W. Dilke* (London, 1917, 2 vols) vol. I, p. 210.

73. Harcourt to Dilke, 10 Oct. 1876: Dilke P. 43890; partially in Gwynn and Tuckwell, *Dilke*, vol. I, pp. 209–10.

74. Ibid., pp. 210–11.

75. Gladstone to Granville, 19 Nov. 1876: Ramm, *Corr.*, vol. I, no. 30; Gladstone to Olga Novikov, 17 Oct. 1876: Morley, *Gladstone*, vol. II, p. 165. Madame Novikov, a fervent pan-Slav propagandist, replied: 'I rather like the idea of treating the Eastern question as a question of fashion, some thing like a chignon, or a crinoline, wh. the upper 10 thousand accept or reject!! Well – it is *loathsome* – to tell the truth, I could not say otherwise!' (Novikov to Gladstone, 18 Oct. 1876: Glad. P. 44268.)

76. Hartington to Granville, 26 Nov. 1876: Gran. P. PRO 30/29/22A/2. Spencer refused to lend his name to the conference because he wanted nothing to do with a debating society outside parliament. Spencer to Granville, 30 Nov. 1876: ibid./29/29A.

77. In general see Shannon, *Bulgarian Agitation*, pp. 251–61. Also D.D., 9 Dec. 1876; and Derby to Salisbury (Private), 7, 14 Dec. 1876: S.P.

78. Hartington to Granville, 18 Dec. 1876: Gran. P. PRO 30/29/22A/2; also, with omissions and changes, in Edmond Fitzmaurice, *The Life of Granville George Leveson Gower Second Earl Granville K.G. 1815–1891* (London, 3rd edn, 1905, 2 vols) vol. II, p. 167.

79. Gladstone to Granville, 7 Oct. 1876: Ramm, *Corr.*, vol. I, no. 18.

80. Beaconsfield to Barrington (Private), 11 Sept. 1876: Disraeli P. 58210.

81. Beaconsfield to M. Corry. 13 Sept. 1876: H.P. B/XVI/B/1.
82. Manners to Beaconsfield (Private), 7 Sept. 1876: ibid./XX/M/196.
83. Beaconsfield to Derby, 6 Sept. 1876: D.P. 16/2/2; also in M & B, vol. VI, p. 53.
84. D.D., 7 Sept. 1876.
85. Derby to Cross (Private), 8 Sept. 1876: Cr. P. 51266.
86. D.D., 10 Sept. 1876; the Queen to Beaconsfield, 13 Sept. 1876: H.P. B/XIX/B/597.
87. *Northcote* to Cross (Private), 3, 8 Sept.: Cr. P. 51265; to W. H. Smith, 5 Sept.: Hamb. P. PS5/15. *Hardy* to Cairns, 29 Aug., 14 Sept.: Cairns P. PRO 30/51/7. *Cross* to Beaconsfield, 13 Sept.: H.P. B/XX/Cr/59; to Derby (Private), 13 Sept.: D.P. 16/2/5. *Cairns* to Hardy (Private), 31 Aug., (Confidential) 16 Sept.: Cran. P. T501/262 (latter also in Gathorne-Hardy, *Cranbrook*, vol. I, pp. 370—1); to Beaconsfield (Confidential), 31 Aug., 16, 18, 21 Sept.: H.P. B/XX/Ca/186, 188—90; to Cross (Private), 11 Sept., (Confidential) 13 Sept.: Cr. P. 51268; to Northcote (Private), 14 Sept.: Idd. P. 50021. *Carnarvon* to Lytton (Private), 31 Aug.: Lyt. P. D/EK/C36; to Northcote (Private, Copy), 30 Aug.: Carn. P. PRO 30/6/7; to Beaconsfield (Private & Confidential), 6 Sept.: H.P. B/XX/He/72; to Salisbury (Private & Personal), 9 Sept.: S.P.; to Hardy (Private & Personal), 12 Sept.: Cran. P. T501/262; to Cairns, (Private) 13 Sept., (Private & Personal) 15 Sept. 1876: Cairns P. PRO 30/51/8.
88. Beaconsfield to Derby, 7 Sept.: D.P. 16/2/2; to Northcote, 11 Sept.: Idd. P. 50017 (also in M & B, vol. VI, p. 62); to Cairns, 12 Sept.: Cairns P. PRO 30/51/1; to the Queen (Confidential), 12 Sept. 1876: RA H9/115.
89. Malmesbury to Cairns, 10 Sept. 1876: Cairns P. PRO 30/51/20.
90. M. Corry to Beaconsfield, 19 Sept. 1876: H.P. B/XVI/B/9.
91. Beaconsfield to Cairns (Confidential), 23 Sept. 1876: Cairns P. PRO 30/51/1.
92. Cairns to Beaconsfield (Confidential), 24, 25 Sept. 1876: H.P. B/XX/Ca/191, 192.
93. Northcote to Beaconsfield (Confidential), 19 Sept.: ibid./N/16; also Northcote to Cross (Private) 20 Sept. 1876: Cr. P. 51265.
94. Hardy to Carnarvon (Private), 25 Sept. 1876: Carn. P. PRO 30/6/12.
95. Richmond to Salisbury, 26 Sept. 1876: S.P.
96. Minute on draft by A. F. O. Liddell, Sept. 1876: H.O. 45/9418/58267.
97. Shannon, *Bulgarian Agitation*, p. 149; Derby to the Queen, 25 Sept. 1876: RA H9/159.
98. Northcote to Beaconsfield, 28 Sept. 1876: H.P. B/XX/N/17.
99. Beaconsfield to the Queen, 25 Sept. 1876: RA H9/163.
100. 'Lady Strangford shrieks, that her appeal is niggardly responded to. If the public knew as much about that lady as Ld. Beaconsfield does, they would wonder she had got so much.' Beaconsfield to the Queen (Confidential), 2 Oct. 1876: ibid. H10/8 [CAB 41/7/16]. Similarly, Beaconsfield to Lady Bradford, 2 Oct. 1876: M & B, vol. VI, pp. 78—9.
101. Beaconsfield to the Queen (Telegram, deciphered), 4 Nov. 1876 (6 p.m.): RA H11/51 [CAB 41/7/20].
102. A. Borthwick to M. Corry, 14 Nov. 1876 (with instruction: 'Please read my note to Ld. B.'): H.P. B/XVI/C/25. On Russia at this time see B. H. Sumner, *Russia and the Balkans 1870—1880* (Oxford, 1937) ch. 6 and pp. 230—1; also Lionel de Rothschild to Beaconsfield, 11, 12 Oct. 1876: H.P. B/XXI/R/222, 223.
103. Beaconsfield to Corry, 15 Nov. 1876: ibid./XVI/B/2.

104. Beaconsfield to Salisbury (Confidential), 3 Sept. 1876: S.P.
105. D.D., 2 Aug. 1876.
106. Ibid., 1 July 1876.
107. Ibid., 24 Oct. 1876.
108. Ibid., 11 Apr. 1876.
109. Ibid., 2 Aug. 1876. 'Schou, whatever else he may be, is on the side of peace.':
   Derby to Beaconsfield, 11 Oct. 1876: H.P. B/XX/S/1167. For a sketch of
   Shuvalov's career and personality see Seton-Watson, *Eastern Question*, p. 40.
110. For example, A. Borthwick to M. Corry, 27 Oct., 13 Nov. 1876: H.P.
   B/XVI/C/23.
111. Lady Janetta Manners witnessed one of Shuvalov's performances when she sat
   next to him for dinner at the Northcotes' in March 1877. The ambassador, who
   'was in a *tremendous* state, clasping his hands, and gesticulating wildly', talked
   about dismembering the Ottoman empire in cooperation with Great Britain.
   She asked him, ' "Who would go shares...." Oh, he said "I am a pig. I am a
   pig that hunts for Truffles. I have found my Truffle, I take it, I give it to Lord
   Derby. It is a Programme, a programme in four points. I hate diplomacy; it is a
   disgusting métier. But my wife would not be so unhappy if it were not for the
   'Beasts and Monsters' that are about." ' All the guests noticed Shuvalov's
   conduct and wondered at the content as well as the form of his remarks. The
   men thought that he was drunk, as 'he kept pegging away' at a large dish of
   brandied cherries 'quite early in the dinner'. Janetta Manners disagreed with
   them, and she was probably right. Lady J. Manners to Salisbury, 25 Mar. 1877:
   S.P.; similarly, Lady J. Manners to Beaconsfield (Private), n.d.: ibid.
   11/XX/M/344.
112. More than two years after Shuvalov's recall from London, newspapers mistakenly reported the death of a cousin for his own. They quickly rectified the
   error, 'much to the relief of M. to whom the news came as a shock'. D.D.,
   23 Feb. 1882.
113. Beaconsfield to Derby (Confidential), 7 Nov. 1876: D.P. 16/2/2; Derby to
   Beaconsfield (Private), 7 Nov., Mary Derby to Beaconsfield (Confidential),
   1 Dec. 1876: H.P. B/XX/S/1182, 1466; Mary Derby to R. A. Cross (Confidential), 12 Dec. [1876]: Cr. P. 51266.
114. See Seton-Watson, 'Russo-British Relations during the Eastern Crisis',
   Slavonic Review, 3—6, 8—12, 14, 17 (Dec. 1924—Dec. 1927).
115. After a Cabinet meeting in mid-November 1876, Richmond remarked: 'I do not
   think I ever saw the For. Secy so "stiff". ...I suspect it will be necessary to
   keep him up [to] the mark. I was surprised to find the Prime Minister side so
   much with him.' Richmond to Cairns (Confidential), 14 Nov. 1876: Cairns
   P. PRO 30/51/3.
116. Salisbury to Carnarvon (Confidential), 13 Sept., to Lytton, 12 Sept. 1876:
   S.P. D/31/3, D/40/58; also Gwendolen Cecil, *Life of Robert Marquis of Salisbury* (London, 1921—32, 4 vols) vol. II, pp. 84—7.
117. Beaconsfield to Salisbury, 10 Nov. 1876: ibid., p. 95.

Notes to Chapter 3: The Stress of Politics

  1. Spencer to Granville, 14 Jan. 1877: Gran. P. PRO 30/29/29A; Derby to
   Salisbury (Private), 11 Jan. 1877: S.P.

2. D.D., 18 Apr. 1877.
3. Beaconsfield to the Queen, 2 Feb. 1877: RA H12/111 [CAB 41/8/3]. D.D., 31 Jan. 1877.
4. S. Northcote to Salisbury (Private), 22 Jan. 1877: S.P.
5. Beaconsfield tc Salisbury (Confidential), 6 Feb. 1877: ibid.; also in M & B, vol. VI, p. 117.
6. D.D., 9 Feb. 1877. See also R.W. Seton-Watson, *Disraeli, Gladstone and the Eastern Question* (London, 1935; 1969 edn) p. 160.
7. D.D., *passim*, and especially 8 Mar. 1876. In that entry Derby welcomed one of the results of the recession of the mid-1870s: 'wages are less extravagantly high in Manchester, and the men more easily managed than in 1871–74'. At that time he had written: 'There is great prosperity and general content in these Lancashire towns. Both at L. pool and in Bury I have been told that work was never more abundant, nor wages higher. But the latter will as usual all go in beer.' Derby to Halifax, 9 Sept. 1871: Hick. P. A4/87.
8. D.D., 9 July 1877. Cf. Robert Blake, *Disraeli* (London, 1966) p. 630. Also Mary Derby to Halifax, 12 Aug. 1877: Hick. P. A4/87a: 'I wonder if you approve of Mr. Smith's appt. I think it useful in many most important ways, but strictly between ourselves it does not seem perhaps just what one expected to find the first Ld. of the Admiralty & the owner of the railroad book stalls in the same person. These are private views – as a Govt. your's did the same about Mr. Goschen. So we won't quarrel!!'
9. D.D., 15 Mar. 1878.
10. Ibid., 7 Apr. 1878.
11. Carn. D., 3 Oct., 14 Nov. 1875.
12. D.D., 21 [sic: 20] Jan. 1877.
13. Salisbury to Lytton (Private), 9 Feb. 1877: S.P. D/40/85. For further quotations and Salisbury's attitude in general see Gwendolen Cecil, *Life of Robert Marquis of Salisbury* (London, 1921–32, 4 vols) vol. II, pp. 128–32.
14. D.D., 4 Apr. 1878.
15. Salisbury to Derby (Private), 15 Feb. 1877: D.P. 16/2/7.
16. Salisbury to Lytton (Private), 2 Mar. 1877: S.P. D/40/89.
17. D.D., 28 June 1877.
18. Beaconsfield to the Queen, 12 July 1877: RA H15/18.
19. R. Bourke to Derby, 9 Mar. 1877: D.P. 16/2/9; W. E. Forster to Duchess of Manchester, 17 Mar. 1877: Dev. P. (unc.); Gladstone to Granville (Private), 17 Mar. 1877: Ramm, *Corr.*, vol. I, no. 51; Derby to Beaconsfield (Private), 15 Mar. 1877: H.P. B/XX/S/1215. Also D.D. 14, 15 Mar. 1877; the Queen to Beaconsfield, 29 Mar. 1877: H.P. B/XIX/B/735. Derby believed that Elliot had 'been very ill used, and that no man could have done the work better. Recollect that it is as the exponent of our policy that he is attacked.' Derby to Northcote (Private), 27 Mar. 1877: Idd. P. 50022.
20. Beaconsfield to the Queen (Confidential), 31 Mar. 1877: RA H12/209 [CAB 41/8/10]; Derby to Beaconsfield, with Minute by M. Corry, 17 Mar. 1877: H.P. B/XX/S/1217; D.D., 17, 19 Mar. 1877.
21. Carn. D., 18 Mar. 1877.
22. Beaconsfield, Memorandum for the Queen, 13 Mar. 1877: RA H12/166 [CAB 41/8/5]. Derby to Beaconsfield, 11 Mar. 1877: H.P. B/XX/S/1212. Also Salisbury to Beaconsfield (Confidential), 12 Mar. 1877: ibid./Ce/202; partially in Cecil, *Salisbury*, vol. II, p. 131. For a summary of the diplomatic situation see William

L. Langer, *European Alliances and Alignments 1871—1890* (New York, 2nd edn, 1950) pp. 114—15.

23. D.D., 13 Mar. 1877.
24. Salisbury to Lytton (Private), 9 Mar. 1877: S.P. D/40/91; partially in Cecil, *Salisbury*, vol. II, p. 130.
25. Harcourt to Hartington, 8 Feb. 1877: Dev. P. 340.698.
26. Granville to J. T. Delane, 9 Feb. 1877: Delane Corr. 22/25.
27. W. H. Dyke to Beaconsfield (Confidential), 22 Feb. 1877: H.P. B/XXI/D/469.
28. Derby to [Beaconsfield] (Private), 10 Feb. 1877: ibid./XX/S/1210. D.D., 10 Feb. 1877.
29. Granville to J. T. Delane, 21 Feb. 1877: Delane Corr. 22/27.
30. Granville to Rosebery (Private), 21 Feb. 1877: R.P. 10074.
31. Ramm, *Corr.*, vol. I, nos 45—50 (24 Feb.—7 Mar. 1877); Hartington to Gladstone (Private), 3 Mar. 1877: Glad. P. 44144 (also in Bernard Holland, *The Life of Spencer Compton Eighth Duke of Devonshire* [London 1911, 2 vols] vol. I, pp. 193—4); Seton-Watson, *Eastern Question*, ch. 5, especially pp. 164—6.
32. Holland, *Devonshire*, vol. I, p. 192; Seton-Watson, *Eastern Question*, pp. 178—80.
33. Beaconsfield to the Queen, 7 Apr. 1877; RA H13/10. The Prime Minister was particularly critical of financial articles in *The Times*: Beaconsfield to Salisbury (Confidential), 1 Apr. 1877: S.P.
34. Beaconsfield to the Queen, 13 Apr. 1877: RA A51/32; partially in *QVL*, vol. II, pp. 527—8.
35. Hartington to Granville, 14 Apr. 1877: Gran. P. PRO 30/29/26B.
36. Beaconsfield to Lady Bradford, 17 Apr. 1877: M & B, vol. VI, pp. 136—7.
37. See Seton-Watson, *Eastern Question*, pp. 181—8.
38. R. Bourke to Beaconsfield, 26 Apr. 1877: H.P. B/XVI/C/17.
39. D.D., 27 Apr. 1877.
40. Hartington to Granville, 1 May 1877: Gran. P. PRO 30/29/26B; Harcourt to Hartington, 30 Apr. 1877: Dev. P. 340.706 (partially in Holland, *Devonshire*, vol. I, p. 196, and in A. G. Gardiner, *The Life of Sir William Harcourt* [London, 1923, 2 vols] vol. I, p. 318).
41. Morley, *Gladstone*, vol. II, p. 171.
42. D.D., 30 Apr. 1877.
43. F. Cavendish to Granville, 2 May 1877: Gran. P. PRO 30/29/26B.
44. See Morley, *Gladstone*, vol. II, pp. 172—3; D.D., 7 May 1877.
45. Harcourt to Hartington (Private), n.d. [Apr. 1877]: Dev. P. 340.704 (partially in Holland, *Devonshire*, vol. I, pp. 195—6, and Gardiner, *Harcourt*, vol. I, p. 318); Granville to Gladstone, 27 Apr., and Gladstone to Granville, 23 May 1877: Ramm, *Corr.*, vol. I, nos 56, 65.
46. Beaconsfield to Northcote, with Minute by M. Corry, 14 May 1877: H.P. B/XVI/B/48.
47. Beaconsfield to the Queen, 15 May 1877: RA A51/44.
48. Chamberlain to J. Collings (Copy), 18 Mar. 1877: JC 5/16/65.
49. Chamberlain to W. T. Stead (Copy), 24 May 1877: ibid. 6/45/5.
50. Gladstone to Granville, 19 May 1877: Ramm, *Corr.*, vol. I, no. 63.
51. Gladstone to Granville, Birmingham, 1 June 1877: ibid., no. 68; see also J. L. Garvin, *The Life of Joseph Chamberlain* (London, 1932—4, 3 vols) vol. I, p. 261.

52. Chamberlain to Stead (Copy), 18 May 1877; JC 6/45/4.
53. J. A. Godley to Granville, 5 June 1877: Gran. P. PRO 30/29/26B.
54. Gladstone to Granville, 23 May 1877: Ramm, *Corr.*, vol. I, no. 65.
55. M. Hicks Beach to the Queen (Copy), 2 June 1877; H.B. P. PCC/67.
56. The former Liberal Lord Chancellor, for example, adhered to the opinion which Hartington had hitherto held: that he would approve of changes in the franchise and of a redistribution of seats only when they appeared 'to be a necessary result of matured public opinion, and ripe social progress'. He was not satisfied that 'to make the agitation for another Reform Bill, at the present time, an article of the Liberal party' was in the interest of either the party or the country. Selbourne to Granville, 6 June 1877: Gran. P. PRO 30/29/26B.
57. G. O. Trevelyan to Hartington (Private), 31[?] May 1877: Dev. P. 340.711.
58. D.D., 1 July 1877.
59. Thomas J. Spinner, Jr, *George Joachim Goschen The Transformation of a Victorian Liberal* (Cambridge, 1973) pp. 57−60.
60. M. Corry to Beaconsfield, 19 Apr. 1877: H.P. B/XVI/B/22. For this memorandum in full see Appendix A. Also D.D., 5 May 1877.
61. Barrington to Beaconsfield (Private), 20 Apr. 1877: H.P. B/XX/Ba/45.
62. Beaconsfield to the Queen, 20 Apr.; also Theodore Martin to the Queen, 21 Apr. 1877: RA H13/30, 31. D.D., 22 Apr. 1877.
63. Corry to Beaconsfield, 21 May 1877: H.P. B/XVI/B/25. See Richard Koebner and H. D. Schmidt, *Imperialism The Story and Significance of a Political Word, 1840−1960* (Cambridge, 1964) p. 128.
64. See J. H. Gleason, *The Genesis of Russophobia in Great Britain* (Cambridge, Mass., 1950).
65. Beaconsfield to the Queen (Secret), 17 Apr. 1877 (7 o'clock): RA H13/24.
66. Bath to Granville, 21 Apr. 1877: Gran. P. PRO 30/29/26B.
67. Cairns to Beaconsfield (Confidential), 24 May 1877; H.P. B/XX/Ca/213; also Cairns to Richmond (Private), 31 May 1877: Goodwood Ms. 869.
68. Beaconsfield to Derby (Confidential), 22 May 1877: D.P. 16/2/3; also in M & B, vol. VI, p. 140.
69. Beaconsfield to Derby (Confidential), 25 May 1877: D.P. 16/2/3 (also in M & B, vol. VI, p. 141); Derby to Beaconsfield (Private), 26 May 1877: H.P. B/XX/S/1235.
70. D.D., 5 May 1877.
71. Ibid., 30 May 1877.
72. Ibid., 30 June 1877.
73. Ibid., 25 Apr. 1877.
74. Beaconsfield to the Queen (Secret), 12 June, also (Telegram, deciphered) 8 June (1 p.m.): RA H14/78, 69. See also the Queen to Beaconsfield (Confidential), 7, 9 June 1877: H.P. B/XIX/B/795, 797; also in M & B, vol. VI, pp. 143−4. D.D., 10 June 1877.
75. Beaconsfield to the Queen, 25 June 1877: CAB 41/8/23; partially in *QVL*, vol. II, p. 544.
76. D.D., 30 May, 17 June 1877.
77. Ibid., 18 June 1877.
78. Beaconsfield to the Queen, 10 July 1877: RA H15/14. Also Beaconsfield to Richmond, 12 July 1877: Goodwood Ms. 865, enquiring on the force of marines in the Mediterranean squadron.
79. Beaconsfield to the Queen, 16 July 1877: RA 012/219.

80. D.D., 3, 4 July 1877.
81. Ibid., 12 July 1877.
82. For example, ibid., 8 July 1877.
83. Ibid., 14 July 1877.
84. Cairns to the Queen, 15 July 1877: RA H15/22; D.D., 14 July 1877.
85. Ibid., 21 July 1877; Beaconsfield to the Queen (Telegram, deciphered), 21 July (2.30 p.m.), 22 July 1877: RA B52/10, 11 [CAB 41/9/3, 4] (also in M & B, vol. vi, pp. 154–5); Hardy to Beaconsfield (Confidential), 22, 23 July 1877: H.P. B/XX/Ha/143, 144. Manners promptly resigned, because he would not countenance the Russians' setting foot in Constantinople; but Beaconsfield prevailed upon him to rescind his decree. J. Manners to Beaconsfield, (Most Confidential) 22, (Secret) 24 July 1877: ibid./M/224; Beaconsfield to Manners, 24 July 1877: M & B, vol. vi, p. 156; see also Charles Whibley, *Lord John Manners and His Friends* (Edinburgh, 1925, 2 vols) vol. ii, pp. 190–2.
86. D.D., 17 July 1877.
87. Ibid., 28 July 1877.
88. Carn. D., 3 Aug. 1877.
89. D.D., 30, 31 July 1877. Lady Derby told Carnarvon that her husband 'was satisfied at the result & at the support which I had given him & which he seems to have appreciated. She was astonished at Salisbury's change of front', attributing it to the Queen's influence. Carnarvon concluded: 'It seems to have been Disraeli's notion that if he could be sure of Salisbury he mt. count upon me: & if this was so all this must have been a gt. disappointment to him.' Carn. D., 3 Aug. 1877.
90. Beaconsfield was delighted at the reports of Turkish success at Plevna (Beaconsfield to the Queen, 1 Aug. 1877: RA B52/16; also in M & B, vol. vi, pp. 160–1). Anti-Turkish Liberals reacted differently. 'This awful defeat of the Russians, combined with the frightful account of the Bashi Bazouks in this days Times... make all honest men unhappy. ...The calamities of the Russians are terrible,' G. O. Trevelyan wrote to his wife (2, 3 Aug. 1877: Trevelyan P. GOT 2).
91. Beaconsfield to Derby (Confidential), 7, 8 Aug. 1877: D.P. 16/2/3.
92. D.D., 2 Aug. 1877.
93. Ibid., 14 Aug. 1877.
94. Beaconsfield, Note on Cabinet, 15 Aug. 1877: RA B52/24 [CAB 41/9/9]; also in M & B, vol. vi, pp. 171–2.
95. Correspondence in RA H15; also M & B, vol. vi, pp. 173–6; *QVL*, vol. ii, pp. 560–7. 'I do not propose to make any communication to Lord Derby, and respectfully suggest to Your Majesty, that complete silence on the subject is best at present.' Beaconsfield to the Queen (Telegram, deciphered), 8 Oct. 1877 (6.5 p.m.): RA H16/110. For Wellesley's official reports to Derby (July–Oct. 1877) see B. H. Sumner, *Russia and the Balkans 1870–1880* (Oxford, 1937) app. 5.
96. Hardy to Cross, 10 Sept. 1877: Cr. P. 51267; Beaconsfield to Cross (Confidential), 16 Sept., enclosing 'Memorandum by the Queen', 7 Sept. 1877: ibid. 51265.
97. Beaconsfield to the Queen, 16 Sept. 1877: RA B52/32.
98. Manners to Beaconsfield (Private), 30 Sept., and Cairns to Beaconsfield (Confidential), 1 Oct. 1877: H.P. B/XX/M/228 and /Ca/220. Beaconsfield to Salisbury

(Confidential), 3 Oct. 1877: S.P. Beaconsfield to Derby, (Confidential) 1 and 13 Sept., 16, 28 Sept. 1877: D.P. 16/2/3; Derby to Beaconsfield (Private), 29 Sept. 1877: H.P. B/XX/S/1267 (all, except 16 Sept., also in M & B, vol. vi, pp. 177−8, 182−3); D.D., 23, 25, 29 Sept. 1877. Beaconsfield to the Queen. (Secret) 3, 4 Oct. 1877: RA B53/14, 16.

99. Cairns, Hardy, Manners, Beach and the Duke of Richmond, the Lord President, backed Beaconsfield. Cairns to the Queen, 7 Oct. 1877: ibid. H16/104. Also D.D., 5 Oct. 1877; Manners to Beaconsfield (Private), 8 Oct. 1877: H.P. B/XX/M/229; Beaconsfield to the Queen, (Telegram, deciphered) 5 Oct., and (Secret) 6 Oct. 1877: RA H16/103 (with some changes, in M & B, vol. vi, p. 183), and RA B53/19 [CAB 41/9/11] (also in M & B, vol. vi, pp. 183−4); Arthur Hardinge, *Life of Henry Howard Molyneux Herbert Fourth Earl of Carnarvon 1831−1890* (London, 1925, 3 vols) vol. ii, pp. 362−3.

100. Salisbury to Carnarvon (Confidential), 14 Oct. 1877: S.P. D/31/55.

101. Carnarvon to Salisbury (Private), 8 Oct. 1877: S.P.; also partially in Cecil, *Salisbury*, vol. ii, p. 161.

102. The Queen to Beaconsfield, 30 Oct. 1877: H.P. B/XIX/B/930; Richmond to Cairns, 2 Nov. 1877: Cairns P. PRO 30/51/4.

103. Beaconsfield to Tenterden (Confidential), 12 Oct.; Derby to Tenterden (Private), 14 Oct. 1877: Tent. P. F.O. 363/1, pt 1, f. 57; pt 2, f. 249.

104. M. Corry to Beaconsfield, 31 Oct. 1877: H.P. B/XVI/B/33; partially in M & B, vol. vi, pp. 195−6.

105. Cross to Derby (Private), 23 Oct. 1877: D.P. 16/2/5; Derby to Cross (Private), 26 Oct. 1877: Cr. P. 51266. On Cross's association with Derby see F. J. Dwyer, 'R. A. Cross and the Eastern Crisis of 1875−8', *Slavonic and East European Review*, 39, 93 (June 1961) 452−3.

106. Beaconsfield to W. H. Smith (Confidential), 23 Oct. 1877: Hamb. P. PS5/54.

107. Beaconsfield to the Queen, 1, (Secret) 3 Nov. 1877: RA B53/32, 35 [CAB 41/9/13]; also in M & B, vol. vi, pp. 193−5. Cf. Andrew Lang, *Life, Letters and Diaries of Sir Stafford Northcote First Earl of Iddesleigh* (Edinburgh, 1890, 2 vols) vol. ii, pp. 105−6; Hardinge, *Carnarvon*, vol. ii, pp. 363−4. D.D., 21 Oct. 1877: for Beaconsfield's description of six parties in the Cabinet, at Woburn Abbey where he also said, perhaps for the benefit of the Derbys, that he had the resignations of Manners and Cairns in his pocket.

108. Derby to Beaconsfield (Private, Copy), 1 Nov. 1877: D.P. 17/2/3.

109. On the same day that Salisbury spoke to Beaconsfield, he wrote to his bellicose Viceroy in India: 'I am closé to the great democracy we all have to obey − and my attention is most drawn to the danger of giving a false direction to his ill-informed and unbridled impulses.' Salisbury to Lytton (Private), 2 Nov. 1877: S.P. D/40/129.

110. Beaconsfield to the Queen (Telegram, deciphered), 5 Nov. 1877 (5.15 p.m.): RA H17/14 [CAB 41/9/14]; also in M & B, vol. vi, p. 195. D.D. 5 Nov. 1877.

111. Beaconsfield to the Queen, 12 Nov. 1877: RA B53/42 [CAB 41/9/15]. D.D., 7, 10, 29 Nov. 1877. Cf. Granville to Gladstone, 21 Nov. 1877: Ramm, *Corr.*, vol. i, no. 92, and n. 1, p. 60.

112. D.D., 14, 20, 21 Nov. 1877; Beaconsfield to Derby (Private), 20 Nov., enclosing Cairns to Beaconsfield (Confidential), 19 Nov. 1877: D.P. 16/2/3; Beaconsfield to the Queen, 28 Nov. 1877: RA B53/53, expressing approval of a Memorandum by John Manners, 26 Nov. 1877: H.P. B/XX/M/234.

113. D.D., 24 Nov. 1877.
114. Ibid., 27 Nov. 1877.
115. Ibid., 26 Nov. 1877.
116. Beaconsfield to the Queen, 4 Dec. 1877 (2.25 p.m.): RA H17/89 [CAB 41/9/16]; Manners to the Queen, 4 Dec. 1877: RA B54/6 (also in M & B, vol. VI, pp. 198–9); D.D., 4 Dec. 1877. Derby, Note, 4 Dec. 1877: H.P. B/XX/S/1280; 'Draft Memorandum to be delivered confidentially to Count Schouvaloff', as 'altered after Cabinet of Dec. 4. 1877' (alterations in Derby's hand): D.P. 16/2/3.
117. D.D., 14, 17, 18 Dec. 1877. Reports of these Cabinet meetings in RA B54/13, 18, 21 [CAB 41/9/18, 19, 21]; also in M & B, vol. VI, pp. 201–2, 204, 206–7. Beaconsfield to the Queen, 18 Dec. 1877: RA B54/19 [CAB 41/9/20]: 'This was cyphered, but not sent, as it was considered dangerous thro' the For. Office to Yr Majesty.' Relative correspondence (14–18 Dec. 1877) in S.P., Idd. P. and H.P. See also 'General Summary of *Cairns resns.* mentioned 18 Dec.': Carn. D., end of 1877; Cecil, *Salisbury*, vol. II, pp. 163–7; Hardinge, *Carnarvon*, vol. II, pp. 364–7.
118. D.D., 6 Dec. 1877.
119. Tenterden, Minute for Derby, 18 Apr. 1877: D.P. 16/2/11.
120. Having heard that Derby was to assist in some partridge driving at Knowsley, Richmond acidly commented: 'I wonder if he will keep a journal of the number of shots.' Five years later he remarked when Derby joined a Liberal government: 'I wonder if Derby will take as copious notes as he did in our time.' Richmond to Cairns, (Private) 10 Sept. 1877, 20 Dec. 1882: Cairns P. PRO 30/51/4.
121. Derby to Beaconsfield (Private), 14 July 1877: H.P. B/XX/S/1250. After resigning from the Cabinet in March 1878, Derby destroyed many papers and letters. He then admitted: 'I am chiefly embarrassed by the minutes, habitually taken, of what has passed in Cabinet, which I know not whether I ought to keep, & yet hardly like to destroy.' (D.D., 30 Mar. 1878). Apparently the only minutes now extant are those of February and March 1878, which Derby kept because of the controversy surrounding his resignation.
122. The Queen to Beaconsfield, 1 Aug. 1877: H.P. B/XIX/B/843; also in Blake, *Disraeli*, p. 627.
123. The Queen, Memorandum (dictated), 9 Aug. 1877: RA H15/113. Also the Queen to Beaconsfield, 26 Aug. 1877: H.P. B/XIX/B/874; Hardy to Carnarvon, Balmoral, 28 Aug. 1877: Carn. P. PRO 30/6/12.
124. Hardy to Cairns (Private), 6 Sept. 1877: Cairns P. PRO 30/51/7.
125. Cross to Hardy, 12 Sept. 1877: Cran. P. T501/259.
126. The Queen to Beaconsfield (Confidential), 4 Oct. 1877: H.P. B/XIX/B/906.
127. D.D., 5 Dec. 1877.
128. Beaconsfield to Salisbury, 8 Dec. 1877: S.P.; Beaconsfield to the Queen, 8 Dec. 1877: RA B54/7 (also in Blake, *Disraeli*, p. 635). D.D., 26 Nov., 8 Dec. 1877.
129. Beaconsfield to Salisbury (Confidential), 24 Dec. 1877: S.P.; also in Blake, *Disraeli*, pp. 636–7, partially in Cecil, *Salisbury*, vol. II, p. 169, and apparently from a draft in H.P., in M & B, vol. VI, p. 210.
130. Dean of Windsor (the Very Reverend G. Wellesley) to the Queen, 27 Dec. 1877, 1 Jan. 1878; Lady Derby to Dean of Windsor, 29 Dec. 1877: RA H18/52, 68, 69.

131. Beaconsfield to the Queen, 3 Jan. 1878: ibid. B54/42. See also Blake, *Disraeli*, p. 635.

132. For a later example see Mary Derby to Halifax (Confidential), 16 Nov. 1878: Hick. P. A4/87a.

133. D.D., 29 Dec. 1877. At Knowsley on 30 December 1877 Derby wrote in his diary that Mary had heard from the palace — about the relations between the Queen and John Brown. He did not mention the letter which she had received from the Dean of Windsor and to which she had replied the previous day. If Derby did not make a deliberate omission from his diary, Mary must have lied to him. Perhaps she did so because he had seen the envelope from Windsor and might, she felt, speculate on its contents. Derby probably had some idea that his wife told Shuvalov more than she should have done.

134. Northcote to Beaconsfield (Most Confidential), 17 Dec. 1877: H.P. B/XX/N/46.

135. Northcote to Salisbury (Confidential), with Note by Salisbury, 18 Dec. 1877: Idd. P. 50019; in general see Cecil, *Salisbury*, vol. II, pp. 163—72.

136. See M & B, vol. VI, pp. 202—4. For the Home Secretary's satisfaction with the police arrangements, Police Orders, 8 Jan. 1878: Mepol. 7/40.

137. Derby to Salisbury (Secret), 23 Dec. 1877: S.P.; also in Blake, *Disraeli*, pp. 635—6, and partially in Cecil, *Salisbury*, vol. II, pp. 170—1, where the commentary is misleading. D.D., 23 Dec. 1877.

138. Disraeli to the Queen (Most Confidential), 14 Apr. 1875: CAB 41/6/25.

139. L. [?] to Granville, 28 Dec. 1877: Gran. P. PRO 30/29/26B.

140. Harcourt to Granville, 24 Dec. 1877: ibid./29A; also in Seton-Watson, *Eastern Question*, p. 253. Granville to Hartington, 26 Dec., Harcourt to Hartington, 27 Dec. 1877: Dev. P. 340.740, 741. Granville to Gladstone, 25 Dec. 1877: Ramm, *Corr.*, vol. I, no. 99.

141. Carn. D., 25 Dec. 1877.

142. D.D., 21 Mar. 1876, 18 Apr. 1877.

143. See Earl of Carnarvon, Introduction to H. L. Mansel, *The Gnostic Heresies of the First and Second Centuries* (London, 1875) pp. xx—xxii.

144. Hardinge, *Carnarvon*, vol. II, p. 369.

145. A. J. Mundella to W. E. Gladstone (Private), 9 Jan. 1878: Glad. P. 44258.

146. Beaconsfield to the Queen, 3 Jan. 1878: RA B54/41 [CAB 41/10/2]; also in M & B, vol. VI, pp. 213—14. For her condemnation of the speech, the Queen to Carnarvon (Copy), 4 Jan. 1878: Carn. P. PRO 30/6/13; also in *QVL*, vol. II, pp. 588—9. In the royal household, Carnarvon was known as the '*wretched* little "Twitters"': Prince Leopold to the Queen, 7 Jan. 1878: RA B54/53. The Permanent Under Secretary at the Foreign Office foolishly thought the speech 'a great success': Tenterden to Carnarvon, 3 Jan. 1878: Carn. P. PRO 30/6/13.

147. Derby to Carnarvon, [3 Jan. 1878]: ibid. D.D., 3 Jan. 1878.

148. Northcote to Carnarvon (Confidential), 3 Jan. 1878: Carn. P. PRO 30/6/13.

149. Chamberlain to W. T. Stead (Private, Copy), 22 Dec. 1877: JC 6/4k/9.

150. A. J. Mundella to Gladstone, 22 Dec. 1877: Glad. P. 44258; partially in W. H. G. Armytage, *A. J. Mundella 1825—1897 The Liberal Background to the Labour Movement* (London, 1951) p. 180.

151. Gladstone to Granville, 5 Sept. 1877: Ramm, *Corr.*, vol. I, no. 84.

152. Gladstone to Bright, 22 Dec. 1877: Bright P. 43385.

153. Gladstone to Chamberlain [Draft], 3 Jan. 1878: Glad. P. 44125.

154. Barrington to Beaconsfield (Private), 26 Dec. 1877: H.P. B/XX/Ba/151.

155. Halifax to Granville, 24 Dec. 1877: Gran. P. PRO 30/29/26B.
156. Gladstone to Granville, 5 Jan. 1878: Ramm, *Corr.*, vol. I, no. 101.
157. Mundella to Gladstone, 26 Dec. 1877: Glad. P. 44258.
158. Derby to Beaconsfield, n.d. [21 Dec. 1877]: H.P. B/XX/S/1268.
159. More than 700 police of all ranks were assigned to Hyde Park on 24 February 1878, more than 1000 on 10 March. Compare these numbers with the 1250 posted between Putney and Mortlake for the annual Boat Race between Oxford and Cambridge on 13 April. Police Orders, 23 Feb., 9 Mar., 10 Apr. 1878: Mepol. 7/40.
160. See Hugh Cunningham, 'Jingoism in 1877—78', *Victorian Studies*, 14, 4 (June 1971); Seton-Watson, *Eastern Question*, pp. 272ff.; E. P. Thompson, *William Morris Romantic to Revolutionary* (London, 1955) pp. 253—60; G. C. Thompson, *Public Opinion and Lord Beaconsfield 1875—1880* (London, 1886, 2 vols) vol. II, pp. 360—9; Bath to Carnarvon, 15 Jan. 1878 (5 p.m.): Carn. P. (BL).
161. Northcote to the Queen, 10 Jan. 1878: RA H18/115.
162. Beaconsfield to the Queen, 11 Jan. 1878: ibid. B54/67. Almost two weeks later Leopold asked Corry: 'Who wrote the *first* article in to-days "Morning Post"? *You* must have *inspired* it at any rate!' Leopold to M. Corry (Private & Confidential), 24 Jan. 1878: H.P. B/XIX/B/1102.
163. Layard to Lytton (Private & Confidential), 2 Jan. 1878: Lyt. P. D/EK/C36.
164. A. B. Paget to H. Ponsonby, 12 Feb. 1878: F.O. 800/3, ff. 355—6.
165. J. C. MacDonald to John MacGregor, 24 Aug. 1877: P.H.S. P. L.B. 19/202.
166. MacDonald to C. Austin, 29 Dec. 1877: ibid./363.
167. Gladstone to Granville, 5 Jan. 1878: Ramm, *Corr.*, vol. I, no. 101, and n. 3.
168. Walter to Delane, 8 Nov. 1877: Walter P. 463.
169. MacDonald to D. M. Wallace, 7 Jan. 1878: P.H.S. P. L.B. 19/369.
170. MacDonald to C. Austin, 1 Feb. 1878: ibid./392.
171. M. Corry to Beaconsfield, (Confidential) 30 Dec. 1877, (Confidential & Personal) 7, 10 Jan. 1878: H.P. B/XVI/B/35—7.
172. D.D., 7 Jan. 1878.
173. Beaconsfield to the Queen, 9 Jan. 1878: RA B54/60 [CAB 41/10/4]; also in M & B, vol. VI, pp. 216—17. First draft of the speech with Derby's emendations, with D. Cab. Min.; with Carnarvon's emendations, in Carn. P. PRO 30/6/13. D.D., 9 Jan. 1878.
174. Northcote to Hardy (Confidential), 9 Jan. 1878: Cran. P. T501/271; Hardy to Northcote (Private), 11 Jan. 1878: Idd. P. 50040.
175. W. H. Smith to Northcote (Private), 12 Jan. 1878, partly destroyed: ibid. 50021.
176. Beaconsfield to the Queen, 12 Jan. 1878: RA B54/69 [CAB 41/10/5]; also in M & B, vol. VI, pp. 219—20. Of this meeting Derby noted in his diary: 'for nearly an hour I thought I had ceased to be a minister: but in the end...I came away well satisfied, for this is the second time in the last few days that I have succeeded in carrying my point against a large majority of my colleagues'. D.D., 12 Jan. 1878. The Queen's private secretary, a Whig, was 'startled' by the Cabinet decision: 'So I went to church with an anxious heart and joined in the War Psalm "Let God Arise" including the words "There is little Benjamin their ruler".' Henry F. Ponsonby to Carnarvon (Private), 13 Jan. 1878: Carn. P. PRO 30/6/13.

177. Carnarvon to Derby (Private), 14 Jan. 1878: D.P. 16/2/4. D.D., 14 Jan. 1878. Carnarvon to Beaconsfield, 15 Jan. 1878: H.P. B/XX/He/88.
178. Derby to Beaconsfield, enclosing Minute (in T. H. Sanderson's hand) signed by Derby, 16 Jan. 1878: ibid./S/1295, 1295a; also in M & B, vol. vi, p. 221.
179. D.D., 1, 16 Jan. 1878.
180. Ibid., 17, 18 Jan. 1878.
181. Hardinge, *Carnarvon*, vol. ii, p. 376.
182. Carnarvon to Hardy (Private), 23 Jan. 1878: Cran. P. T501/262.
183. Carnarvon to Smith (Private, Copy), Smith to Carnarvon (Private), 23 Jan. 1878: Carn. P. PRO 30/6/13.
184. Derby to Beaconsfield, 23 Jan., Carnarvon to Beaconsfield, 24 Jan. 1878: H.P. B/XX/S/1302 (also in M & B, vol. vi, p. 228), /He/93. Derby apparently withheld his letter until the 24th: Beaconsfield to the Queen, 24 Jan. 1878: RA B55/45; also in M & B, vol. vi, p. 229.
185. Balfour, Memorandum, 8 May 1880: Balfour P. 49688.
186. Derby to Carnarvon, 25 Jan. 1878 (2 letters): Carn. P. PRO 30/6/13.
187. Beaconsfield to Derby (Confidential), 24 Jan. 1878: D.P. 16/2/3; Derby to Beaconsfield, 24, 25 Jan. 1878: H.P. B/XX/S/1304—5. The Queen to Beaconsfield, 24 Jan. 1878: ibid/XIX/B/1108; also, without emphases pointed against Derby, in M & B, vol. vi, pp. 229—30. The Queen had wanted Beaconsfield himself to assume the Foreign Office, in fact if not formally: the Queen to Beaconsfield (Very Confidential), 14 Jan. 1878: H.P. B/XIX/B/1062. According to one of her sons, 'she *literally* clapped her hands with pleasure' at the news of Derby's resignation. Leopold to M. Corry (Private & Confidential), 24 Jan. 1878: ibid./1102.
188. Northcote to Beaconsfield (Confidential), 24 Jan. 1878: ibid./XX/N/60.
189. Northcote to Beaconsfield (Most Confidential), 25 Jan. 1878: ibid./62.
190. W. H. Dyke to Beaconsfield (Confidential), 25 Jan. 1878: ibid./S/1308.
191. Copy in RA H19/37.

Notes to Chapter 4: The Politician as Diplomatist
1. R. A. Cross to the Queen (Confidential), 11 Feb. 1878: RA H20/47. Beaconsfield to the Queen, 9, 10 Feb. 1878: ibid. B56/32, 34; also in M & B, vol. vi, pp. 244—7 (with reference to the 'cowardice' of Derby and Carnarvon deleted); Gwendolen Cecil, *Life of Robert Marquis of Salisbury* (London, 1921—32, 4 vols) vol. ii, pp. 196—9. D.D., 8, 10, 11 Feb. 1878.
2. Donald Cameron to [?] (Copy), 14 Feb. 1878: RA B56/80, apparently in Cairns's hand and forwarded to the Queen by Beaconsfield.
3. Carn. D., 13 Feb. 1878.
4. Ibid., 13 Mar. 1878.
5. Derby to Beaconsfield, 19 Mar. 1878: H.P. B/XX/S/1331; D. Cab. Min., 18, 20 Mar. 1878.
6. Salisbury to Beaconsfield (Secret), 19 Mar. 1878: H.P. B/XX/S/1331a.
7. Beaconsfield to Derby, 19 Mar. 1878: D.P. 16/2/3.
8. D.D., 19, 24 Mar. 1878.
9. On this decisive Cabinet meeting, see Beaconsfield to the Queen (Secret),

27 Mar. 1878 (2 letters): RA B57/21; D. Cab. Min., D.D., 27 Mar. 1878 (also in M & B, vol. VI, pp. 262−6); and Derby's account as related to Carnarvon, in Carn. D., 4 Apr. 1878.

10. Salisbury to Lytton, 29 Mar. 1878: S.P. C/4. Salisbury had used the argument in Cabinet that intervention in Syria would convey an impression of British strength to the natives in India. D. Cab. Min., 16 Mar. 1878.

11. On the subsequent controversy over this Cabinet meeting between Derby and his former colleagues see Derby to Granville (Private), 16, 18, 25 June, 19, 24 July 1878: Gran. P. PRO 30/29/26A/2; Derby to Northcote, (Private) 19, 21 July 1878: Idd. P. 50022; D.D., 20, 22 July 1878. As to seizing Cyprus, Northcote emphasized on 19 July: 'Now I can say with the utmost confidence that no such resolution as this was ever agreed to by the Cabinet. That some proposals of this kind were discussed is quite true. But it was not agreed that anything should be done in this direction beyond making inquiries upon certain points. What I believe to be the real explanation of the painful divergence between your recollection and that of your colleagues is, − that you from the first put an erroneous construction on what passed.' A few days later Northcote asserted: 'I have just come across two notes, written in the Cabinet Room on the 27th March, which conclusively prove that no decision was then arrived at.' Northcote to Derby. (Private, [Draft]) 19, (Confidential, Copy) 22 July 1878: Idd. P. 50022. See also M & B, vol. VI, pp. 267−8, 273−9; but Buckle, obligated to Lord Sanderson, Derby's former private secretary, for some of his information, made out the best case he could for Derby. See also Nancy E. Johnson (ed.), *The Diary of Gathorne Hardy, later Lord Cranbrook, 1866−1892: Political Selections* (Oxford, 1981) 19 July 1878; Harold Temperley, 'Disraeli and Cyprus' and 'Further Evidence on Disraeli and Cyprus', *English Historical Review*, 46 (Apr. and July 1931); and Dwight E. Lee, 'A Memorandum Concerning Cyprus, 1878', *Journal of Modern History*, 3, 2 (June 1931).

12. A. J. Balfour, Memorandum on Conservative government's foreign policy, 8 May 1880: Balfour P. 49688.

13. The Queen to Beaconsfield (Secret), 27 Mar. 1878 (6.15 p.m.): H.P. B/XIX/B/1241; also in M & B, vol. VI, p. 263, with omission of quoted words, as well as the remark that Lady Derby 'was doing immense harm & counteracting the decisions of the Gov't.'.

14. Tenterden to Salisbury (Private), 31 Mar. 1878: S.P. Also Tenterden to A. H. Layard (Private, Copy), 31 Jan. 1876: Tent. P. F.O. 363/2, ff. 117−18.

15. D.D., 1 Apr. 1878. Beaconsfield asserted that the heads of the two great departments of expenditure, the army and navy, must sit in the House of Commons. Beaconsfield to the Queen, 2 Apr. 1878: RA B57/34; other parts in M & B, vol. VI, p. 282.

16. Northcote to Beaconsfield, (Confidential) 1, 2 Apr.: Idd. P. 50018; (Confidential) 29 Apr. 1878: H. P. B/XX/N/75.

17. The Queen to Constance Stanley (Copy), 2 Apr.; C. Stanley to the Queen, 3 Apr. 1878: RA B29/67.

18. W. H. Dyke to Beaconsfield (Confidential), 28 Mar. 1878: H.P. B/XXI/D/474.

19. Salisbury to the Queen, 1 May 1878: RA H22/1. See Arthur J. Marder, Documents, 'British Naval Policy in 1878', *Journal of Modern History*, 12, 3 (Sept. 1940) 367−73.

20. Salisbury to Lytton, 1 Mar. 1878: S.P. C/4.
21. See Cecil, *Salisbury*, vol. ii, p. 226ff.
22. Salisbury to W. H. Smith, 23 Apr. 1878: Hamb. P. PS6/197.
23. W. H. Smith to G. P. Hornby (Private & Confidential, Copy), 20 Apr. 1878: ibid./83; also in Viscount Chilston, *W. H. Smith* (London, 1965) p. 116.
24. Richmond to Salisbury (Private), 29 Apr. 1878: S.P.
25. Salisbury to Cross (Private), 30 Apr. 1878: Cr. P. 51263; partially in Cecil, *Salisbury*, vol. ii, pp. 253−4.
26. Referring to a speech by John Bright, Salisbury added: 'I believe Bright is going to have an attack of softening of the brain again.' Salisbury to Cranbrook, 3 May 1878: Cran. P. T501/267. On speeches at the end of April and beginning of May 1878 by Cross, Cranbrook, Bright and Joseph Chamberlain see R. W. Seton-Watson, *Disraeli, Gladstone and the Eastern Question* (London, 1935; 1969 edn) pp. 391−4. Cross had not 'been selected as the apologist of official policy in the north of England' (ibid., p. 393), for he urgently requested, on the day before his address at Preston, that Salisbury provide him with information: Secretary of State to Private Secretary or Under Secy of State, Home Office (Telegram), 29 Apr. 1878: S.P. E.
27. Cranbrook to Cross (Private), 2 May 1878: Cr. P. 51267.
28. On Austrian policy see Cecil, *Salisbury*, vol. ii, pp. 245−50; M. D. Stojanovic, *The Great Powers and the Balkans 1875−1878* (Cambridge, 1939) pp. 245−55. Salisbury complained: 'I am in Derby's old difficulty that Beust mis-repeats everything both Andrassy & I tell him.' Salisbury to Northcote (Private), 28 Apr. 1878: Idd. P. 50019.
29. Northcote to Salisbury (Private), 26 Apr. 1878: S.P.
30. Beaconsfield to the Queen, 24 Apr. 1878: RA B57/56; partially in M & B, vol. vi, p. 281.
31. Salisbury to Northcote (Private), 20 Apr. 1878: Idd. P. 50019.
32. Salisbury to Odo Russell (Draft telegram, 'Personal & Most Secret'), 6 Apr.; Russell to Salisbury, (Telegram, No. 22, Personal, Private & Secret) 7, (Telegram, Personal) 9 Apr. 1878: S.P.; all in *QVL*, vol. ii, pp. 612−14, with the omission at the end of the first telegram of these words: '& prefix the word "personal" to your telegrams in reply'. Here was an early indication of the way in which Salisbury liked to conduct delicate diplomatic negotiations.
33. Salisbury to the Queen, 1 May 1878: RA H22/1.
34. For details of these diplomatic dealings see B. H. Sumner, *Russia and the Balkans 1870−1880* (Oxford, 1937) ch. 17 and app. 8; Seton-Watson, *Eastern Question*, pp. 408−19, 421−9; Dwight E. Lee, *Great Britain and the Cyprus Convention Policy of 1878* (Cambridge, Mass., 1934) pp. 82−7; and W. N. Medlicott, *The Congress of Berlin and After* (London, 2nd edn, 1963) pp. 21−6.
35. The original British proposal had been for a conference in Vienna: D.D., 4, 6 Feb. 1878. Tenterden had volunteered to assist Lyons: Tenterden to Derby (Private & Personal), 19 Feb. 1878: D.P. 16/2/11.
36. Northcote, Notes, [27, 28 May 1878]: H.P. B/XX/N/79, 80.
37. Beaconsfield to the Queen, 31 May 1878: RA B57/70; also in M & B, vol. vi, pp. 306−7. The Queen had not wanted Beaconsfield to go to Berlin. She adduced reasons of health, and of state: 'I dont believe that *without fighting*, and giving these detestable Russians a good beating, *any* arrangement will be

lasting, or that we shall ever be friends.' The Queen to the Prince of Wales (Copy), 30 May 1878: RA B57/69; partially in M & B, vol. VI, p. 306.

38. Cairns to Salisbury (Confidential), 30 Apr. 1878: S.P. E.

39. Chamberlain to W. T. Stead (Private, Copy), 30 Mar. 1878: JC 6/4k/19.

40. Chamberlain to J. Collings, 2 Apr. 1878: ibid. 5/16/81; also, with omissions, in J. L. Garvin, *The Life of Joseph Chamberlain* (London, 1932−4, 3 vols) vol. I, p. 248.

41. Goschen to Hartington (Private), n.d. [May 1878]: Dev. P. 340.754. Also T. Paine to Granville, City of London Club, 9 May 1878: Gran. P. PRO 30/29/26A/2.

42. Carn. D., 1 Apr. 1878.

43. Granville to Hartington, 10 Apr. 1878: Dev. P. 340.752; also in Edmond Fitzmaurice, *The Life of Granville George Leveson Gower Second Earl Granville K.G. 1815−1891* (London, 3rd edn, 1905, 2 vols) vol. II, pp. 175−6. See also Granville to Gladstone, 9, 11 Apr., Gladstone to Granville, 12 Apr. 1878: Ramm, *Corr.*, vol. I, nos 106−8; Bernard Holland, *The Life of Spencer Compton Eighth Duke of Devonshire* (London, 1911, 2 vols) vol. I, p. 208.

44. Northcote to Beaconsfield, 8 May 1878: H.P. B/XX/N/76.

45. Hartington to Harcourt, 8 May 1878: Harcourt P. 78. See also Holland, *Devonshire*, vol. I, pp. 208−9; A. G. Gardiner, *The Life of Sir William Harcourt* (London, 1923, 2 vols) vol. I, pp. 328−9; Halifax to H. Ponsonby, 18 May 1878: Hick. P. A4/86.

46. Argyll to Halifax, 16 May 1878: ibid./82.

47. A. D. Elliot, *The Life of George Joachim Goschen First Viscount Goschen 1831−1907* (London, 1911, 2 vols) vol. I, pp. 190−2. See also Thomas J. Spinner, Jr, *George Joachim Goschen The Transformation of a Victorian Liberal* (Cambridge, 1973) pp. 56−7.

48. Carn. D., 19 June 1878.

49. J. C. MacDonald to D. M. Wallace, 22 Feb. 1878: P.H.S. P. 19/417.

50. See Appendix C.

51. Chamberlain to Collings, 5 Apr. 1878: JC 5/16/82; also, with omissions, in Garvin, *Chamberlain*, vol. I, pp. 248−9.

52. Derby to Granville (Private), 2, also 5, June 1878: Gran. P. PRO 30/29/26A/2; also in Seton-Watson, *Eastern Question*, p. 514.

53. George Gissing, *New Grub Street* (1881).

54. This paragraph based on Northcote to Beaconsfield (Confidential), 29 June, 4 July 1878: H.P. B/XX/N/85, 86; Tenterden to Corry (Private), 26 June 1878: ibid./XXI/T/107. Beaconsfield to Tenterden (Private), 2 July; Tenterden to Beaconsfield (Private, Copy), 4 July 1878: Tent. P. F.O. 363/1, pt 1, ff. 63−8, 59−62. Cross to Salisbury (Private), 26 July [sic: June], 3 July 1878: S.P. E; Tenterden to Salisbury (Private), 27 June, Beaconsfield to Salisbury, 1 July 1878: S.P. Salisbury to Cross (Confidential), 15 June 1878: Cr. P. 51263. See also Cecil, *Salisbury*, vol. II, pp. 262−3, 282, 285, 289; Seton-Watson, *Eastern Question*, pp. 419−21; M & B, vol. VI, pp. 303, 320−1; Lee, *Cyprus Convention*, pp. 88−9; A. W. Ward and G. P. Gooch (eds), *The Cambridge History of British Foreign Policy 1783−1919* (Cambridge, 1922−3, 3 vols) vol. III, pp. 591−2; Charles Marvin, *Our Public Offices* (London, 1879) especially p. 265ff.

55. R. Montgelas to M. Corry, 18 June 1878: H.P. B/XVII/88.
56. Cranbrook to Salisbury (Confidential), 20 June 1878: S.P. E.
57. Cross to Salisbury, 21 June 1878: ibid.; Manners to Beaconsfield (Private), 20 June 1878: H.P. B/XX/M/247.
58. Northcote to Salisbury (Confidential), 26 June 1878: S.P.
59. Manners to Beaconsfield (Private), 3 July 1878: H.P. B/XX/M/249.
60. W. H. Dyke to Beaconsfield (Confidential), 25 June; to Corry (Private), 28 June 1878: ibid./XXI/D/478. Also Northcote to Beaconsfield (Confidential), 29 June 1878: ibid./XX/N/85.
61. Cross to Salisbury (Secret & Personal, Telegram), 25 June (6 p.m.); Tenterden to Salisbury (Private, Telegram, deciphered), 24 June 1878 (4.30 p.m.): Tent. P. F.O. 363/4.
62. By contrast, Beaconsfield was not worried about the political consequences of the European settlement: 'I feel confident when the hour arrives, that I shall be able to show, that the establishment of the Balkan frontier, & all its accessories, has materially strengthened the Ottoman Dominion, & was surely no mean diplomatic triumph.' Beaconsfield to Tenterden (Private), 2 July 1878: ibid./1, pt 1, ff. 63−8 (also partially in Medlicott, *Congress of Berlin*, p. 107). Beaconsfield thanked Tenterden for supplying him with 'your "Confidential Notes on the Treaty of San Stefano", which is my Vade Mecum, & is of inestimable use to me'. Tenterden had intended these notes 'to be a complete "crib" to all the questions arising under the Treaty'. (Tenterden to M. Corry, 7 June 1878: H.P. B/XXI/T/106.)
63. Beaconsfield to Salisbury, 1 July 1878: S.P.
64. Salisbury to Beaconsfield, 2 July 1878: ibid. D/20/228; also in Cecil, *Salisbury*, vol. ii, p. 289.
65. Medlicott, *Congress of Berlin*, p. 29; ch. Seton-Watson, *Eastern Question*, pp. 431−2.
66. On the gathering and its deliberations see Medlicott, *Congress of Berlin*, ch. 2; Sumner, *Russia and the Balkans*, ch. 18.
67. Salisbury to Cross, 20 June 1878: Cr. P. 51263. See Medlicott, *Congress of Berlin*, pp. 103−4; Sumner, *Russia and the Balkans*, pp. 539−45.
68. Cross to Salisbury (Secret & Personal, Telegram), 25 June 1878 (6 p.m.): Tent. P. F.O. 363/4; also partially in Medlicott, *Congress of Berlin*, p. 105. Northcote objected to the 'heavy burden which the necessity for keeping a squadron in the Black Sea may entail on us'. Northcote to Beaconsfield (Private), 22 June 1878: H.P. B/XX/N/84; to Salisbury (Confidential), 25 June 1878: S.P. Turkish opposition had, in any case, doomed the proposal. Salisbury to Tenterden (Personal & Secret, Telegram), 25 June; Cross to Salisbury (Personal & Secret, Very Pressing, Telegram), 25 June (3.30 p.m.); Salisbury to Cross (Personal & Secret, Telegram, deciphered), 25 June 1878 (11 p.m.): Tent. P. F.O. 363/4. In general see Lee, *Cyprus Convention*, pp. 91−7.
69. Cross to Salisbury, 6 July 1878: S.P. E.
70. By article xi of the first memorandum, the British government had agreed 'à ne pas contester le désir de l'Empereur de Russie d'acquérir le port de Batoum et de garder ses conquetes en Arménie'. For the final negotiations regarding Batum see Salisbury to Cross, 10 July 1878: S.P. E; also in Cecil, *Salisbury*, vol. ii, pp. 292−4.

71. Northcote to Beaconsfield, (Confidential) 8, (Private) 20 and 22 June 1878: H.P. B/XX/N/82, 83.

72. Northcote to Salisbury (Private), 20 June 1878: S.P.; partially in Cecil, *Salisbury*, vol. II, p. 288.

73. Salisbury to Northcote (Private), 23 June 1878: Idd. P. 50019; partially in Cecil, *Salisbury*, vol. II, p. 288. Salisbury to his wife on the same day described Northcote as 'in considerable tremor − being frightened out of his life by the Jingo manifestations at home'. (Ibid., p. 286.)

74. Northcote to Salisbury (Confidential), 26 June 1878: S.P.

75. Salisbury to A. H. Layard (Personal, Telegram), 27 June 1878: Tent. P. F.O. 363/4.

76. Salisbury to Northcote (Private), 3 July 1878: Idd. P. 50019.

77. Cross to Tenterden, 6 July; also a memorandum on taking possession of Cyprus marked 'Mr. Cross, Secret & Personal', 30 June 1878: Tent. P. F.O. 363/1, pt 2, ff. 226−7, 224−5.

78. Northcote to Beaconsfield (Private), 9 July 1878: H.P. B/XX/N/87. See also Lee, *Cyprus Convention*, pp. 99−101; Cecil, *Salisbury*, vol. II, p. 294; Medlicott, *Congress of Berlin*, p. 114.

79. Cross to Salisbury, 10, 12 July 1878: S.P. E.

80. Northcote to Beaconsfield (Private), 10 July 1878: H.P. B/XX/N/88. Also Northcote to Salisbury (Confidential), 12 July 1878: S.P.

81. W. H. Dyke to Beaconsfield (Private), 9 July 1878: H.P. B/XXI/D/480.

82. Manners to Beaconsfield (Private), 11 July 1878: ibid./XX/M/250.

83. Lennox was in such bad odour at court that a few months earlier Beaconsfield had instructed Lord Barrington (20 Mar. 1878: Disraeli P. 58210) to give him an intimation, 'very quietly', that the Queen had no desire to see him: 'The Queen told me today, that she thought Lord Henry had better have a cold, & not attend the Drawing Room tomorrow.' For a comment on Lennox's indiscretion see H. Childers to Halifax, 18 Apr. 1880: Hick P. A4/90.

84. Henry Lennox to M. Corry (Confidential), 1 July 1878: H.P. B/XX/Lx/530; also partially in Hugh Cunningham, 'Jingoism in 1877−78', *Victorian Studies*, 14, 4 (June, 1971) 448. Cf. M & B, vol. VI, p. 345.

85. Northcote to Corry (Private), 12 July 1878: H.P. B/XX/N/89.

86. Northcote to Salisbury (Confidential), 12 July 1878: S.P.

87. See *The Times*, 16 July 1878.

88. Corry to Barrington (Telegram), 13 July 1878: Disraeli P. 58210.

89. Corry to Barrington (Private), 13 July 1878: ibid. Cf. Cecil, *Salisbury*, vol. II, p. 296.

90. See M & B, vol. VI, pp. 345−6.

91. *The Times*, 17 July 1878.

92. Police Orders, 15 July 1878: Mepol. 7/40.

93. Carn. D., 16 July 1878.

94. Corry to the Queen (Telegram), 16 July 1878 (5.32 p.m.): RA B59/39.

95. Barrington to Beaconsfield (Private), 8 July 1878: H.P. B/XX/Ba/66.

96. Cross to Salisbury, 16 July 1878: S.P. E. Cross added: 'I have not advised any declaration of war! with any country in your absence and I hope you will find all official matters in order.' As for Cyprus, Salisbury was bitterly opposed to assigning the island to the jurisdiction of the Colonial Office, preferring the India Office. 'If you get your officers from the Indian service you have an

enormous choice from a first rate service, well accustomed to deal with Orientals,' he had advised Cross: 'If you go to the Colonial Office – you have to choose from a service too often recruited from broken down political hacks & people "who have deserved well of the party".' Salisbury to Cross (Private), 12 July 1878; also a second letter of the same date: Cr. P. 51263. Cross had considered that the War Office should administer Cyprus 'at the first'. Note by Cross on Northcote to Cross (Private), 9 July 1878: ibid. 51265.

97. Beaconsfield to Richmond (Confidential), 17 July 1878: Goodwood Ms. 865. The occasion was to celebrate the laying of the cornerstone of the City Carlton's new building on a site secured through the Grocer's Company. Richmond had tried to use the excuse of being delayed at a Cabinet meeting for missing the function. For a report of the banquet see *The Times*, 18 July 1878.

98. Salisbury to Northcote, (Private) 5, 22 Aug. 1878: Idd. P. 50019 (also in Cecil, *Salisbury*, vol. II, pp. 306–7, 309–11). Also, enclosed with the former, A. H. Layard to Sutherland (Copy), 24 July; Northcote to Salisbury, 22 Aug., to Beaconsfield and to Sutherland, 29 Aug. 1878: Idd. P. 50053. In general see Lee, *Cyprus Convention*, especially pp. 66–8, 125–44, and app. 7.

99. J. C. MacDonald to F. Eber, 20 July 1878: P.H.S. P. L.B. 19/576.

100. T. Chenery to Granville, 6 Aug. 1878: Gran. P. PRO 30/29/26A, pt 2.

101. T. Chenery to M. Corry, 29 July 1878: H.P. B/XX/A/138 (on the appointment of the Marquis of Lorne as Governor General of Canada).

102. MacDonald to J. Walter, 26 Aug. 1878: Walter P. 467.

103. See Seton-Watson, *Eastern Question*, pp. 504–9.

104. W. H. Dyke to Beaconsfield (Confidential), 19 July 1878: H.P. B/XXI/D/481; also partially in M & B, vol. VI, p. 369. Dyke added: 'Derby is most severely condemned, and has hung himself Politically instead of Physically as you once suggested.'

105. Dyke, Memorandum (Confidential), 26 Aug. 1878: H.P. B/XXI/D/484.

106. See Bruce Waller, *Bismarck at the Crossroads The Reorientation of German Foreign Policy after the Congress of Berlin 1878–1880* (London, 1974) p. 51.

107. Salisbury to H. McLeod, 18 July 1878: S.P. D/43/64.

108. Salisbury to Cranbrook (Private), 7, 9 Aug. 1878: Cran. P. T501/269.

109. Gladstone to W. T. Stead (Private), 24 July 1878: Glad. P. 44303.

110. See *The Times*, 29 July 1878.

111. M. Corry to the Queen, 29 July 1878: RA B58/50; also in M & B, vol. VI, pp. 360–1, but with the reference to the Apsley House banquet omitted.

112. Salisbury's speech at the Mansion House, 3 Aug. 1878: *The Times*, 5 Aug. 1878.

113. See especially ibid., 15, 31 May 1878. Also R. A. Cross to the Queen, 16 May 1878: RA B29/94.

Notes to Chapter 5: Popular Politics

1. See W. N. Medlicott, *The Congress of Berlin and After* (London, 2nd edn, 1963) chs 3–10; M & B, vol. VI, ch. 10; Gwendolen Cecil, *Life of Robert Marquis of Salisbury* (London, 1921–32, 4 vols) vol. II, ch. 9; Ronald Robinson and John Gallagher, *Africa and the Victorians* (London, 1961) ch. 3.

2. Beaconsfield to Salisbury (Confidential), 17 Sept. 1878: S.P.; also in Trevor Lloyd, *The General Election of 1880* (Oxford, 1968) p. 141. Similarly, Beacons-

field to Cranbrook (Confidential), 17 Sept. 1878: M & B, vol. vi, p. 381.

3. Beaconsfield to the Queen, 5 Oct. 1878: RA B59/4. Beaconsfield added: 'The commercial depression has now lasted five years.'
4. Salisbury to Beaconsfield, (Private) 24 Feb., (Confidential) n.d. [Feb.] 1880: S.P. D/20; Beaconsfield to Salisbury, (Confidential) 26, 28 Feb. 1880: S.P.; Salisbury to A. Paget, 27 Feb. 1880: ibid. (Draft).
5. Beaconsfield to Salisbury (Confidential), 1 Oct. 1879: S.P.; also in M & B, vol. vi, pp. 489—90.
6. F. Greenwood, Memorandum submitted to Lord Beaconsfield, 20 Dec. 1878: H.P. B/XX/A/99.
7. Beaconsfield to Salisbury (Private), 22 Dec. 1878: S.P.
8. Beaconsfield to Cairns (Private & Confidential), 23 Dec. 1878: Cairns P. PRO 30/51/1.
9. Salisbury to Beaconsfield (Private), 23 Dec. 1878: S.P. D/20; Cairns to Beaconsfield (Private & Confidential), 24 Dec. 1878: H.P. B/XX/Ca/241.
10. Beaconsfield to Salisbury, 23 Dec. 1878: S.P.
11. Salisbury to Beaconsfield (Private), 24 Dec. 1878: ibid. D/20.
12. Northcote to Beaconsfield, 23 Dec. 1878: in E. J. Feuchtwanger, *Disraeli, Democracy and the Tory Party* (Oxford, 1968) p. 88.
13. Beaconsfield to Salisbury, 24 Dec. 1878: S.P.
14. Salisbury to Beaconsfield, (Private) 25, (Confidential) 27 Dec. 1878: ibid. D/20.
15. R. A. Cross to A. F. O. Liddell (Telegram), 26 Dec. 1878; Precis of replies for England and Wales, and for Scotland, n.d.: H.O. 45/9471/79559/4, 9 (5—8 and 10 destroyed in Mar. 1879).
16. Beaconsfield to the Queen, 21 Jan. 1879: RA B60/9.
17. F. Greenwood to Beaconsfield, 21 Jan. [1879]: H.P. B/XX/A/100.
18. Cairns to Richmond (Private), 1 Apr. 1879: Goodwood Ms. 869.
19. The rate of unemployment for unions making returns rose from 1.7 per cent in 1874 to 4.7 in 1877, climbed the next year to 6.8, and in 1879 to 11.4, the highest figure for two decades and unequalled again until after the First World War. B. R. Mitchell and Phyllis Deane, *Abstract of British Historical Statistics* (Cambridge, 1962) pp. 64—5.
20. Mary Derby to Halifax, 17, 30 Jan. 1879: Hick. P. A4/87a.
21. Beaconsfield to the Queen, 18 Apr. 1879: RA B60/48.
22. Dyke to Beaconsfield (Confidential), 8 Sept. 1878: H.P. B/XXI/D/485.
23. Dyke to Beaconsfield (Confidential), 11 Jan. [1879]: ibid./490.
24. Dyke to Beaconsfield (Confidential), 28 July 1879: ibid./491.
25. M. Corry to Beaconsfield, 28 Sept. 1879: ibid./XX/Co/129. Corry concluded: 'I wish I could share all his view as to the result!' Some years later, he underlined this sentence and noted: 'I never, for a moment, had but one opinion, wh. I told Lord B.! R[owton].' At the time, Corry had advised Beaconsfield (17 Sept. 1879: ibid./128) that a renewal of hostilities in Afghanistan would provide 'an opportunity for going to the country, before the bad harvest and the impending reduction of wages tell their tale'.
26. Dyke to Beaconsfield, 20 Oct. 1879, enclosing Dyke, 'Return showing the Number of Circulars, issued by the Secretary of the Treasury during the years 1874-5-6-7&8 — requesting the attendance of members in the House of Commons and the result', 26 Aug. 1879: ibid./XXI/D/506, 506a. According to Dyke's table, the ministry, which had begun with a working majority of fifty in the House of Commons, had secured majorities of one hundred on 40 per cent

of 929 government divisions between 1874 and 1878 and of sixty or more on nearly 70 per cent of them.

27. 'The truth is that the Liberal Party are desperately demoralised & broken: the leaders have lost all courage & I suspect all heart & faith in themselves': Carn. D., 9 Aug. 1878.

28. Gladstone to W. T. Stead (Private), 4 July 1878: Glad. P. 44303; also in W. T. Stead, *The M.P. for Russia Reminiscences & Correspondence of Madame Olga Novikoff* (London, 1909, 2 vols) vol. I, pp. 512-13.

29. Gladstone to Halifax, 12 July 1878: Hick. P. A44/88.

30. Cardwell to Halifax (Private), 12 July 1878: ibid./154.

31. Barrington to Beaconsfield (Private), 11 July 1878: H.P. B/XX/Ba/67.

32. *The Times*, 22 July 1878.

33. Argyll to Gladstone, 7 Sept. 1878, also 5 Feb. 1879: Glad. P. 44104.

34. Argyll to Gladstone, 27 Aug. 1879: ibid. See also Gladstone to Granville, and Granville to Gladstone, [Sept. 1878]: Ramm, *Corr.*, vol. I, nos 121, 122.

35. Hartington to Granville, 28 Sept.; 24, 29 Nov. 1878: Gran. P. PRO 30/29/26A/2; /22A/2. On British policy toward Afghanistan see M & B, vol. VI, ch. 10; and Maurice Cowling, 'Lytton, the Cabinet, and the Russians, August to November 1878', *English Historical Review*, 298 (Jan. 1961).

36. Hartington to Granville, 5 Oct. 1878: Gran. P. PRO 30/29/26A/2.

37. *The Times*, 11 Nov. 1878; Ramm, *Corr.*, vol. I, nos 131-6 (14-20 Nov. 1878).

38. Grey to Granville, 14 Nov. 1878: Gran. P. PRO 30/29/26A/2. Lord Bath warned Granville (25 Nov. 1878: ibid.): 'You may depend on it that Gladstone is the only man capable of rallying the country, and the Liberal party has no prospects of success till it has conceded to him the nominal as he now holds the virtual leadership.'

39. E. Perry to Granville (Private), 11 Oct. 1878: ibid.

40. Halifax to Granville, 11 Dec. 1878: ibid. Cf. Somerset to Granville, 7 Dec. 1878: ibid.

41. Forster to Gladstone, 2, also 15, Sept. 1878: Glad. P. 44157; former also in T. Wemyss Reid, *Life of the Right Honourable William Edward Forster* (London, 4th edn, 1888, 2 vols). vol. II, pp. 212-13.

42. Hartington to Chamberlain [Draft], 20 Dec. 1878: Dev. P. 340.781. Hartington crossed through the sentence quoted, perhaps because it revealed his feelings all too clearly. See also Bernard Holland, *The Life of Spencer Compton Eighth Duke of Devonshire* (London, 1911, 2 vols) vol. I, pp. 245-8; J. L. Garvin, *The Life of Joseph Chamberlain* (London, 1932-4, 3 vols) vol. I, pp. 267-8.

43. Hartington to Granville, 28 Dec. 1878: Gran. P. PRO 30/29/22A/2.

44. Hartington to Harcourt, 2 Jan. 1879: Harcourt P. 78. See also A. G. Gardiner, *The Life of Sir William Harcourt* (London, 1923, 2 vols) vol. I, pp. 345-6.

45. Granville to Hartington, also Forster to Hartington, 30 Dec.; Hartington to Chamberlain [Draft], 29 Dec. 1878: Dev. P. 340.786, 785; 784 (last also in Holland, *Devonshire*, vol. I, pp. 247-8).

46. Harcourt to Hartington, 3 Jan. 1879: Dev. P. 340.789.

47. Adam to Hartington, 27 Dec. 1878, 16 Jan. 1879: ibid. 783, 791.

48. Beaconsfield to the Queen, 4 Oct. 1879: RA B62/19.

49. D.D., 22 Jan. 1880.

50. Mundella to Rosebery, 8 Apr. 1879: R.P. 10075. See also Granville to Fitzwilliam, 1 Feb. 1880: Edmond Fitzmaurice, *The Life of Granville George Leveson Gower Second Earl Granville K.G. 1815-1891* (London, 3rd edn,

1905, 2 vols) vol. II, pp. 191–2. Fitzwilliam had strongly opposed the atrocities agitation.

51. See R. W. Seton-Watson, *Disraeli, Gladstone and the Eastern Question* (London, 1935; 1969 edn) pp. 543–4. Cf. G. Salisbury to Beaconsfield, n.d. [Oct. 1879 ?]: H.P. B/XX/Ce/352: 'Manchester was a great success. I do not believe there are any liberals there.'

52. Bright to Hartington, 20 Oct. 1879: Dev. P. 340.841.

53. R. N. Philips to Hartington, 13 Oct. 1879: ibid. 839.

54. In general see Cornelius O'Leary, *The Elimination of Corrupt Practices in British Elections 1868–1911* (Oxford, 1962) ch. 5; William B. Gwyn, *Democracy and the Cost of Politics in Britain* (London, 1962) p. 51; Lloyd, *General Election of 1880*, pp. 73–7, and also ch. 5.

55. U. Kay Shuttleworth to Hartington, 8 Nov. 1878; William Rathbone to Hartington, 16 Jan. 1879; R. Brett to Hartington, 4 Feb. 1879: Dev. P. 340.771, 790, 799. Granville, Notes for speech, n.d. [Oct. 1879 ?]: Gran. P. PRO 30/29/22A/7. Hartington to Granville, 22 Aug., 21 Sept., 28 Oct. 1879: ibid./2. 'He talks in a slow drawling way,' Derby noted of Hartington, 'as if the exertion of opening his mouth were disagreeable.' D.D., 24 Oct. 1879.

56. Stanley to Beaconsfield, 24 July 1879: H.P. B/XXI/S/550.

57. Granville to Hartington, 18 June 1879: Gran. P. PRO 30/29/22A/4.

58. Derby to Hartington (Private), 21 Mar. 1880: Dev. P. 340.909. Mary Derby to Halifax, 26 Mar. 1880: Hick. P. A4/87a.

59. Derby to Hartington, 10 Oct. 1879: Dev. P. 340.837; Harcourt to Frank Hill (Private, Copy), 15 Oct. 1879: Harcourt P. 208 (also partially in Gardiner, *Harcourt*, vol. I, p. 356); D.D., 11 Oct. 1879. Nathaniel Rothschild to Beaconsfield, 22 Oct. [1879]: H.P. B/XXI/R/253; Mary Derby to Halifax, (Private & Confidential) 15 Oct. 1879, 19 Jan. 1880: Hick. P. A4/87a. Also Mary Derby to Harcourt, 18, 20 Jan. 1880: Harcourt P. 209; Mary Derby to Granville, 23 Mar. 1880: Gran. P. PRO 30/29/278; and Lloyd, *General Election of 1880*, pp. 119–20.

60. Chamberlain to J. T. Bunce (Copy), 16 May 1879: JC 5/8/43; Granville to Hartington, 12 Oct. 1879: Dev. P. 340.838; Hartington to Harcourt, 12 Oct. 1879: Harcourt P. 78; Harcourt to Granville, 13 Oct. 1879: Gran. P. PRO 30/29/29A.

61. James G. Kellas, 'The Liberal Party in Scotland 1876–1895', *Scottish Historical Review*, 44, 137 (Apr. 1965) 2–3, 6, n. 4.

62. Adam to Rosebery, n.d. [Dec. 1878 ?]: R.P. 10074; also in R. R. James, *Rosebery* (London, 1963) p. 93.

63. Wolverton to Rosebery, 11 Dec. 1878: R.P. 10074 (also in James, *Rosebery*, p. 93); John Reid to Rosebery, and Ralph Richardson to Rosebery, 24 Dec. 1878: R.P. 10074. Richardson gave Rosebery these figures on 1 January 1879 (ibid. 10075): Total voters – 2929; Liberals – 1462; Conservatives – 959; Doubtful – 434; Dead – 28; Unaccounted for – 46.

64. Hartington to Gladstone, 31 Jan. 1879: Glad. P. 44145.

65. Granville to Gladstone, 14 Jan. 1879: Ramm, Corr., vol. I, no. 140.

66. Correspondence in R.P. 10075 and 10076. The total declared cost of the Liberal campaign was £2600, of which Rosebery contributed at least £1000. Reid to Rosebery, 18 Apr., 18 May 1880: ibid. 10075, 10076.

67. Gladstone to Rosebery, 21 Aug., 2 Sept. 1879: ibid. 10022.

68. Reid to Rosebery, 5, 17 Oct. 1879: ibid. 10075.
69. Reid to Rosebery, 16 Oct. 1879: ibid.
70. Rosebery wanted crowds to view Gladstone in daylight as much as possible. Rosebery to Gladstone, 29 Oct. 1879: Supp. Glad. P. 56444.
71. Gladstone to Rosebery, 14 Nov. 1879: R.P. 10022.
72. Gladstone to Rosebery, 17 Nov. 1879: ibid.
73. See W. E. Gladstone, *Midlothian Speeches 1879* (Leicester, 1879; 1971 edn). On the first Midlothian campaign in general see Morley, *Gladstone*, vol. II, ch. 6; James, *Rosebery*, pp. 91–9; Philip Magnus, *Gladstone A Biography* (London, 1954; 1970 edn) pp. 256–67; Robert Kelley, 'Midlothian: a Study in Politics and Ideas', *Victorian Studies*, 4, 2 (Dec. 1960).
74. D.D., 30 Nov. 1879.
75. F. Cavendish to Hartington, Hawarden, 9 Feb. 1879: Dev. P. 340.802.
76. Granville to Hartington, 29 Oct. 1879: Fitzmaurice, *Granville*, vol. II, pp. 182–3.
77. Gladstone to Bright, 28 Nov. 1879: Morley, *Gladstone*, vol. II, pp. 207–8.
78. Bath to Carnarvon, 23 Nov. 1879: Carn. P. (BL).
79. Granville to Hartington, 14 Oct. 1879: Dev. P. 340.840. Probably because he knew of the Queen's displeasure, Gladstone had added it to the list of reasons which he gave Bright, in his letter of 28 November 1879, for not seeking the party leadership.
80. Barrington to Beaconsfield (Private), 29 Nov. 1879: H.P. B/XX/Ba/83. At West Calder on 27 November 1879 Gladstone had accepted, in principle, the right of the state 'to buy out the landed proprietors as it may think fit': Gladstone, *Midlothian Speeches*, p. 102.
81. Bath to Carnarvon, 30 Nov. 1879: Carn. P. (BL).
82. Spencer to Granville, 26 Nov. 1879: Gran. P. PRO 30/29/29A.
83. Hartington to Rosebery, 3 Dec. 1879: R.P. 10075.
84. Hartington to Granville, 2, also 3 and 7, Dec. 1879: Gran. P. PRO 30/29/22A/2 (correspondence largely in Fitzmaurice, *Granville*, vol. II, pp. 183–5, and Holland, *Devonshire*, vol. I, pp. 258–61). For the impact of the Midlothian campaign on Hartington and his doubts about the leadership see Dev. P. 340.851–62.
85. Forster to Granville, 9, (Private) 14 Dec. 1879: Gran. P. PRO 30/29/22A/8; also in Fitzmaurice, *Granville*, vol. II, pp. 186–8.
86. Barrington to Beaconsfield (Private), 15 Dec. 1879: H.P. B/XX/Ba/85. See also Morley, *Gladstone*, vol. II, pp. 227–8.
87. W. T. Arnold [to Forster] (Copy), 14 Dec., enclosed with Forster to Hartington, 17 Dec. 1879: Dev. P. 340.861, 860.
88. Wolverton to Gladstone, 20, 17 Dec. 1879: Morley, *Gladstone*, vol. II, pp. 209–10.
89. Chamberlain to Harcourt, 4 Nov. 1879, 25 Jan. 1880: Harcourt P. 59; latter, and Harcourt to Chamberlain, 24 Jan. 1880, in Garvin, *Chamberlain*, vol. I, p. 288. Also Harcourt to Chamberlain, 3 and 6 Nov. 1879: JC 5/38/3–4.
90. Spencer to Granville, 12 Feb., 18 Mar. 1880: Gran. P. PRO 30/29/29A.
91. Halifax to Granville, 2 Feb. 1880: ibid./27B.
92. Gladstone to Granville, 18 Feb. 1880: Ramm, *Corr.*, vol. I, no. 174.
93. Cross to Salisbury, 15 Feb. 1880: S.P. E.; Salisbury to Cross (Private), 16 Feb. 1880: Cr. P. 51263.

94. See W. E. Gladstone, *Political Speeches in Scotland*, March and April 1880 (Edinburgh, rev. edn, 1880).
95. Desirous of Bright's support, Gladstone tried clumsily to compliment him by remarking that 'now men anxious to make reproach would perhaps say Bright is like Gladstone, who some years back would have said Gladstone is like Bright'. Gladstone to Bright, 12 Apr. 1880: Bright P. 43385.
96. Bright to Chamberlain, 18 Apr. 1880: Garvin, *Chamberlain*, vol. I, p. 294.
97. Ripon to Halifax, 12 Apr. 1880: Hick. P. A4/89.
98. See Morley, *Gladstone*, vol. II, pp. 229–36; Holland, *Devonshire*, vol. I, pp. 270–9; Fitzmaurice, *Granville*, vol. II, pp. 193–4.
99. Derby to Gladstone, 24 Apr. 1880 (4 p.m.): Glad. P. 44141, in reply to Gladstone to Derby (Copy), 23 Apr. 1880 (10.30 p.m.): Supp. Glad. P. 56445. Also Derby to Granville (Private), 14 Apr., 17 May 1882: Gran. P. PRO 30/29/22A/4.
100. Gladstone to Mundella (Secret, Copy), Mundella to Gladstone, 27 Apr. 1880: Glad. P. 44258.
101. Dudley W. R. Bahlman (ed.), *The Diary of Sir Edward Walter Hamilton 1880–1885* (Oxford, 1972, 2 vols) vol. I, p. 4 (29 Apr. 1880).
102. Chamberlain to Dilke (Private), 4 Apr. 1880: Dilke P. 43885; see also Garvin, *Chamberlain*, vol. I, pp. 290–303, and Stephen Gwynn and G. M. Tuckwell, *The Life of the Rt Hon. Sir Charles W. Dilke* (London, 1917, 2 vols) vol. I, pp. 303–10.
103. Bath to Carnarvon, 28 Apr. 1880: Carn. P. (BL).
104. Cranbrook to Cairns (Private), 6 Apr. 1880: Cairns P. PRO 30/51/7. Cranbrook was at least pleased that, despite the influence of Lord and Lady Derby, R. A. Cross had retained his seat in Lancashire: 'Thank God that you have triumphed over your opponents and the pitiful sneak at Knowsley who has in my judgment been as unscrupulous as treacherous. It would have given me a real pang to have seen you made a victim of Ahab and Jezebel.' Cranbrook to Cross, 8 Apr. 1880: Cr. P. 51267.
105. Richmond to Cairns, 3 Apr. 1880: Cairns P. PRO 30/51/4; Richmond to Salisbury, 10 Apr. 1880: S.P.
106. Salisbury to Lady Janetta Manners, 18 Apr. 1880: ibid. D/48/10.
107. Beaconsfield to Salisbury, 2 Apr. 1880: S.P.; partially in Robert Blake, *Disraeli* (London, 1966) p. 719.
108. Salisbury to Beaconsfield (Private), 7 Apr. 1880: S.P. D/20.
109. R. Bourke to Salisbury (Private), 9 Apr. 1880: S.P.; also Bourke to Beaconsfield, 4 Apr. 1880: H.P. B/XII/K/20.
110. G. Salisbury to Beaconsfield, 17 Apr. 1880: ibid./XX/Ce/335. Algernon Cecil thought that in the Manchester area 'the election was lost owing to the Radical proclivities of the large number of 12 pounders who have been added to the Register during the last 3 or 4 years. There are miles of new streets just outside of Manchester & other Boroughs whose occupants have I now find been completely neglected by our Registration Agents. I don't think we have lost any of our old supporters. When the County & Borough Franchise is [sic] assimilated...these suburban voters may very possibly strengthen instead of weaken the Conservative Party, as they are a very different class from the Working men householders in the Country.' A. Cecil to W. H. Smith, 9 Apr. 1880: Hamb. P. PS6/530.

111. Beaconsfield to W. H. Smith, 7 Aug. 1880: ibid./635.
112. See Feuchtwanger, *Tory Party*, p. 143ff.; Northcote to Beaconsfield, (Private) 7 July 1880, 8 Jan. 1881: Idd. P. 50018 (both also in Feuchtwanger, *Tory Party*, pp. 56, 59−60); John Manners to Northcote (Confidential), 16 Nov. 1880: Idd. P. 50041.
113. Rowton to the Queen (Draft), 19 May 1880: H.P. B/XII/J/103c; also in M & B, vol. VI, pp. 575−7.
114. Beaconsfield to Lytton (Confidential), 31 May 1880: Lyt. P. C/EK/C36.
115. Richmond to Cairns, 16 Apr. 1880: Cairns P. PRO 30/51/4.
116. A. J. Balfour to Uncle Robert [Salisbury] (Copy), 8 Apr. 1880: Balfour P. 49688.
117. Salisbury to Beaconsfield (Confidential), 10 Apr. 1880: H.P. B/XX/Ce/140.
118. Salisbury to R. C. Conybeare, 23 Apr. 1880: S.P. D/16/3. The Reverend Charles Conybeare had written to Salisbury the previous day (ibid. E): 'I am hoping that you will not resign till Parliament meets. We are henceforth to be under demagogue government; and it would be a good lesson for such in the future, I think, if Gladstone were now to be brought to book in the House for all that he dared to say on the hustings, but would not dare to utter there. I think his words after the contest was over, wishing all to be forgotten in pious forgiveness of his enemies, ultra Pecksniffian.' Conybeare enclosed a poem of his own devising:

> O high-church Cleon, leathern-lunged,
>   Our demagogue Dictator,
> Sole Saviour to the Daily News
>   And to the weeks Spectator;
> Friend of each sacerdotalist
>   Ally of each dissenter,
> Of Quaker, and of Pansclavist,
>   Of Paddy the no-renter;
> In office when you eat your words,
>   − A pretty lot I tell ye −
> You'll find the honey from your mouth
>   But bitter in your belly.

119. D.D., 21 July 1877.
120. Carnarvon to Derby (Private), 13 Nov. 1879: D.P.
121. See O'Leary, *Elimination of Corrupt Practices*, ch. 6.
122. Morley to Joseph Chamberlain, 16 Oct. 1878: JC 5/54/228.
123. For example, Spencer to Granville, 28 Aug., 15 Oct., 13 Nov. 1879: Gran. P. PRO 30/29/29A.
124. D.D., 19 Aug. 1877.

Notes to Chapter 6: Imperialism in Egypt

 1. See C. W. Hallberg, *The Suez Canal: Its History and Diplomatic Importance* (New York, 1931) pp. 224−7, and H. L. Hoskins, *British Routes to India* (London, 1928; 1966 edn) pp. 454−6.

2. Lyons to Clarendon (Private), 9 June 1870: Clarendon Corr. F.O. 361/1.
3. Gladstone to Granville, 24 Aug. 1873: Ramm, *Corr.*, vol. II, no. 882.
4. Lowe to Granville, 18 Aug. 1870: Gran. P. PRO 30/29/66. Regarding a proposed sale of the canal company's shares to the British government in 1871 see Tenterden to M. Corry (Private), 8 Mar. 1876: H.P. B/XXI/T/87.
5. Disraeli to Derby, 23 Apr. 1874: D.P. 16/2/1, Derby to Disraeli (Private), 24 Apr. 1874: H.P. B/XX/S/905 (both also in M & B, vol. v, pp. 412−13); Lyons to Derby, 11 July 1874: Lord Newton, *Lord Lyons   A Record of British Diplomacy* (London, n.d.) p. 348.
6. Disraeli to the Prince of Wales (Confidential), 11 Dec. 1875 (with postscript of 16 Dec.): RA 012/127. For background and official details regarding the purchase see Turkey: Suez Canal, Aug.−Dec. 1875: F.O. 78/2432.
7. Carn. D., 17 Nov. 1875.
8. Northcote to Derby (Confidential), 18 Nov. 1875: D.P. 16/2/6.
9. Carn. D., 22, 25 Nov. 1875.
10. M. Corry, Memorandum of conversation with Baron Rothschild, 19 Feb. 1876: H.P. B/XX/Co/114; also see M & B, vol. v, pp. 447−8.
11. Northcote to L. Rothschild, 15, also 30 Dec.; Note on Alfred Rothschild's visit to the Treasury, 17 Dec. 1875: Idd. P. 50052. Also Northcote to M. Corry, 22 Nov. 1875: ibid. 50017; Northcote to Derby (Private), 13 Dec. 1875: D.P. 16/2/6. Although the Rothschilds's commission of 2½ per cent 'startled' officials at the Treasury (Northcote to Disraeli [Confidential], 24 Nov. 1875: Idd. P. 50017), it probably represented but a fraction of their total profit on the shares transaction. The revelation of the purchase sent the Egyptian loan of 1873, quoted at less than 55 on 15 November 1875, over 70 on 26 November. (L. H. Jenks, *The Migration of British Capital to 1875* [London, 1927; 1938 edn] p. 410, n. 53; listing of foreign stocks in *The Times*, 16, 27 Nov. 1875.) Philip Rose, Disraeli's solicitor and investment counsellor, who speculated on foreign loans, 'knew before the world did what was going on'. He was of the opinion that 'Rothschilds alone must have benefitted largely, as they bought to the extent of millions of Egyptian stock'. (Sir Philip F. Rose to W. F. Monypenny, 14 Jan. 1907; in reply to Monypenny's enquiry of 12 Jan. about Rose's father's involvement in the purchase of the canal shares: H.P. R/V/A/33, 32a. Philip Rose to Corry [Private], 29 Nov. 1875; also Emile Erlanger to P. Rose, 27 Oct. 1876: ibid. B/XX/R/77, 92.)
12. Carn. D., 4, 16, 18 Nov. 1875; also Arthur Hardinge, *Life of Henry Howard Molyneux Herbert Fourth Earl of Carnarvon 1831−1890* (London, 1925, 3 vols) vol. II, p. 95. One example of George Ward Hunt's incompetence was his remark at the Lord Mayor's banquet concerning the ramming of the *Vanguard* by the *Iron Duke* in fog off Wicklow: 'If the "Iron Duke" had sent an enemy's ship to the bottom we should have called her one of the most formidable ships of war in the world; and all that she has done is actually what she was intended to do, except, of course, that the ship she struck was unfortunately our own property, and not that of an enemy.' *Annual Register, 1875*, p. [131].
13. Richmond to Disraeli (Confidential), 5 Dec. 1875: H.P. B/XX/Le/93.
14. Northcote had suggested to Disraeli on 25 November that he 'get a correct story into the Times tomorrow morning'. The Prime Minister immediately telegraphed to instruct one of his private secretaries, Algernon Turnor, to give the news to *The Times*. Northcote [to Disraeli], n.d.; Disraeli to A. Turnor,

25 Nov. 1875: Idd. P. 50017, ff. 125, 128. 'It appears to be quite time,' Turnor ejaculated, 'as I met Lord Roseberry [sic] 5 minutes ago & he was acquainted with the rumours.' Turnor to Derby (Private), 25 Nov. 1875: D.P. 16/2/1. Also Carn. D., 26 Nov. 1875.

15. J. T. Delane to William Stebbing, 25 Nov. 1875: Delane Corr., unindexed letters, 1865−75 (photocopy). Thomas Chenery, who succeeded Delane as editor two years later, and James Macdonell were writing leading articles. See those on the shares purchase in *The Times*, 26, 27 Nov. 1875.

16. Carlingford to Hartington, 19 Dec. 1875: Dev. P. 340.625.

17. F. Cavendish to Hartington, 30 Jan. 1876: ibid. 656.

18. Kimberley to Halifax, 10 Dec. 1875: Hick. P. A4/151.

19. Halifax to Gladstone, 11 Dec. 1875: Glad. P. 44186.

20. Hartington to Granville, 15, 28 Nov. 1875: Gran. P. PRO 30/29/22A/2. Also Hartington to Gladstone, 30 Nov. 1875: Glad. P. 44144.

21. Barrington to Disraeli (Private), 28 Nov. 1875: H.P. B/XX/Ba/30.

22. Granville to Gladstone, 28, 29 Nov., 1 Dec. 1875: Ramm, *Corr.*, vol. II, nos 1020−2 and notes. Granville to Halifax, 1 Dec. 1875: Hick. P. A4/85; Cardwell to Halifax, 29 Nov. 1875: ibid./154.

23. Gladstone to Halifax, 20 Dec. 1875: ibid./88.

24. Kimberley to Halifax, 15 Dec. 1875: ibid./151.

25. Gladstone to Granville, 28 Nov. 1875: Ramm, *Corr.*, vol. II, no. 1019. Also Gladstone to Hartington (Copy), 13 Dec. 1875: Glad. P. 44144, and Hick. P. A4/88.

26. Bright to Granville (Private), 5 Jan. 1876: Gran. P. PRO 30/29/22A/2.

27. Gladstone to Hartington (Private), 14 Feb. 1876: Dev. P. 340.657.

28. Barrington to Disraeli (Private), 6 Feb. 1876: H.P. B/XX/Ba/33.

29. Hartington to Gladstone, 15, 18 Feb. 1876: Glad. P. 44144. See also Hoskins, *Routes to India*, pp. 466−8.

30. See in general David S. Landes, *Bankers and Pashas in Egypt* (London, 1958), and Jenks, *British Capital*, pp. 311−20.

31. Roughly calculated from ibid., apps C and D, and B. R. Mitchell and Phyllis Deane, *Abstract of British Historical Statistics* (Cambridge, 1962) p. 334.

32. A. E. Crouchley, *The Economic Development of Modern Egypt* (London, 1938) pp. 136−9; Mitchell and Deane, *Statistics*, p. 228; E. R. J. Owen, *Cotton and the Egyptian Economy 1820−1914* (Oxford, 1969) pp. 110−12, 141, 277.

33. Crouchley, *Egypt*, p. 138; figures on cotton derived from Owen, *Cotton*, p. 177, and Mitchell and Deane, *Statistics*, pp. 298, 304.

34. Owen, *Cotton*, pp. 136−7.

35. B.T. 13/8 E2559 (1875), E3134 (1876), and 13/10 E4476 (1879).

36. Salisbury to Disraeli (Private), 26 Nov. 1875: H.P. B/XX/Ce/203.

37. Northcote to Disraeli (Confidential), 23 Nov. 1875: Idd. P. 50017. For North-cote's attitude toward the purchase see Andrew Lang, *Life, Letters and Diaries of Sir Stafford Northcote First Earl of Iddesleigh* (Edinburgh, 1890, 2 vols) vol. II, pp. 82−5. Lang failed to distinguish between purchase of the canal shares and of the Khedive's reversionary rights. When, within a week of selling his holding in the canal company, Ismail made 'an offer of his right to 15 per cent on the net profits...for £2,000,000', the Cabinet turned it down. Northcote to Carnarvon, 3 Dec. 1875: Idd. P. 50052. Also Derby to Cairns (Private), 6 Dec. 1875: Cairns P. PRO 30/51/8; in reply to Cairns to Derby (Private),

4 Dec. 1875: D.P. 16/2/1. See Hoskins, *Routes to India*, pp. 464–5.
38. Derby to Disraeli, 3 Dec. 1875: H.P. B/XX/S/991.
39. Carnarvon to Disraeli, 29 Nov. 1875: ibid./He/51.
40. Disraeli to Derby, 2 Dec. 1875: D.P. 16/2/1.
41. Barrington, Memorandum, 23 Oct. 1876: Disraeli P. 58210; Beaconsfield to Derby, 22 Oct. 1876: D.P. 16/2/2; both also in M & B, vol. vi, pp. 83–4, 99–100.
42. Northcote to Derby (Confidential), 29 Apr. 1877: D.P. 16/2/6. Also Northcote to Beaconsfield (Confidential), 24 Apr., enclosing G. J. Goschen to Northcote (Confidential, Copy), 23 Apr. 1877: H.P. B/XX/N/27, 27a (copy of latter also in D.P. 16/2/6). Northcote to Cairns (Private & Confidential), 24 Apr. 1877: Cairns P. PRO 30/51/5. For British opposition to a neutralization of the canal, Derby to Odo Russell (Confidential, Draft), 3 May 1877: F.O. 64/874, no. 163.
43. D.D., 16 June 1877.
44. Ibid., 1 May 1877.
45. Beaconsfield to the Queen (Secret), 6 Mar. 1878: RA B56/118; partially in M & B, vol. vi, p. 254.
46. D. Cab. Min., 6 Mar. 1878.
47. Edward Whitley to Sandon, 1 Jan. 1878: in E. J. Feuchtwanger, *Disraeli, Democracy and the Tory Party* (Oxford, 1968) p. 218. Some months later the rumour spread that the Comptroller General of the National Debt Office, Sir Charles Rivers Wilson, was to become Ismail's Minister of Finance. Northcote informed Salisbury ([Confidential], 27 June 1878: S.P.): 'Goschen tells me that Egyptians went up on the report that Mrs. Rivers Wilson had ordered 25 cool dresses!'
48. Salisbury to Northcote (Private), 18 Apr. 1878: Idd. P. 50019; Salisbury to H. C. Vivian, 3 May 1878: Gwendolen Cecil, *Life of Robert Marquis of Salisbury* (London, 1921–32, 4 vols) vol. ii, p. 330.
49. Northcote to Salisbury (Private), 2 May 1878: S.P.
50. Salisbury to Northcote (Private), 4 May 1879: Idd. P. 50019.
51. Northcote to Salisbury (Confidential), 12 May 1879: ibid. 50053. A year earlier, shortly before the signing of the Cyprus convention, Northcote had instructed Rivers Wilson: 'Anything you can tell us about the Harbour of Alexandria will be acceptable. We cannot help thinking that there must be room for some arrangement which would benefit the Harbour itself, which is of importance to us, and the finances of Egypt, on which it must be somewhat of a burden.' Northcote to Wilson, 22 May 1878: ibid. Also Northcote to Salisbury (Confidential), 20 May 1878: S.P.
52. Beaconsfield to the Queen, 21 Feb. 1879: RA B60/27; also in C. J. Lowe, *The Reluctant Imperialists British Foreign Policy 1878–1902* (London, 1967, 2 vols) vol. ii, p. 13. Beaconsfield asserted: 'Now, the advantage of Cyprus may be recognised. In 4 & 20 hours, almost in a night, a couple of Yr Majestys ships might carry a couple of thousand men from that island to Alexandria!' Also Salisbury to F. Lascelles (Private), 28 Mar. 1879: F.O. 800/8 (also in Cecil, *Salisbury*, vol. ii, pp. 349–50); Northcote to Rivers Wilson, 8 May 1879: Idd. P. 50053.
53. Salisbury to Northcote (Private), 13 June 1879: ibid. 50019; partially in John Marlowe, *Cromer in Egypt* (London, 1970) pp. 42–3. Sir Henry Bartle Frere, the high commissioner for South Africa and governor of the Cape Colony, had instigated the Zulu war.

54. Northcote to Salisbury (Confidential, Copy), 24 June 1879: Idd. P. 50019.
55. The acting British agent and consul general in Egypt had suggested this course more than two months earlier: F. Lascelles to Salisbury (Private, Copy), 5 Apr. 1879: F.O. 800/8. On the diplomacy of Egyptian finance in general see William L. Langer, *European Alliances and Alignments 1871—1890* (New York, 2nd edn, 1950) pp. 257—62, and Agatha Ramm, 'Great Britain and France in Egypt, 1876—1882', in Prosser Gifford and Wm. Roger Louis (eds), *France and Britain in Africa Imperial Rivalry and Colonial Rule* (New Haven, Conn., 1971) pp. 77—81; also W. N. Medlicott, *Bismarck, Gladstone, and the Concert of Europe* (London, 1956) pp. 118—19.
56. Salisbury to F. Lascelles (Private), 8 Aug. 1879: F.O. 800/8.
57. Ramm, 'Great Britain and France in Egypt', in *Britain and France in Africa*, pp. 82—6. For accounts of activities in Egypt during the period of the dual control by two British proconsuls see Earl of Cromer, *Modern Egypt* (London, 1908, 2 vols) vol. I, chs 2—10, and Viscount Milner, *England in Egypt* (London, 13th edn, 1926) chs 2—4. Also Edward Malet, *Egypt 1879—1883* (London, 1909). For the personal involvement of C. Rivers Wilson with Egyptian finance see his *Chapters from My Official Life* (London, 1916) chs 9—17, 20.
58. Beaconsfield to Salisbury, 24 June 1879: S.P.; also in M & B, vol. VI, p. 445. For interpretations stressing the importance of the bondholders see J. A. Hobson, *Imperialism A Study* (London, 1902) ch. 4, and P. T. Moon, *Imperialism and World Politics* (New York, 1926; 1930 edn) p. 223ff.; cf. D. C. M. Platt, *Finance, Trade, and Politics in British Foreign Policy 1815—1914* (Oxford, 1968) p. 154ff.
59. Tenterden to [Salisbury], 'Egypt', 10 Nov.; also 'Rothschild Loan', 2 Nov. 1879: S.P.
60. Hartington to Granville, 4, 10 Nov. 1878: Gran. P. PRO 30/29/22A/2.
61. Chamberlain to W. T. Stead (Copy), 10 Aug. 1878: JC 6/4k/24.
62. Chamberlain to C. Dilke, 9 Feb. 1879: Dilke P. 43885; partially quoted and misinterpreted in Stephen Gwynn and G. M. Tuckwell, *The Life of the Rt Hon. Sir Charles W. Dilke* (London, 1917, 2 vols) vol. I, p. 273.
63. Derby to Granville (Private), 17 Apr. 1879: Gran. P. PRO 20/29/27A. Lord Spencer wrote to Granville on 14 April 1879 (ibid./29A), shortly after Ismail's dismissal of his British and French ministers: 'What a nasty mess this Egyptian business is, without knowing what engagements have been made it seems a strong order to get an hereditary Viceroy dismissed & all engagements as to succession broken because he dismisses 2 foreign Ministers. If Government do it & go on interfering "crescendo" it would have been better to have annexed Egypt instead of Cyprus & given Crete to France or find out some other sop.'
64. Chamberlain to Stead (Copy), 21 Dec. 1877: JC 6/4k/8.
65. Northbrook to Hartington (Private), 25 Sept.; also Baring to Northbrook, 29 Dec. 1879: Dev. P. 340.834, 866.
66. Bleichröder to Beaconsfield, 8 June 1880; H.P. B/XXI/B/551; Odo Russell to Tenterden, 10 Apr. 1880: Tent. P. F.O. 363/3; Philip Currie to Salisbury, 31 Jan. 1880: S.P. E; A. H. Layard to Tenterden (Private), 27 Apr. 1880: S.P. E; A. H. Layard to Tenterden (Private), 27 Apr. 1880: Tent. P. F.O. 363/2, ff. 228—30. On Gladstone's petulant criticism of Austria during the second Midlothian campaign see Argyll to Gladstone, 22 Mar. 1880: Glad. P. 44104; Edmond Fitzmaurice, *The Life of Granville George Leveson Gower Second Earl Granville K.G. 1815—1891* (London, 3rd edn, 1905, 2 vols) vol. II, pp. 200—6;

and Medlicott, *Concert of Europe*, pp. 30, 60–2. When the British ambassador in Vienna sent two telegrams describing the Emperor's reaction to Gladstone's condemnation of Austrian policy, Northcote compounded the difficulties of the situation. In 'a comedy of errors', he publicly read a paraphrase of the ciphered message rather than the one *en clair*. H. Elliot to Tenterden (Private), 26 Mar.; Tenterden to Elliot (Private, Copy), 6 Apr. 1880: Tent. P. F.O. 363/1, pt 2, ff. 342–3, 345–6. Also Northcote to Salisbury (Private), 20 Mar. 1880: S.P.; Salisbury to Northcote (Private), 20 Mar. 1880: Idd. P. 50020; Salisbury to A. J. Balfour (Private), enclosing 'Memo.', 18 Mar. 1880: Balfour P. 49688; and W. E. Gladstone, *Political Speeches in Scotland*, March and April 1880 (Edinburgh, rev. edn, 1880) pp. 277–80, app. 3.

67. Dufferin to Salisbury (Private), 8 Apr. 1880: S.P. E.
68. E. Hamilton to Rosebery (Confidential), 26 July 1880; R.P. 10031; cf. Dudley W. R. Bahlman (ed.), *The Diary of Sir Edward Walter Hamilton 1880–1885* (Oxford, 1972, 2 vols) vol. I, pp. 24, 29–30 (13, 28 July 1880).
69. Rowton to Beaconsfield, 12 July 1880: H.P. B/XX/Co/139.
70. See Medlicott, *Concert of Europe*, ch. 6.
71. Harcourt to Gladstone, 20 Oct. 1880: Glad. P. 44196.
72. Gladstone to Granville, 14 Oct. 1880: Ramm, *Corr.*, vol. I, no. 346.
73. Gladstone to W. T. Stead (postcard), 4 June 1897: Glad P. 44303.
74. Bleichröder to Beaconsfield, 6, also 11, Oct. 1880: H.P. B/XXI/B/553, 554.
75. See Medlicott, *Concert of Europe*, chs 7 and 9. Bleichröder misleadingly informed Beaconsfield on 1 March 1881 (H.P. B/XXI/B/556): 'Our relations with the other Powers continue very good, with Russia too, altho' for the present there is no question of alliances.'
76. Beaconsfield to the Queen, 14 June, also 16 July, 1880: RA B64/3, 4.
77. On the Egyptian background see Alexander Schölch, *Ägypten den Ägyptern! Die politische und gesellschaftliche Krise der Jahre 1878–1882 in Ägypten* (Freiburg i. Br., n.d.).
78. E. B. Malet to Tenterden, 2 Aug. 1881: Tent. P. F.O. 363/2. On the role, probably exaggerated, of Malet and other officials see Alexander Schölch, 'The "Men on the Spot" and the English Occupation of Egypt in 1882', *Historical Journal*, 19 (Sept. 1976).
79. Gladstone to Halifax, 18 Sept. 1881: Hick. P. A4/88.
80. See Gladstone to Granville, 4 Jan. 1882: Ramm, *Corr.*, vol. I, no. 599; Bahlman, *Hamilton*, vol. I, pp. 214–15, 219, 235–6, 256–7, 276, 279–80, 289 (22 Jan., 4 Feb., 12 Mar., 20 Apr., 21 and 31 May, 13 June 1882).
81. Joseph Chamberlain, *A Political Memoir 1880–92*, C. H. D. Howard (ed.) (London, 1953) p. 71.
82. See D. M. Schreuder, *Gladstone and Kruger Liberal Government and Colonial 'Home Rule' 1880–85* (London, 1969) chs 4–5, particularly pp. 176–80, 304–5.
83. On the political and diplomatic reaction of the British government to events in Egypt see Ronald Robinson and John Gallagher, *Africa and the Victorians* (London, 1961) pp. 94–121; Ramm, 'Great Britain and France in Egypt', in *France and Britain in Africa*, pp. 89–114; Langer, *Alliances and Alignments*, pp. 265–78; and Paul Knaplund, *Gladstone's Foreign Policy* (London, 1935; 1970 edn) pp. 167–89.
84. Hartington to Ripon, 2 June 1882: Ripon P. 43568.

85. E. W. Hamilton to Gladstone, 1 June 1882: Hamilton P. 48607A, reporting the views of Wilfrid Blunt.

86. Granville to Hartington, 29 May; Gladstone to Granville, n.d. [30(?) May], enclosed with Granville to Hartington (Private), [30?] May 1882: Dev. P. 340. 1243, 1244—5.

87. Dilke to Ripon, 18, also (Secret) 24—5, May 1882: Ripon P. 43528.

88. Gladstone, Cabinet Minutes, 31 May 1882: Glad, P. 44643.

89. Ibid., 21 June 1882 (also in Ramm, *Corr.*, vol. I, no. 730); Robinson and Gallagher, *Africa*, p. 108.

90. Northbrook to Hartington (Private), 19 June 1882: Dev. P. 340.1247.

91. Gwynn and Tuckwell, *Dilke*, vol. I, pp. 460 note; 462.

92. Dilke, 'Reparation', n.d. [23(?) June 1882]: Dev. P. 340.1248; see also Gwynn and Tuckwell, *Dilke*, vol. I, p. 463.

93. Gladstone to Granville, 1 July 1882: Ramm, *Corr.*, vol. I, no. 736.

94. Gladstone to Granville, 25 July 1882: ibid., no. 784 and n. 3. Lord Derby later doubted that the government had done all it might have 'to get at some terms with Arabi'. Mary Derby to Halifax, 30 July 1882: Hick. P. A4/87a.

95. Sir Cooper Key, Memorandum on the despatch of Turkish troops to Egypt (Private & Confidential), enclosed with Hartington to Ripon, 16 June 1882: Ripon P. 43568.

96. Gladstone to the Queen, 3—4 July 1882 (1.15 a.m.): CAB 41/16/33.

97. Gladstone to Granville, 21 (early), 24 June 1882: Ramm, *Corr.*, vol. I, nos 728, 731.

98. See, for example, Bahlman, *Hamilton*, vol. I, p. 337 (10 Sept. 1882).

99. Childers to Halifax (Secret), 3 July 1882: Hick. P. A4/90: in reply to Halifax to Childers, 2 July 1882: Spencer Childers, *The Life and Correspondence of the Right Hon. Hugh C. E. Childers 1827—1896* (London, 1901, 2 vols) vol. II, p. 89.

100. Childers to Halifax (Private), 7 July 1882: Hick. P. A4/90; Gladstone to the Queen, 5 July 1882: CAB 41/16/34.

101. A. Grey to Halifax, 28 June 1882: Hick. P. A4/84. Grey added that only the incompetence of the opposition, led by Northcote, kept the ministry in office. Among Liberals, he punned: 'The feeling at present is, it is better to be ruled by a grand old man who makes mistakes, than by a grand old woman.'

102. Gladstone to Granville, 1 July 1882: Ramm, *Corr.*, vol. I, no. 736.

103. Gladstone, Memorandum on Suez Canal (Copy), 5 July 1882: Glad. P. 44766; also, without pencilled note at end, in Ramm, *Corr.*, vol. I, no. 741.

104. Chamberlain to T. H. S. Escott, 20 June 1882: Escott P. 58777.

105. Bahlman, *Hamilton*, vol. I, pp. 294, 296 (25, 26 June 1882).

106. Grey mistakenly assumed that the safety of Europeans in the east necessitated the action. A. Grey to Halifax, 13 July 1882: Hick. P. A4/84. Gladstone knew that the use of force by the British warships was more likely to lead to a 'massacre' than to prevent one: Gladstone to the Queen, 15 June 1882: CAB 41/16/29. In general see Mary Rowlatt, *Founders of Modern Egypt* (Bombay, 1962).

107. Dilke to Ripon, 13 July 1882: Ripon P. 43528.

108. E. W. Hamilton to Rosebery (Secret), 14 July 1882: R.P. 10031; Gladstone to Bright (Copy), 12 July 1882: Bright P. 43385; Bahlman, *Hamilton*, vol. I, pp. 306—7, 308 (14, 17 July 1882).

109. Dilke to Ripon, 20 July 1882: Ripon P. 43528; Gladstone to the Queen, 18 July

1882: CAB 41/16/37; Gwynn and Tuckwell, *Dilke*, vol. I, p. 470; S. Childers, *Childers*, vol. II, pp. 90—6.

110. Gladstone to Granville, 20 July 1882: Ramm, *Corr.*, vol. I, no. 772.

111. Childers to the Queen, 20 July 1882: S. Childers, *Childers*, vol. II, pp. 96—7.

112. Gladstone to Granville (Immediate), 21 July 1882: Ramm, *Corr.*, vol. I, no. 775 and n. 3.

113. Gladstone to Granville, 23 July 1882: ibid., no. 780 and n. 1; *Hansard* 272, cols. 1574—90, 24 July 1882. Salisbury commented: 'Tomorrow we have an Indian troop vote. Poor Lord Beaconsfield! if he could have lived to see Gladstone suing the Turk for assistance in maintaining British interests — sending for Indian troops — & using Cyprus as a place of arms.' Salisbury to Janetta Manners, 24 July 1882: S.P. D/48/63.

114. Granville to Gladstone, 23 July 1882: Ramm, *Corr.*, vol. I, no. 781 and n. 3; Bahlman, *Hamilton*, vol. I, p. 311 (25 July 1882); Ramm, 'Great Britain and France in Egypt', in *France and Britain in Africa*, p. 110.

115. Dilke to Ripon, 27 July 1882; Ripon P. 43528.

116. Gladstone to Granville, 13 July 1882 (9.45 p.m.): Ramm, *Corr.*, vol. I, no. 758.

117. Bahlman, *Hamilton*, vol. I, p. 311 (25 July 1882); Gladstone to the Queen, 24 July 1882; CAB 41/16/39; Ramm, 'Great Britain and France in Egypt', in *Britain and France in Africa*, pp. 110—11.

118. See Ampthill to Granville, 15 July 1882: Fitzmaurice, *Granville*, vol. II, pp. 268—9. Also Hugh G. MacDonell to Tenterden (Private), 30 Aug. 1882: Tent. P. F.O. 363/2, ff. 356—9.

119. Granville to Gladstone, Gladstone to Granville, 25 June 1882: Ramm, *Corr.*, vol. I, no. 732 and n. 4, no. 733 and n. 2. Also Dilke to Ripon, 29 June 1882: Ripon P. 43528; Gwynn and Tuckwell, *Dilke*, vol. I, pp. 463—4; Chamberlain, *Memoir*, p. 73.

120. Granville to Halifax, 26/27 July 1882: Hick. P. A4/85; Granville to Gladstone, 28 July 1882: Ramm, *Corr.*, vol. I, no. 793. Also see Fitzmaurice, *Granville*, vol. II, pp. 270—1.

121. Hartington to Ripon, 28 July 1882: Ripon P. 43568.

122. Dilke to Ripon, 4 Aug. 1882: 43528; Gladstone to the Queen, 3 Aug. 1882: CAB 41/16/43. See also Gwynn and Tuckwell, *Dilke*, vol. I, pp. 474—5.

123. Hartington to Ripon, 4 Aug. 1882: Ripon P. 43569.

124. Hartington to Ripon, 11 Aug. 1882: ibid.; Gladstone to Granville, 10 Aug. 1882: Ramm, *Corr.*, vol. I, no. 798 and n. 1. Bahlman, *Hamilton*, vol. I, p. 316 (6 Aug. 1882): 'There is also further good news: — It is thought we shall be able to stave off intervention in Egypt altogether, even if the Sultan issues the necessary proclamation against Arabi, which is doubtful.' See also Alfred Lyall, *The Life of the Marquis of Dufferin and Ava* (London, 1905, 2 vols) vol. II, pp. 20—31.

125. Salisbury to Cairns (Private), 21 July 1882: Cairns P. PRO 30/51/6.

126. G. Hamilton to Salisbury, 4 Aug. 1882: S.P. E.

127. Salisbury to G. Hamilton (Confidential), 6 Aug. 1882: ibid. D/27/4. See in general Cecil, *Salisbury*, vol. III, pp. 50—5.

128. Dilke to Ripon, 4 Aug. 1882: Ripon P. 43528. See also Gwynn and Tuckwell, *Dilke*, vol. I, p. 448; Bahlman, *Hamilton*, vol. I, p. 316 (6 Aug. 1882).

129. G. Hamilton to Salisbury, 8 Aug. 1882: S.P. E.

130. Richmond to Cairns (Confidential), 6, also 13, Aug. 1882: Cairns P. PRO

30/51/4. More than a year later Richmond groused to Cairns ([Confidential], 1 Nov. 1883: ibid.): 'Our leader was to my mind much too rash and hot headed and did not seem to know the meaning of the word "compromise". I do not wish to pass such another three weeks as I did last [sic] August.'

131. Salisbury to R. A. Cross, 10 Aug. 1882: Cr. P. 51263. See also Bahlman, *Hamilton*, vol. I, p. 317 (11 Aug. 1882).

132. Derby to Granville (Private), 24 Sept. 1882: Gran. P. PRO 30/29/22A/4.

133. *Hansard* 272, col. 171, 12 July 1882.

134. R. Churchill to Northcote, 16 Oct. [1882]: Idd. P. 50021.

135. See Chamberlain, *Memoir*, pp. 74, 80–1; and John V. Crangle, 'The Decline of Anti-Imperialism in the Age of Disraeli and Gladstone', *Quarterly Review of Historical Studies*, 13, 2 (1973–4) 72–3, and 'The British Peace Movement and the Anglo–Egyptian War of 1882', ibid., 15, 3 (1975–6).

136. Gladstone to Bright, 24 Sept. 1882: Bright P. 43385 (also partially in Morley, *Gladstone*, vol. II, pp. 325–6); Gladstone to Granville, 22 Sept. 1882 (2 letters): Ramm, *Corr.*, vol. I, nos 835–6.

137. Bright to Gladstone (Copy), 11 Oct. 1882: Bright P. 43385; Gladstone to Granville, 3 Oct., and Granville to Gladstone, 13 Oct. 1882: Ramm, *Corr.*, vol. I, nos 857, 867.

138. See Malet, *Egypt*, pp. 456–525; Lyall, *Dufferin*, vol. II, pp. 34–6; Cromer, *Modern Egypt*, vol. I, pp. 334–7; Schölch, *Ägypten*, pp. 259–60. Lord Dufferin, the ambassador to Turkey who was acting as special commissioner in Egypt, hoped that the government approved of 'the way in which we got rid of Arabi's trial'. Dufferin to Hartington (Private), 12 Dec. 1882: Dev. P. 340.1288.

139. Chamberlain to Bright, (Private) 31 Dec. 1882, 14 Jan. 1884: Bright P. 43387. Bright to Chamberlain, 4 Jan. 1883: Chamberlain, *Memoir*, pp. 79–80.

140. *Hansard* 272, col. 1575, 24 July 1882; see Mitchell and Deane, *Statistics*, p. 428.

141. Ripon to Hartington, 17 Mar. 1882: Dev. P. 382.133.

142. Ripon to Hartington (Printed), 26 July 1882: ibid. 160; also 161, 163ff. On the philosophy which inspired this plea see Anthony Denholm, 'Lord Ripon and Liberal Party Indian Policy 1859–1909', *Quarterly Review of Historical Studies*, 16, 1 (1976–7).

143. Dilke to Ripon, 27 July 1882: Ripon P. 43528; Gladstone to Ripon, 6 Sept. 1882: ibid. 43515. Hartington argued that if India did not share the expenses of this war, 'she can never be asked to pay for anything except her own frontier wars'. Hartington to Ripon, 4 Aug. 1882: ibid. 43569.

144. Ripon to Hartington, 4 July 1882: Dev. P. 382.155.

145. Hartington to Ripon, 28 Sept., also 30 Aug. and 4 Sept. 1882: Ripon P. 43569. Despite the opinion of the Lord Chancellor and the Attorney General that parliament must sanction the use of Indian troops in Egypt, Hartington had asserted that the session was too far advanced to allow time for a debate, which 'would have been more likely to have provoked than to have averted hostile criticism'. (26 July–23 Aug. 1882: Dev. P. 340.1255–60).

146. Dilke to Ripon (Secret), 16 Feb. 1883: Ripon P. 43528. Also Gladstone to the Queen, 1 Dec. 1882: CAB 41/16/58; Hartington to Ripon, 1 Dec. 1882: Ripon P. 43569; Bahlman, *Hamilton*, vol. I, pp. 341, 355, 362, 369 (16 Sept., 2 and 19 Nov., 3 Dec. 1882), and vol. II, p. 464 (28 July 1883); Granville to Gladstone, 14 Feb., Gladstone to Granville (Immediate), 28 July 1883: Ramm, *Corr.*, vol. II, nos 980, 1072. Fawcett had consistently objected to the 'mean-

ness...involved in making India pay for a so-called "spirited foreign policy"'. Fawcett to Gladstone, 21 Dec. 1878: Glad. P. 44156.

147. Bahlman, *Hamilton*, vol. I, pp. 324−5, 338−41 (25 Aug., 15−16 Sept. 1882).

148. See J. L. Garvin, *The Life of Joseph Chamberlain* (London, 1932−4, 3 vols). vol. I, p. 453.

149. See N. W. Summerton, 'Dissenting Attitudes to Foreign Relations, Peace and War, 1840−1890', *Journal of Ecclesiastical History*, 28, 2 (Apr. 1977) 167−70.

150. Granville to Halifax, 22 Sept. 1882: Hick. P. A4/85.

151. Salisbury to Northcote (Private), 29 Sept. 1882: Idd. P. 50020. Also Cairns to Cranbrook, 20 Sept. 1882: Cran. P. T501/262.

152. Northcote to W. H. Smith (Private), 28, 21 Sept. 1882: Hamb. P. PS8/48/46.

153. Bahlman, *Hamilton*, vol. I, p. 346 (7 Oct. 1882).

154. See ibid., pp. 339−40 (15 Sept. 1882), and Holland, *Devonshire*, vol. I, p. 368. Cf. Laurence Senelik, 'Politics as Entertainment: Victorian Music-Hall Songs', *Victorian Studies*, 19, 2 (Dec. 1975) 162, and Morley, *Gladstone*, vol. II, p. 360.

Notes to Conclusion

1. D.D., 2 Dec. 1882.

2. Ibid., 1 Dec. 1882.

3. Ibid., 1 Jan. 1883.

4. Ibid., 17 Nov. 1881, 21 Jan. 1882.

5. According to 'Votes of Members in Office Session 1881', Gladstone had voted on 116 of 212 occasions. 'Good Conduct List': Hamilton P. 48607A.

6. 'Tenure of Office &c Comparative Table', Dec. 1882: Glad. P. 44766.

7. D.D., 14 Feb. 1885.

8. Dilke to Ripon, 18 Jan. [1883]: Ripon P. 43528.

9. Dudley W.R. Bahlman (ed.), *The Dairy of Sir Edward Walter Hamilton 1880−1885* (Oxford, 1972, 2 vols) vol. II, p. 434 (11 May 1883).

10. Herbert Gladstone to Bright (Private), 15 Oct. 1883: Bright P. 43385. See also Bahlman, *Hamilton*, vol. II, p. 502 (10 Nov. 1883).

11. John Morley, *Recollections* (London, 1917; 1918 edn, 2 vols) vol. I, p. 198; Andrew Jones, *The Politics of Reform 1884* (Cambridge, 1972) pp. 3−4.

12. Gladstone to Granville, 8 Dec. 1883: Ramm, *Corr.*, vol. II, no. 1162.

13. Gladstone to the Queen, 4 Jan. 1884: CAB 41/18/2.

14. See Charles Seymour, *Electoral Reform in England and Wales* (Newton Abbot, Devon, 1915; 1970 edn) ch. 15; and Neal Blewett, 'The Franchise in the United Kingdom 1885−1918', *Past & Present*, 32 (Dec. 1965).

15. See Seymour, *Electoral Reform*, ch. 16; Henry Pelling, *Social Geography of British Elections 1885−1910* (London, 1967) pp. 8−9.

16. See J. A. Thomas, *The House of Commons 1832−1901 A Study of Its Economic and Functional Character* (Cardiff, 1939) pp. 13−22; also W. L. Guttsman, *The British Political Elite* (London, 1965 edn) pp. 89−91, 104.

17. Mallet to John Bright, 16 Apr. 1872: Bright P. 43389.

18. Mallet to Salisbury (Private), 2 Sept.; Salisbury to Mallet (Private), 11 Sept. 1878: S.P.; ibid. D/45/53. Salisbury recognized the national importance of a strong economy: 'that is her weak point,' he declared of Russia in 1885: '& if we become her chronic enemy it is to that weak point that our efforts must be addressed. We must lead her into all the expense that we can, in the conviction

that with her the limit of taxation has been almost reached, & that only a few steps much push her into the revolution over which she seems to be constantly hanging.' Salisbury to Robert Morier, 15 Sept. 1885: S.P. C/6/180.

19. C. M. Kennedy, 'Memorandum. For Mr. Bourke, in reply to his request for further information in regard to Memm. of Novr. 20. 1877', 10 Mar. 1879: F.O. 800/4. On 'governmental machinery for overseas trade' see D. C. M. Platt, *Finance, Trade, and Politics in British Foreign Policy 1815–1914* (Oxford, 1968) app. 1.

20. Francis N. Rowsell to W. H. Smith (Private & Confidential), 30 Dec. 1878: Hamb. P. PS6/279.

21. See Platt, *British Foreign Policy*, especially pp. 362–8. A specific example of intervention was Salisbury's attempt to induce the Rumanian government to allow Armstrong's to join the international competition for a contract to supply guns for the fortifications of Bucharest: Eric Barrington to Percy Sanderson, 7 Aug., Arthur Hardinge to Sanderson, 19 Aug. 1885; F.O. 800/21. Sir Julian Pauncefote, the Permanent Under Secretary of State at the Foreign Office, 1883–9, was favourably inclined toward imperial expansion by his earlier experiences at the Colonial Office and as a conveyancing barrister at Hong Kong. See R. B. Mowat, *The Life of Lord Pauncefote* (London, 1929) pp. 13–39; and for some evidence of his business interests during his decade in the Far East: Jardine, Matheson & Co. archive, University Library, Cambridge.

22. Based upon figures in B. R. Mitchell and Phyllis Deane, *Abstract of British Historical Statistics* (Cambridge, 1962) pp. 283, 319, 325.

23. Kimberley to Ripon (Private), 4 Oct. 1880: Ripon P. 43522. For confirmation of Ripon's assertion see Brian L. Blakeley, *The Colonial Office 1868–1892* (Durham, N.C., 1972) p. 63.

24. Julian Pauncefote, 'Notes on the North Borneo Charter' (F.O. Confidential Print, 'Final Revise'), 19 Jan. 1882: Glad. P. 44628.

25. Granville to R. Morier (Draft), F.O. Confidential Print, 7 Jan. 1882: ibid.

26. See Granville to Gladstone, 16 Dec. 1881; Gladstone to Granville, 20 Jan., 18 Mar. 1882: Ramm, *Corr.*, vol. I, nos 589, 610, 655. For a detailed account of the granting of the charter see L. R. Wright, *The Origins of British Borneo* (Hong Kong, 1970) pp. 142–70.

27. See John S. Galbraith, *Mackinnon and East Africa 1878–1895 A Study in the 'New Imperialism'* (Cambridge, 1972) p. 75. The example of the Borneo charter also inspired German colonialists: Henry A. Turner, Jr, 'Bismarck's Imperialist Venture: Anti-British in Origin?', in Prosser Gifford and Wm. Roger Louis (eds), *Britain and Germany in Africa Imperial Rivalry and Colonial Rule* (New Haven, Conn., 1967) p. 69.

28. D.D. 30 Nov. 1881.

29. Lord Sanderson, Memorandum, 21 Feb. 1907: G. P. Gooch and Harold Temperley (eds), *British Documents on the Origins of the War 1898–1914* (London, 1926–38, 11 vols in 13) vol. III, p. 430.

30. Bahlman, *Hamilton*, vol. II, p. 592 (9 Apr. 1884).

31. Salisbury to R. A. Cross (Private), 5 Jan. 1884: Cr. P. 51263. Also, for the views of the Conservative leadership, Salisbury to Cairns (Private), 28 Jan. 1884, 20 Feb. 1885: Cairns P. PRO 30/51/6; Salisbury to Carnarvon (Private), 1 Feb. 1885: S.P. D/31/81; W. H. Smith to Northcote, 6 Dec. 1883, and Cairns to Northcote, 13 Feb. 1885: Idd. P. 50021; S. Northcote to H. S. Northcote (Private), 27 Jan. 1884: ibid. 50032; R. Bourke to Salisbury, 2 Feb. 1884: S.P.

32. Rosebery to Granville (Copy), 12 Nov. 1884: R.P. 10081. Concerning Egypt, Rosebery, whose wife was the former Hannah Rothschild, added: 'You can guess the extreme delicacy of my relation to that question, for though I am not a member of the House of Rothschild, I am allied to it as closely as possible by kinship and friendship.' See also Joseph Chamberlain, *A Political Memoir 1880–92*, C. H. D. Howard (ed.) (London, 1953) pp. 83–5.
33. Rosebery to Gladstone, [Copy] 1, [Draft] 8 Feb. 1885: R.P. 10023.
34. Stephen Gwynn and G. M. Tuckwell, *The Life of the Rt Hon. Sir Charles W. Dilke* (London, 1917, 2 vols) vol. I, p. 546. Also Granville to Gladstone, 7 Jan. 1885: Ramm, *Corr.*, vol. II, no. 1536.
35. W. H. Smith to Northcote (Private), 22 Feb. 1885, partly destroyed: Idd. P. 50021. Goschen, who had been solicitous of the interests of the Egyptian bondholders, took advantage of the popular indignation at the death of General Charles Gordon at Khartoum to canvass railway projects in the Sudan. Goschen to Northcote (Private), 5 Mar., Northcote to Goschen (Private, Copy), 6 Mar. 1885, partly obliterated: ibid. See also Thomas J. Spinner, Jr, *George Joachim Goschen The Transformation of a Victorian Liberal* (Cambridge, 1973) pp. 104–5.
36. J. L. Simmons to W. H. Smith, 4, 24 Mar.; cf. (Confidential) 19 June 1885: Hamb. P. PS9/14, 15, 31. W. H. Smith reported that Pauncefote had told him, regarding the Suez canal, that 'it was of the highest importance that we, the Opposition, should maintain a firm and decided attitude or the Gov[ern]ment would concede...everything'. Smith to Northcote (Confidential), 21 July 1883, partly destroyed: Idd. P. 50021. The military attaché at Berlin exclaimed: 'Great God, was there ever a Ministry that has done us so much harm & made us look so mean abroad? It is enough to make one turn Yankee!' Lt. Col. L. V. Swaine to H. Ponsonby (Private), 16 May 1885: F.O. 800/3, ff. 168–71.
37. A. Cooper Key to Northbrook (Confidential), printed, 19 Jan. 1884: Glad. P. 44629; underlining added in ink, probably by Gladstone, to this and other references to an indefinite period of occupation.
38. Bahlman, *Hamilton*, vol. II, pp. 619, 546 (18 May, 23 Jan. 1884); Gladstone to Granville, 12 Sept. 1883, 10 Jan. 1885: Ramm, *Corr.*, vol. II, nos 1100, 1539.
39. E. W. Hamilton to Gladstone, 28 May, Gladstone to Hamilton, 29 May 1884: Hamilton P. 48607A; Gladstone to Granville, 22 Mar., 28 May 1884: Ramm, *Corr.*, vol. II, nos 1261, 1309.
40. Gladstone to Bright (Secret), 28 May 1884: Bright P. 43385. See also Bahlman, *Hamilton*, vol. II, pp. 626–7 (29 May 1884).
41. Ibid., p. 729 (11 Nov. 1884).
42. Gladstone to Halifax, 22 Nov. 1884: Hick. P. A4/88.
43. Bahlman, *Hamilton*, vol. II, pp. 760, 769 (1, 11, 12 Jan. 1885).
44. Gladstone to Rosebery, 8 Feb. 1885: R.P. 10023. Cf. Gladstone to Granville, 31 May 1885: Ramm, *Corr.*, vol. II, no. 1674.
45. For a classic account of the diplomatic complexities of colonialist expansion between 1882 and 1885 see William L. Langer, *European Alliances and Alignments 1871–1890* (New York, 2nd edn, 1950) ch. 9.
46. Gladstone to Granville, 19 Sept., Granville to Gladstone, 20 Sept. 1884: Ramm, *Corr.*, vol. II, nos 1434, 1438. In general see Wm. Roger Louis, 'Great Britain and German Expansion in Africa, 1884–1919', in *Britain and Germany in Africa*, pp. 3–10.

47. Minute by Granville, 'Egyptian Loan', [? Aug. 1885]: H.B. P. PC/PP/52.
48. Gladstone to Granville, 6 Mar. 1885: Ramm, *Corr.*, vol. ii, no. 1591.
49. See Edmond Fitzmaurice, *The Life of Granville George Leveson Gower Second Earl Granville K.G. 1815-1891* (London, 3rd edn, 1905, 2 vols) vol. ii, pp. 433-4; A. B. Cooke and John Vincent, *The Governing Passion Cabinet Government and Party Politics in Britain 1885-86* (Brighton, 1974) pp. 208-9.
50. Rosebery to Herbert Bismarck (Private, Copy), 22 Feb. 1885: R.P. 10004; Bahlman, *Hamilton*, vol. ii, p. 872 (30 May 1885). Further correspondence between Rosebery and H. Bismarck, 25 Feb.-11 June 1885 in R.P. 10004; also Rosebery to Granville (Confidential), 23 June 1885, enclosing notes of an interview with O. Bismarck: ibid. 10083.
51. Baron Ludwig von Plessen to Salisbury (Private), 15 Aug. 1885: S.P. G.
52. Iddesleigh to Salisbury (Private), 23 Aug. 1885: S.P.
53. Salisbury to Iddesleigh (Private), 24 Aug. 1885: Idd. P. 50020.
54. R. Bourke to Salisbury, 28 Sept. 1885: S.P.
55. O. Bismarck to Salisbury, 8 July 1885: ibid. G.
56. Minute by Granville, 'Egyptian Loan', [? Aug. 1885] (also Note by R. Welby, '1885 Egyptian Loan', n.d.): H.B. P. PC/PP/52; Beach to Salisbury (Copy), 13, 16 July 1885: ibid. PCC/30. See also John Clapham, *The Bank of England A History* (Cambridge, 1944, 2 vols) vol. ii, p. 316.
57. C. Rivers Wilson and R. Welby, Memorandum, 21 July 1885: H.B. P. PC/PP/52. On the relationship between Bismarck and Gerson von Bleichröder, see Fritz Stern, *Iron and Gold Bismarck, Bleichröder, and the Building of the German Empire* (London, 1977).

Note to Appendix A
1. Montagu Corry to Beaconsfield, 19 [sic: 20] Apr. 1877: H.P. B/XVI/B/22.

Note to Appendix B
1. W. H. Dyke to Beaconsfield (Confidential), Treasury, S.W., 23 Jan. 1878: H.P. B/XXI/D/471.

Notes to Appendix C
1. J. C. MacDonald to F. Eber, 28 Apr. 1877: P.H.S. P. L.B. 19/1. MacDonald's opinion was particularly valuable not only because, from the mid-1870s, he appointed the foreign correspondents but also because the proprietor of *The Times*, John Walter, implicitly trusted him. See *The History of 'The Times'* (London, 1935-52, 4 vols in 5) vol. ii, pp. 503-5.
2. MacDonald to Eber, 22 Sept. 1877: P.H.S. P. L.B. 19/229.
3. MacDonald to Eber, 18 Mar. 1878: ibid./435.
4. MacDonald to D. M. Wallace, 19 Mar. 1878: ibid./438.
5. MacDonald to Eber, 14 May 1878: ibid./502.
6. MacDonald to Wallace, 1 June 1878: ibid./528.
7. MacDonald to Wallace, 5 July 1878: ibid./562.
8. MacDonald to Eber, 11 Dec. 1878: ibid./721.

Index

SHL
BIBL.
WITHDRAWN
UNIV.

Gladstone's "Bulgarian Atrocities"

Daily News

Disraeli's Letters